MULTICULTURAL EDUCATION SERIES

James A. Banks, Series Editor

Talkin Black Talk

Language, Education, and Social Change

Edited by
H. Samy Alim
and John Baugh

Teachers College, Columbia University
New York and London

Published by Teachers College Press, 1234 Amsterdam Avenue, New York, NY 10027

Library of Congress Cataloging-in-Publication Data

Talkin black talk : language, education, and social change / H. Samy Alim and John Baugh, editors.
    p. cm. -- (Multicultural education series)
  Includes bibliographical references and index.
  ISBN-13: 978-0-8077-4746-9 (pbk : alk. paper)
  ISBN-13: 978-0-8077-4747-6 (cloth : alk. paper)
  1. Black English—United States. 2. Black English—Social aspects. 3. African Americans—Languages. 4. English language—Social aspects—United States.
5. Language and education—United States. 6. Sociolinguistics—United States.
I. Alim, H. Samy. II. Baugh, John, 1949– III. Title: Talking black talk.
  PE3102.N42T35   2007
  427'.97308996073—dc22   2006028928

978-0-8077-4746-9 (paper)
978-0-8077-4747-6 (cloth)

Printed on acid-free paper
Manufactured in the United States of America

14   13   12   11   10   09   08   07   8   7   6   5   4   3   2   1

Poem for Black English *by June Jordan*
(Dedicated to Dr. Geneva Smitherman)

You don' never write me off
because you ignorant
don' know nobody got my
name
my low lights
softstone hometown
street
my rollin high Apollo style
my sweet
two babies wait
for food I ain' figured
out about
yet
but you bet
I will
I'll get
them somethin serious goin on
just let
me sit here
half a minute
on the sidewalk
next to Willie's
Burgers
watch that ole man
suited up besides
the blues
can' touch that faithful
finery
can' mess up walk-to-Jesus shoes
he clean
he shine and shave and lose
a weeklong shuffle
steppin
close to music
from the signifyin red
dress of some woman
do not care
the world stay blind
to all the glory all the heavy
invitation of a red dress radiate
a whole day
that she wear no stretch no
stress
she overturn the law
of gravity
she dare you
don' believe it
yeah
she dare you!

Contents

Part I:
Language, Literacy, and Liberation

Part II
Culture, Communication, and Consciousness

Part III
Toward Linguistic Emancipation

Series Foreword

The nation's deepening ethnic texture, interracial tension and conflict, and the increasing percentage of students who speak a first language other than English make multicultural education imperative in the 21st century. The U.S. Census (2000) estimates that people of color made up 28% of the nation's population in 2000 and predicts that they will make up 38% in 2025 and 50% in 2050 (El Nasser, 2004).

American classrooms are experiencing the largest influx of immigrant students since the beginning of the 20th century. About a million immigrants are making the United States their home each year (Martin & Midgley, 1999). Almost four million (3,780,019) legal immigrants settled in the United States between 2000 and 2004. Only 15% came from nations in Europe. Most (66%) came from nations in Asia; from Mexico; and from nations in Latin America, Central America, and the Caribbean (U.S. Department of Homeland Security, 2004). A large but undetermined number of undocumented immigrants also enter the United States each year. The influence of an increasingly ethnically diverse population on U.S. schools, colleges, and universities is and will continue to be enormous.

Schools in the United States are characterized by rich ethnic, cultural, and linguistic diversity. American schools are more diverse today than they have been since the early 1900s, when a flood of immigrants entered the United States from Southern, Central, and Eastern Europe. In the 30-year period between 1973 and 2004, the percentage of students of color in U.S. public schools increased from 22 to 43%. If current trends continue, the number of students of color might equal or exceed the number of White students in U.S. public schools within one or two decades. Students of color already exceed the number of White students in six states: California, Hawaii, Louisiana, Mississippi, New Mexico, and Texas (Dillon, 2006).

Linguistic and religious diversity are also increasing among U.S. students. In 2000, about 20% of the school-age population spoke a language at home other than English (U.S. Census Bureau, 2000). Harvard professor Diana L. Eck (2001) calls the United States the "most religiously diverse nation on earth" (p. 4). Islam is now the fastest-growing religion in the U.S. as well as in several European nations such as France and the United Kingdom (Cesari, 2004). Most teachers now in the classroom and in teacher education programs are likely to have students from diverse ethnic, racial, linguistic, and religious groups in their classrooms during their careers. This is true for both inner-city and suburban teachers.

An important goal of multicultural education is to improve race relations and to help all students acquire the knowledge, attitudes, and skills needed to participate in cross-cultural interactions and in personal, social, and civic actions that will help make our nation more democratic and just. Consequently, multicultural education is as important for middle-class White suburban students as it is for students of color who live in the inner-city. Multicultural education fosters the public good and the overarching goals of the commonwealth.

The major purpose of the *Multicultural Education Series* is to provide preservice educators, practicing educators, graduate students, scholars, and policy makers with an interrelated and comprehensive set of books that summarizes and analyzes important research, theory, and practice related to the education of ethnic, racial, cultural, and linguistic groups in the United States and the education of mainstream students about diversity. The books in the *Series* provide research, theoretical, and practical knowledge about the behaviors and learning characteristics of students of color, language minority students, and low-income students. They also provide knowledge about ways to improve academic achievement and race relations in educational settings.

The definition of multicultural education in the *Handbook of Research on Multicultural Education* (Banks & Banks, 2004) is used in the *Series*: Multicultural education is "*a field of study designed to increase educational equity for all students that incorporates, for this purpose, content, concepts, principles, theories, and paradigms from history, the social and behavioral sciences, and particularly from ethnic studies and women's studies*" (p. xii). In the *Series*, as in the *Handbook*, multicultural education is considered a "metadiscipline."

The dimensions of multicultural education, developed by Banks (2004b) and described in the *Handbook of Research on Multicultural Education*, provide the conceptual framework for the development of the publications in the *Series*. They are: *content integration, the knowledge construction process, prejudice reduction, an equity pedagogy,* and *an empowering school culture and social structure.* To implement multicultural education effectively, teachers and administrators must attend to each of the five dimensions of multicultural education. They should use content from diverse groups when teaching concepts and skills; help students to understand how knowledge in the various disciplines is constructed; help students to develop positive intergroup attitudes and behaviors; and modify their teaching strategies so that students from different racial, cultural, language, and social-class groups will experience equal educational opportunities. The total environment and culture of the school must also be transformed so that students from diverse groups will experience equal status in the culture and life of the school.

Although the five dimensions of multicultural education are highly interrelated, each requires deliberate attention and focus. Each publication in the *Series* focuses on one or more of the dimensions, although each book deals with all of them to some extent because of the highly interrelated characteristics of the dimensions.

The rich cultural, ethnic, social-class, and linguistic diversity of students in U.S. schools presents serious challenges to teachers and other educators. It also provides rich opportunities to create a nation-state in which diversity is valued and greatly enriches American society. Schools should prepare students from all racial, ethnic, cultural, and language groups to become effective and reflective citizens of the national civic culture and community. This goal should be attained in ways that are consistent with the idealized values of U.S. society, which include civic equality, recognition (Gutmann, 2004), and cultural democracy (Ramírez & Castañeda, 1974). Honoring these values requires that we help students from diverse groups to become effective citizens of the United States and the world without alienating them from their home cultures or violating their cultural and language identities (Wong Fillmore, 2005). As the authors of this informative and timely book, *Talkin Black Talk*, make clear, language is an important part of a student's identity. When teachers reject students' languages, they reject an important part of their identities; deny them language rights, recognition, and cultural democracy; and prevent them from attaining cultural empowerment.

In the past, U.S. schools tried to make students effective citizens of the nation-state by alienating them from their home and community cultures. Forcing students to become alienated from their home and community cultures in order to obtain an education violates some of the fundamental principles of a democratic and just society. Students should be able to maintain those aspects of their home and community cultures that help them to function effectively in their cultural community and that provide them with a sense of kinship and belonging.

Assimilationists worry that students who maintain attachments to their community cultures and languages may not develop sufficiently strong attachments to the nation-state or become effective participants in the civic culture and community. Kymlicka (2004) states that assimilationists have "a zero sum conception of identity" (p. xiv). However, Kymlicka goes on to point out that identities are usually "multiple, nested, and overlapping. Members of minority groups are likely to become more attached to their country, not less, when it affirms the legitimacy of their ethnic identity and the value of their cultural heritage" (p. xiv). Rather than being harmful to a nation-state, citizens who have clarified cultural identifications and are rooted in their home and community cultures and languages are better able to be effective citizens than are individuals who have confused and ambivalent cultural identifications and attachments or who have been forced to become alienated from their home and community cultures and languages (Banks, 2004a).

Teachers and schools should respect African American English not only because it is the home and community language of many African American students, but also because—as the authors of this book point out—it is an indigenous American language that enriches American culture and language discourse. Consequently, it is important for all students to become acquainted with the history, formation, and current usage of African American Language in Black communities—especially in churches— as well as with the ways that it has been incorporated into Western popular culture in the United States and around the world. Teachers should teach all students about the "rich and diverse linguistic practices" of African American English (Alim, this volume, p. 25). Teachers should make pragmatic use of African American English by employing it as a vehicle to help its speakers to learn Standard American English. In Chapter 3 of this book, LeMoine and Hollie describe creative and engaging strategies for training educators to teach Standard American English to speakers of African American English while respecting their home language and culture. However, Alim challenges educators (in Chapter 1) to go beyond using African American English as a vehicle to teach Standard American English. He argues convincingly that because of its "rich and diverse linguistic practices" African American English should be studied because of the status it deserves in the curriculum and the contribution it can make to the liberal and humanistic education of all students (p. 25).

Historically in U.S. schools, teachers have tried to help students acquire Standard American English by attempting to eradicate their home and community languages and forcing them to experience self-alienation from their home cultures and languages. The school often taught students contempt for their family cultures and languages (Greenbaum, 1974). Greenbaum states that the school provided students with *shame* and *hope*. It taught students to be ashamed of their home cultures and languages, and, in exchange, offered them hope for assimilation into the mainstream culture. This strategy worked much more effectively for White European immigrants than it did for people of color (Roediger, 2005). Cultural assimilation did not assure people of color a place at the table or structural inclusion into mainstream U. S. society (Painter, 2005).

The "No Spanish Rule" was common in schools in Southwestern states such as Texas, Arizona, and New Mexico during the 1950s and 1960s (Carter, 1970).

Mexican American students who spoke Spanish in the classroom were punished, sometimes severely. African American students were also discouraged or prohibited from speaking their home language during instruction. Yet, research indicates that the most effective way to teach students a second language or variety of a language is to use their home language as a building block to help them learn the second language or language variety— not to try to eradicate their first language or language variety (Bhatia & Ritchie, 2004; Cummins, 2000).

Talkin Black Talk contains information, perspectives, and insights that will help educators and other professionals who work with youth to implement language education programs that respect the cultural rights of speakers of African American English as well as help them to learn Standard American English. It also provides educators with the information needed to help all students to understand the complexity of African American English and its contribution to Stanford American English, to U.S. society, and to popular culture around the world. This book deserves to be read widely and carefully not only because of the research and insights it contains, but also because of its vision of schools as places where all students have cultural freedom and the right to learn in their home and community languages, as well as the right to acquire the knowledge and skills needed to be effective citizens of the United States and the world.

James A. Banks
Series Editor

REFERENCES

Banks, J. A. (2004a). Introduction: Democratic citizenship education. In J. A. Banks (Ed.), *Diversity and citizenship education: Global perspectives* (pp. 3–15). San Francisco: Jossey-Bass.

Banks, J. A. (2004b). Multicultural education: Historical development, dimensions, and practice. In J. A. Banks & C. A. M. Banks (Eds.), *Handbook of research on multicultural education* (2nd ed., pp. 3–29). San Francisco: Jossey-Bass.

Banks, J. A., & Banks, C. A. M. (Eds.). (2004). *Handbook of research on multicultural education* (2nd ed.). San Francisco: Jossey-Bass.

Bhatia, T. K., & Ritchie, W. C. (Eds.). (2004). *The handbook of bilingualism.* Malden, MA: Blackwell Publishing.

Carter, T. P. (1970). *Mexican Americans in school: A history of educational neglect.* New York: College Entrance Examination Board.

Cesari, J. (2004). *When Islam and democracy meet: Muslims in Europe and the United States.* New York: Pelgrave Macmillan.

Cummins, J. (2000). *Language, power and pedagogy: Bilingual children in the crossfire.* Clevedon, England: Multicultural Matters.

Dillon, S. (2006, August 27). In schools across U. S., the melting pot overflows. *The New York Times,* vol. CLV [155] (no. 53,684), pp. A7, 16.

Eck, D. L. (2001). *A new religious America: How a "Christian country" has become the world's most religiously diverse nation.* New York: HarperSanFrancisco.

El Nasser, H. (2004, March 18). Census projects growing diversity: By 2050: Population burst, societal shifts. *USA Today,* p. 1A.

Greenbaum, W. (1974). America in search of a new ideal: An essay on the rise of pluralism. *Harvard Educational Review, 44,* 411–440.

Gutmann, A. (2004). Unity and diversity in democratic multicultural education: Creative and destructive tensions. In J. A. Banks (Ed.), *Diversity and citizenship education: Global perspectives* (pp. 71–96). San Francisco: Jossey-Bass.

Kymlicka, W. (2004). Foreword. In J. A. Banks (Ed.), *Diversity and citizenship education: Global perspectives.* San Francisco: Jossey-Bass.

Martin, P., & Midgley, E. (1999). Immigration to the United States. *Population Bulletin, 54* (2), 1–44. Washington, D.C.: Population Reference Bureau.

Painter, N. I. (2005). *Creating Black Americans: African American history and its meanings, 1619 to the present.* New York: Oxford University Press.

Ramírez, M. & Castañeda, A. (1974). *Cultural democracy, bicognitive development, and education.* New York: Academic Press.

Roediger, D. R. (2005). *Working toward Whiteness: How America's immigrants became White: The strange journey from Ellis Island to the suburbs.* New York: Basic Books.

United States Census Bureau. (2000). *Statistical abstract of the United States* (120th edition). Washington, D. C.: U.S. Government Printing Office.

United States Department of Homeland Security. (2004). *Yearbook of immigration statistics, 2004.* Washington, DC: Office of Immigration Statistics, Author. Retrieved September 6, 2006 from *www.uscis.gov/graphics/shared/statistics/yearbook/Yearbook2004.pdf*

Wong Fillmore, L. (2005). When learning a second language means losing the first. In M. M. Suárez-Orozco, C. Suárez-Orozco, & D. B. Quin (Eds.), *The new immigration: An interdisciplinary reader* (pp. 289–307). New York: Routledge.

Acknowledgments

It is difficult to fully convey our gratitude and appreciation to everyone who has helped us formulate and complete this book. Dr. Geneva Smitherman, to whom this volume is dedicated, is one of those rare individuals who has achieved legendary status within her active professional career. As a scholar-activist, she is the embodiment of the struggle for equal language rights. The collection of essays produced for this book seeks to celebrate her formidable interdisciplinary contributions, and to do so in a representative—and yet accessible—manner.

We owe tremendous thanks to many outstanding scholars whose technical studies are either directly or indirectly related to Dr. G's legacy. More specifically, we have benefited greatly from intellectual insights from Arnetha Ball, Walter Edwards, Nicholas Faraclas, Maisha Fisher, Michele Foster, Keith Gilyard, Lisa Green, Kris Gutierrez, LaMonda Horton-Stallings, Austin Jackson, Jamila Jones, David Kirkland, Carol D. Lee, Margaret Lee, Haki Madhubuti, Ernest Morrell, Marjorie Orellana, Dennis Preston, Elaine Richardson, John Rickford, Ernie Smith, James G. Spady, Julie Sweetland, Orlando Taylor, Teun A. van Dijk, Toya Wyatt, and George Yancy.

The preceding scholars represent a broad range of academic disciplines, including comparative cultural studies, education, English, linguistics, literature, speech pathology, and urban studies, among other fields concerned with language usage among American slave descendants of African origin. Like Dr. G, these scholars have produced essential studies of Black American speech and writing in schools and society, and readers of this volume would be well advised to consult their extensive writings as a complement to the essays contained herein.

Special commendation is due to the late poet-professor June Jordan, who penned her devoted contribution to this book, knowing full well that it would be among her last published poems. June Jordan was an eloquent Black language speaker who soldiered forth in pursuit of the language rights of Black speakers throughout the world. Her spirit and inspired words launch this text. She loved Black people, Black language, and Black culture, and she fought with all her might for those who refuse to give up their language, who knowingly disturb the peace with a verbal innovation and inventiveness that has influenced language users worldwide. June was a visionary who recognized that control of one's language constitutes control of one's destiny. As a poet, author, and scholar she valued the linguistic legacy of slavery. Without question, completion of this book is, in part, dedicated to her memory and undying commitment to her family, her students, and the social change that she and Dr. G have shared as their lifework.

We were encouraged to pursue this project from the outset by James A. Banks, who, as editor of this series, has shared his wisdom and guidance in close collaboration with Brian Ellerbeck, of Teachers College Press, who has been a stickler for major and minor procedural and logistic details. Their comments have greatly enhanced this work. In addition, it is impossible to overstate the masterful editorial effort that Aaron Welborn has provided to this work. Quite frankly, we could not have completed this book without his patience, insight, and constant encouragement. He has provided us, and each contributing author, with insights that consistently lead to greater clarity and an unflinching concern for you, the reader. Recognizing our desire to reach a broad interdisciplinary audience, he has employed the grace of a diplomat and the iron will of a steadfast taskmaster. He routinely anticipated problems that had escaped our attention, and did so with concern for each author's contribution, while simultaneously considering matters pertaining to cohesion of the overall text.

We would be remiss if we did not thank our families for their consistent love and patience throughout all phases of this project; they continually replenished our inspiration. Last, we are delighted to formally acknowledge Dr. Geneva Smitherman's extensive and exhaustive offerings. Her beneficence in helping us ensure the accuracy of several large-to-small details throughout the book has been a godsend. Few other people we have ever known have been as kind or generous as she has been to us, and for that we are more than honored: We remain eternally grateful.

Talkin Black Talk

Language, Education, and Social Change

Black Language, Education, and Social Change

Continuing the Struggle for Equal Language Rights 50 Years After Brown

H. Samy Alim and John Baugh

This case is a judicial investigation of a school's response to language, a language used in informal and casual oral communication among many Blacks but a language that is not accepted as an appropriate means of communication among people in their professional roles in society. . . . The problem posed by this case is one which the evidence indicates has been compounded by efforts on the part of society to fully integrate Blacks into the mainstream of society by relying solely on simplistic devices such as scatter housing and busing of students. . . . Some evidence suggests that the teachers in the schools which are "ideally" integrated such as King do not succeed as well with minority Black students in teaching language arts as did many of the teachers of Black children before integration. The problem, of course, is multidimensional, but the language of the home environment may be one of the dimensions. It is a problem that every thoughtful citizen has pondered, and that school boards, school administrators and teachers are trying to solve.

—Judge Charles W. Joiner, "Memorandum Opinion and Order" in *Martin Luther King Elementary School Children v. Ann Arbor School District Board*, decided July 12, 1979

The crisis is not about education at all. It is about power. Power is threatened whenever the victim—the hypothetical victim, the victim being in this case, someone defined by others—decides to describe himself. It is not that he is speechless, it is that the world wishes that he were.

—James Baldwin during the National Invitational Symposium on the *King* decision, 1981

✯   ✯   ✯

As researchers concerned with educational issues, the year 2004 gave us pause to reevaluate the successes and failures of 50 years of court-ordered desegregation since *Brown v. Board of Education of Topeka, Kansas* (1954). For scholars of literacy and educational linguistics, the year 2004 was cause for a double pause, if you will, and a timely moment to revisit 25 years of language and racial politics in the United States since the "Black English case" (*Martin Luther King Junior Elementary School Children, et al., v. Ann Arbor School District Board,* 1979). Just as the American Educational Research Association chose *Brown* as the primary subtheme for its 2004 annual conference, the organizers of "New Ways of Analyzing Variation" (an annual conference for sociolinguists), which was actually held in Ann Arbor, chose *King* as its primary conference theme. We join these scholars in a collective effort to provide valuable insight into future directions for educational and linguistic research.

Taking an action-oriented approach toward social change, the contributors of this volume are taking part in an agenda that works toward obtaining equal language rights for all citizens of the world. As Ball (2006) asked: What needs to happen before the close of another half century in order for us to realize the full potential of *Brown*? For scholars of color, reexamining and continuing the struggle for equal language rights is not merely a professional exercise without personal meaning. So, before we begin, let's just be clear, fam—our children ain't got another 50 years. As people of color continue to struggle for equal language rights in the United States, we are calling for an agenda that focuses on preparation, pedagogy, and policy. In our view, three major action points should be placed high on the language education agenda for the coming half century: (1) the development of teacher education programs in language and literacy; (2) the development of new language pedagogies; and (3) the development of comprehensive, systemic reform in language education policy. Each of the contributors in this volume addresses one or more of these three central themes.

This book draws attention to two historically neglected dimensions of the Black American experience—the linguistic legacy and the related educational legacy of the African slave trade, or what Smitherman (2000) calls the African Holocaust. Sociolinguistic research (Alim, 2004b; Baugh 1983, 1999b, 2000a; Labov, 1972; Rickford & Rickford, 2000; Smitherman, 2000; Wolfram & Thomas, 2002) has shown that the linguistic legacy of slave descendants of African origin differs from that of *every other* immigrant group in the United States. Despite this unique linguistic heritage, or perhaps because of it, the law has never fully addressed the language issues faced by many Black Americans. As involuntary immigrants (Ogbu, 1978, 1992), Black Americans differ from voluntary immigrants in that, in addition to suffering the cruel and obvious indignities of chattel slavery, they were abruptly cut off from their linguistic heritage.

This historical dimension of the struggle for Black linguistic emancipation is crucial to understanding contemporary issues. While delivering the keynote address during the National Invitational Symposium on the *King* decision in February 1980, in Detroit, Michigan, late great Black American author James Baldwin captured the essence of this view: "I want to suggest to you that history is not the past. It is the present. We carry our history with us. We *are* our history. If we pretend otherwise, to put it very brutally, we literally are criminals" (quoted in Smitherman, 1981, p. 55). Making the link between Black Language (BL, alternatively known as African American Vernacular English, African American Language, Black English, and Ebonics) and the survival of African people in the "North American wilderness," Baldwin testifies to the *deep* meaning of BL, connecting it to the very peculiar experience of the African slave trade and to the strength of African resilience:

> I tell you something else, a *very* important matter. The language forged by Black people in this country, on this continent, as the choir just told you [referring to Smitherman's Tennessee Baptist Church choir's rendition of Black history in song], got us from one place to another. *We* described the auction block. We described what it meant to be there. We survived what it meant to be torn from your mother, your father, your brother, your sister. We described it. We survived being described as mules, as having been put on earth only for the convenience of white people. We survived having *nothing* belonging to us, not your mother, not your father, not your daughter, not your son. And *we* created the only language in this country. (quoted in Smitherman, 1981, p. 56)

As Baugh (2000a) writes elsewhere, not only were enslaved Africans "isolated from other speakers of their native language, which was a practice employed by slave traders to prevent revolts," but they were also simultaneously "denied statutory access to schools, literacy or judicial relief in the courts." Through the manipulation and control of language and literacy, European slavemasters provided the sociolinguistic conditions that fostered the development of a unique Black Language in the United States.

While the Black population in the United States is far more diverse than is often noted, the languages of most Black slave descendants in the Americas do share two very important points. First, all of the "New World" hybrid languages are the result of contact between African and European languages (Ibo and English, for example). Second, all these languages, without exception, have been viewed as lesser versions of their European counterparts, to put it mildly, or have suffered under the laws, practices, and ideologies of linguistic supremacy and White racism

(Alim, 2004a). It is the ideology and practice of linguistic supremacy—that is, the false, unsubstantiated notion that certain linguistic norms are inherently superior to the linguistic norms of other communities, and the practice of mapping those "superior" norms onto "the language of school," "intellectual pursuits," "economic mobility" and "success"—that we seek to eradicate in this work. Our collective aim is to recognize the unique linguistic and educational legacies of the African slave trade and to produce a social action agenda based on teacher preparation, pedagogy, and policy to address the long-neglected sociolinguistic reality of Black Americans.

In addressing this unique sociolinguistic situation, particularly within the educational context, we must begin with the question: When did speaking BL come to be seen as a problem? Public discourse about the language education of Black youth in the United States often incites discourse about racism and race relations, pointing to the fact that racism is still a significant issue in American schooling. In the minds of many Americans, it is not uncommon for linguistic concerns to become intertwined with issues of race. In practice, linguistic "firestorms" (the "Black English case" and the Ebonics controversy, for instance) often reveal a complex array of strategies that perpetuate racist myths about Black people (Ronkin & Karn, 1999).

In the following section, we take some time to reflect on the *Brown* decision, which was mainly about race, in relation to the so-called Black English case, which was mainly about language. While these two cases have often been discussed separately in the scholarly literature (Alim, 2005; Ball & Alim, 2006; Baugh, 1998, 2006), a joint discussion of the cases should prove useful in providing access to equal educational opportunity for all students.

(RE)SEGREGATED SCHOOLS AND SPEECH COMMUNITIES: BROWN AND KING IN COMPARATIVE PERSPECTIVE

Brown v. Board, which many refer to as "the single most honored opinion in the Supreme Court's corpus" (Balkin, 2001), effectively overruled *Plessy v. Ferguson* (1896), which required separate but equal facilities for Blacks and Whites. In the years of struggle leading up to the case, many Blacks and their supporters, fully aware that White facilities were usually better funded and better resourced by local and state governments, argued that the doctrine of "separate but equal" was inherently unequal and that *de jure* segregation helped to reinforce the ideology of White supremacy. As we witnessed only one decade ago in the heated Ebonics controversy of Oakland, California, in 1996–1997, race and schooling remains a cause of concern for (as linguist Geneva Smitherman once said) "ey'body and they momma." But, quiet as it's kept, and amid the controversial firestorms surrounding Blacks and their language, ain't nobody talkin about how America done become a resegregated society (Orfield & Yun, 1999).

King was a federal court case on behalf of 15 Black, economically oppressed children residing in a low-income housing project on Green Road in Ann Arbor, Michigan. The plaintiffs, in brief, argued that the school board had not taken the social, economic, cultural, and linguistic backgrounds of the students into account while attempting to teach them how to read in "standard English" (Smitherman, 1981). Thus, they argued, the students were denied access to equal educational opportunity, also a primary concern for *Brown*. While school desegregation rulings have sometimes mentioned the effects of language, and while language education rulings have sometimes mentioned the effects of desegregation, both types of cases lie right at the nexus of language and racial politics in U.S. education.

The resegregation of American society—not just of Blacks and Whites, but of all communities from one another, particularly Blacks and Latinos—has resulted in a situation in which most Black and Brown children attend racially segregated schools (*de facto* segregation is in full effect, y'all, and in almost every major urban area). As noted by Balkin (2001), the increasing resegregation of U.S. cities is strongly correlated with poverty levels: "Although only 5 percent of segregated white schools are in areas of concentrated poverty, over 80 percent of Black and Latino schools are" (p. 6). Turner Middle School, in Southwest Philly, a school in which Alim taught in the late 1990s, was at the time of his tenure 99.4% Black, with many students living below the poverty line. Alim has also taught in "diverse" California schools where not a single White student attended. Teachers throughout the U.S. can testify to the presence of *de facto* segregation, as there has been a gradual relaxing of the need to comply with court-ordered desegregation since the 1970s (Prince, 2006; see also Balkin's [2001] discussion of *Board of Education of Oklahoma City v. Dowell* [1991], *Freeman v. Pitts* [1992], and *Missouri v. Jenkins* [1995]).

What might resegregation have to do with language education? In the context of a resegregated society, sociolinguists such as William Labov and Wendell A. Harris (1986) argued that Black and White speakers of English were not participating in the same processes of linguistic change. If true, this meant that rather than Black and White dialects of English converging, they were actually diverging. In the press, this had immediate and "newsworthy" social implications, as Americans in the post–civil rights era had come to see themselves as citizens of a nation devoted to equal opportunity for all. So, whereas the Kerner Commission (the National Advisory Commission on Civil Disorders) feared the development of "two separate societies, one Black, the other White," some sociolinguists feared the development of two separate languages, one Black, the other White (see Fasold's 1987 special issue of *American Speech*). This, they argued, would mean that the language of some Blacks in resegregated America would be growing further and further away from the "language of schooling," possibly halting Black American educational progress.

In the *King* decision, Judge Joiner explicitly made the connection between language barriers and segregation. *King* represents the first test of applicability of 1703(f), the language provision of the 1974 Equal Educational Opportunity Act, to speakers of BL (Smitherman, 1981, 2000). The critical clause reads:

> No state shall deny equal educational opportunity to an individual on account of his or her race, color, sex, or national origin, by . . . the failure by an educational agency to take appropriate action to overcome language barriers that impede equal participation by its students in its instructional programs. (20 U.S.C. 1703[f])

In his "Memorandum Opinion and Order," Judge Joiner sought to go beyond *Brown*'s use of social science research: "The court believes that research results . . . are better received as evidence in the case, on the record and subject to cross-examination, than simply by reading the reports and giving consideration to what appears in those reports as was done in *Brown v. Board of Education*, 347 U.S. 483 (1954)" (quoted in Smitherman, 1981, p. 342). It is clear from the ruling that Judge Joiner relied heavily on the research results of educational psychologists and linguists. He ruled:

> The evidence clearly suggests that no matter how well intentioned the teachers are, they are not likely to be successful in overcoming the language barrier caused by their failure to take into account the home language system, unless they are helped by the defendant to recognize the existence of the language system used by the children in their home community and to use that knowledge as a way of helping the children to read standard English.
>
> The failure of the defendant Board to provide leadership and help for its teachers in learning about the existence of "Black English" as a home and community language for many Black students and to suggest to those same teachers ways and means of using that knowledge in teaching the Black children code switching skills in connection with reading standard English *is not rational in light of existing knowledge on the subject.* (quoted in Smitherman, 1981, p. 355, emphasis added)

In the aftermath of the *King* decision, in which Judge Joiner deemed the failure of the school board to use existing knowledge to teach the language arts to be "irrational," and the Oakland "Ebonics controversy" (Baugh, 2000a;

Rickford & Rickford, 2000), in which the majority of the American public deemed statements such as the judge's to be irrational, it seem like what go 'round come 'round and, like Hip Hop brothas Brand Nubian once said, "back around again." The cycle of hysteria that surrounds the right of Black students to their own language begs two important questions for scholars: (1) What are the "rational" ways in which teachers can take BL into account when teaching Black students? and (2) What is the state of "existing knowledge" on the subject? The contributors to this volume attempt to answer those questions. This book combines the most recent knowledge on the subject with cutting-edge pedagogical approaches that not only take the language of students into account, but also recognize the relationship between language and the larger sociopolitical and sociohistorical phenomena that maintain unequal power relations in a still-segregated society. As Jimmy Baldwin aptly put it, "The crisis is not about education at all. It is about power."

CONTINUING THE STRUGGLE FOR EQUAL LANGUAGE RIGHTS

In this volume, we have pulled together top scholars and practitioners in the areas of sociolinguistics, literature, literacy, and education to produce research that contributes to the continuing struggle for equal language rights. We open the book with "Poem for Black English," by celebrated Black Arts Movement poet, professor, and political activist June Jordan. Because June writes as only June can, her words bounce right off the paper. Like that wild No Limit souljah Mystikal warned, "*Watch* yo-self!" Like the BL that she writes in, June's spirit continues to live on, despite all the efforts made to diminish her vitality, energy, and enthusiasm for the struggle. June's contributions to the struggle for the language and educational rights of Black children, of *all* children, are consistent with the goals of this volume.

Part I, Language, Literacy, and Liberation, presents research on language pedagogy and planning, with a focus on new approaches to the education of linguistically marginalized youth. The section begins with H. Samy Alim's chapter, "The Whig Party Don't Exist in My Hood": Knowledge, Reality, and Education in the Hip Hop Nation, which focuses on the development of innovative language pedagogies, such as Da Bomb Squad Comprehensive Literacy Program and Hiphopography: The Ethnography of Hip Hop Culture and Communication. Seeking both a corrective to eradicationist language pedagogy and an interrogation of dominant language ideologies, Alim challenges researchers and educators to "go beyond the clichéd 'taking them from where they're at and leading them somewhere else' approach, lest we unwittingly offer a strawberry-flavored, culturally sensitive pill for our children to swallow, the end result of which would ultimately be the same sickness—the devaluation of their language and culture." The following chapter, by Charles DeBose, The Ebonics Phenomenon, Language Planning, and the Hegemony of Standard English, continues the metadiscursive examination of scholarship on BL, and the interrogation of Standard English hegemony, by viewing sociolinguistic research as engagement in language planning. "Although scholars of AAL [African American Language] have acted with varying degrees of intention and consciousness as agents of language planning," DeBose writes, "their behavior nevertheless qualifies as LP [Language Planning], to the extent that they promote claims that are contrary to established social meaning."

Following DeBose, Chapters 3 and 4 present classroom-based instructional approaches to language and literacy development taking place in California schools. Chapter 3, Developing Academic English for Standard English Learners, by scholar-practitioners Noma LeMoine and Sharroky Hollie, begins with a discussion of the development of the Academic English Mastery Program in Los Angeles, which "serves more than 50 schools, thousands of teachers, and tens of thousands of students—including African Americans, Mexican Americans, Hawaiian Americans, and Native Americans—referred to in the program as Standard English Learners (SELs)." The chapter, which provides important information about teacher attitudes and professional development, outlines six critical instructional approaches to language and literacy development. In Chapter 4, The Art and Science of Teaching Narrative Reading Comprehension: An Innovative Approach, Angela Rickford discusses the challenges of teaching reading comprehension in a state where "ethnically diverse students now comprise the majority in public schools," and many of them "enter school speaking myriad languages and dialects, and while they must learn to read English, it is often not their mother tongue." Rickford explores simple but powerful ways to help teachers achieve their goals when teaching narrative reading and comprehension and help students engage meaningfully with narrative, whether they're reading for pleasure or for school.

In Part II, Culture, Communication, and Consciousness, we continue the theme of liberation and open with Geneva Smitherman's classic piece of literary criticism (first printed in 1973), The Power of the Rap: The Black Idiom and the New Black Poetry, which analyzes the politics and poetics of writer Don L. Lee (now Haki Madhubuti). In a conversation about the relevance of Smitherman's work during a conference in 2000 at Howard University, Madhubuti called Smitherman "a powerful woman" who had "made some significant contributions in the area of language, in legitimizing and pushing our own language" (unpublished interview, 2000). Writing specifically for this volume, he states:

She was a "public intellectual" before they were recognizable in the Black world. Her defense of Black Language and Black people is often a lonely one and predates the current debate on Ebonics by at least 15 years. She was among the first group of Black scholars out of the 1960s along with Addison Gayle Jr., Darwin T. Turner, and Stephen Henderson to seriously consider and write about the poets of the Black Arts Movement (BAM, 1965–1975). . . . Her comments on BAM poets, including my work, displayed both a caring sensibility and an intellectual dissection that encouraged all of us. She was one of the few Black scholars who embraced us while others were running toward whiteness or Eurocentrism in all of its various permutations.

It must be noted that Dr. G is a word warrior and a product of the Black Arts Movement. BAM created an environment where it was possible for all of us to grow and make our contributions. Most certainly BAM liberated us psychologically from our Eurocentric perspective and allowed and encouraged us to create new African-centered paradigms. This new thinking placed Dr. Smitherman right in the center of controversy, for she was taking on the cornerstone of Western civilization—its language. (Madhubuti, unpublished manuscript, 2005)

In Smitherman's essay, she deconstructs the role of BL in Black poetry and links language to the movement for social change in the world. This pioneering work, with a new introductory poem by Haki Madhubuti, has obvious implications for the Hip Hop Cultural Movement, discussed by H. Samy Alim in Chapter 1.

In Chapter 6, Sounds Bouncin Off Paper: Black Language Memories and Meditations, Sonia Sanchez, another leading figure in the Black Arts Movement and considered by many to be the mother of the movement, discusses BL in educational, cultural, historical, and literary contexts—always centering her discussion within the Black community. Passionately written in a flowing, conversational mode, Sanchez's contribution makes interesting links between BL and Black literary and musical traditions, as well as new and innovative cultural forms, such as Hip Hop Culture. Throughout the chapter, Sanchez makes reference to her innovative pedagogy of poetry, which predated contemporary calls to use the student's "home language" in classroom instruction, a subject tackled in the first and last sections of the volume. In Chapter 7, African American Communicative Practices: Improvisation, Semantic License, and Augmentation, Arthur Spears writes about the radical difference between the language use of Black Americans and that of other Americans, Whites in particular, emphasizing the idea that the principal differences between Black ways of speaking and other forms of American speech lie in communicative practices. As he writes, "Some of the most interesting and distinctive features of African American English (AAE) grammar are to be uncovered in the kinds of African American discourses considered unsuitable for drawing rooms where hegemonic, Eurocentric norms prevail, but accepted without comment (even with satisfaction) by those who have been entertained and enlivened by Black talk." The chapters in Part II, as Spears points out about his project, are all efforts to describe and theorize Black American culture and communicative practices in macro and micro terms.

Part III, Toward Linguistic Emancipation, includes several chapters on the local and global dimensions of the struggle for equal language rights. In Chapter 8, Linguistic Emancipation in Global Perspective, John Baugh and Geneva Smitherman summarize some of the most critical research conducted from the *King* case to the present, framed within a global perspective, and conclude with a call for scholarly responsibility on language matters within and beyond the African Diaspora. Ever mindful of "linguistic oppression and the social dislocation that feeds it," as well as of the issues of educational malpractice (Baugh 1995, 1999b), linguistic profiling (Baugh, 2000b), and the continued denial of individuals' right to their own language (Smitherman, 2000a), they seek to overcome the racially motivated existence of linguistic barriers. In Chapter 9, If Our Children Are Our Future Why Are We Stuck in the Past? Beyond the Anglicists and the Creolists and Toward Social Change, Sonja Lanehart provides a controversial, yet complementary, perspective, as she delivers a straightforward, no-holds-barred manifesto about what she perceives to be the most valuable aspect of research on BL—it's consequentiality. In particular, Lanehart questions the efficacy and intentions of the long-standing debate about the history and evolution of BL, "when right now we have African American children who are discriminated against because of their language—the essence of who they are—and graduating with high school diplomas they cannot read."

Recalling DeBose's chapter on language planning and the "Ebonics phenomenon" (Chapter 2), Chapter 10, by influential South African scholar-activist Neville Alexander, titled Mother-Tongue Education and the African Renaissance, with Special Reference to South Africa, focuses specifically on the difficulties of language medium policy and mother-tongue education (MTE) in post-apartheid South Africa. A larger, more pressing issue for him and for other South African scholars (in fact, for all scholars of the postcolonial world) is how exactly we go from the current dominance of colonial languages in Africa to that future scenario where indigenous languages are dominant. Given the varying points of view on this question, Alexander recognizes that answering it would involve many aspects of language planning, language-policy development, and language policy implementation. He concludes with what he views as a rhetorical question: "Is it better for a new government committed to social transformation to perpetuate an educational system based on a language that is effectively foreign to most of its citizens, or should it turn the system around over time in order to base it on the mother tongues of the people?" With the current debates around

BL and bilingual education in the United States, Neville's question is one for all of us to consider.

The contributors to this volume recognize that they are producing knowledge in a world that is hostile to people and languages "of color." We also recognize that our scholarship has the potential to contribute to an action-oriented agenda for social change. This is a time when the George W. Bush administration's No Child Left Behind is seen by many policy analysts as No Children of Color Left—period. This scholarship has policy implications that, if implemented, would secure federal funding for the gamut of linguistically and culturally diverse students who face "language barriers" that limit their chances at educational success. Now, more than ever, it is time to forge a language-policy alliance between scholars and advocates for all linguistically and culturally diverse students, particularly Blacks and Latinos, who compose the two most numerous, and often most vocal, constituencies in the United States. Together, both groups can present a united front that calls for the formulation of a national language policy for all students who speak a language variety other than Standard English. That includes, for example, Vietnamese English learners in the San Francisco Bay Area, Jamaican Creole speakers in the Bronx, Chicano English speakers in East Los Angeles, isolated White Appalachian English speakers in the mountains of the Northeast, Gullah speakers on the Carolina Sea Islands, Lumbee English speakers in southeastern North Carolina, Arabic-dominant Palestinian English learners in New Jersey, and the millions of undocumented students of various immigrant backgrounds in America's schools.

Importantly, a broad-based coalition made up of such members could argue for the cultural, social, and economic value of additive language policies that foster the development of "standard English" *and* the home languages of the students. By denying various communities the use of their home languages in school, advocates for "English Only" are actually stripping America's linguistically diverse students of opportunities to participate in the global economy, where diverse linguistic and cultural resources are seen as assets, not handicaps.

Much more attention needs to be given to the English Plus proposal developed by Geneva Smitherman and later adopted by the Conference of College Composition and Communication. The English Plus proposal includes three main objectives: (1) reinforce the need for and teaching of Standard English as the language of wider communication; (2) reinforce and reaffirm the legitimacy of nonmainstream languages and dialects and promote mother-tongue language as a coequal language of instruction along with the language of wider communication; and (3) promote the acquisition of one or more foreign languages, preferably choosing from those spoken by persons in the third world, one possibility being Spanish, because of its widespread use in this hemisphere.

As Smitherman once noted, regarding the need for scholars of color to produce research with the goal of social transformation:

> Speaking as a mother (now grandmother) and as an educational activist for
> Black and Latino youth, I see such efforts as English Plus, the Ebonics move-
> ment, etcetera, as strategies, tactics in the struggle for equity for our people.
> The question is, What tactics can we develop to redress the disempower-
> ment of our communities, especially our youth? The intellectual production
> of knowledge—that comes out of places like Stanford, University of Pennsyl-
> vania, Michigan State, Harvard, etc.—can aid or deter community struggles
> for empowerment because the state apparatus calls on the works of scholars
> and intellectuals to confirm the agenda of the state, which includes educa-
> tional policies and practice. (Personal communication, November 15, 1999)

As *Brown* turns 50, *King* turns 25, and Ebonics turns 10, it is our collective hope
that the work presented in this volume will aid community struggles for empowerment, particularly the struggle for equal education and language rights.

Part I

LANGUAGE, LITERACY, AND LIBERATION

CHAPTER 1

"The Whig Party Don't Exist in My Hood"

Knowledge, Reality, and Education in the Hip Hop Nation

H. Samy Alim
(Dedicated to Bankie Santana)

The Ebonics community has a rich oral heritage. It is characterized by fondness for and agility in verbal play, as evidenced in today's Hip Hop Culture and Rap music. Twenty-first century language and literacy lessons should not only address the totality of language in life but should also allow for edu-tainment.

—Geneva Smitherman,
"Language Policy and Classroom Practices"

Right now, it is almost IMPOSSIBLE for you not to see how strong rap has gotten, you know what I'm sayin? It's like our brothers and sisters, our youths, and some of our adults their ear is PINNED to rap music right now. And if you really wanna get our message out and really wanna start teachin, we need to start doin that. We really need to start usin our methods, you know what I'm sayin? The Last Poets did it with poetry. And even in our history from ancient African civilizations, poets went from village to village and that's how stories and messages and lessons were taught, you know what I'm sayin? And so like you say, history repeats itself. And so it was obvious for us to pick it up, you know? Being the race that we are, being the strong race that we are, we picked it up, we picked up those positive vibes and we started rappin and so I think it is, it's a very good medium.

—Tupac Shakur,
The Rose That Grew from Concrete

✯   ✯   ✯

You can hear the urgency in the brotha's voice. The Late Great Tupac Shakur was as stressed as the stressed syllables in his raps. Tupac saw, as the Rza of the Mighty Wu-Tang Clan did, that "there's no room for ignorance no more" (Spady, Dupres, & Lee, 1995). What these cats is fightin for is the right to be educated. As I write this, the public school system continues to fail students of color. In particular, educational systems continue to struggle with ways to develop language and literacy skills in diverse populations. Educators and researchers note that for many linguistic- and cultural-minority students, the primary discourses in the communicative spaces of their homes, peer groups, and community settings differ from the academic discourse operative in schools (Ball, 1995; Gee, 1996). In an effort to bridge this gap, much research has been conducted on speakers of Black Language (BL), in particular, yet the educational standing of Black students has not improved, in relative terms. In fact, social psychologist Claude Steele (1992, cited in Rickford, 1999) notes that Black students fall further and further behind their White counterparts with each successive year they stay in school. Both linguists and educators believe language is a crucial factor (Adger, Christian, & Taylor, 1999).

Many scholars, using an ethnography-of-communication framework, have attempted to drive home the main message that students on the margins of school success often possess "different, not deficient," language and literacy practices in their home communities. This "mismatch," they argue, is one cause of schools' failure to reach these pupils. Most notable in this area is Heath's (1983) classic, decade-long study of how families from Black and White working-class communities socialized their children into different "ways with words," or varying language and literacy practices, some of which were closer to school norms than others. Subsequently, scholars have taken on research agendas that aim to "bridge" the out-of-school language and literacy practices of Black students with classroom practice (Ball, 2000; Dyson, 2003; Foster, 2001; Lee, 1993), while others have examined the inventive and innovative language and literacy events of Black youth involved in Hip Hop Culture (Alim, 2004b, 2004c), spoken-word poetry (Fisher, 2003), and other verbal activities (Mahiri & Sutton, 1996; Richardson, 2003, 2006), as well as the relationship between literacy and popular culture, more generally (Duncan-Andrade, 2005).

Recognizing the linguistic discrimination and linguistic profiling (Baugh, 2000a) practiced by American institutions (educational, occupational, and legal), researchers consider their primary concern to be the development of "academic" discourse, or "standard" English skills, in students who speak language varieties that vary from "mainstream" norms. If we are to make a noteworthy educational contribution, we also need an approach that considers the sociocultural contexts within which BL is spoken. Such an approach would foreground issues of cultural and personal identity, educational and linguistic ideologies, and diverse language practices.

This chapter is intended as a resource—a written teacher workshop, if you will—for all teachers of students whose linguistic and cultural experiences have yet to be validated in the school setting. *Teachers* here refers to traditional teachers in the classroom, as well as those who teach in the homes, mosques, churches, streets, and other community sites of learning. What will Smitherman's "twenty-first century language and literacy lessons" look like? As evidenced by the Ebonics controversy, most attempts at using BL in the classroom have met with resistance from all parties (Baugh, 2000a; Rickford & Rickford, 2000; Simpkins & Simpkins, 1981; Smitherman, 1981), with one notable exception—*the students*. The language and literacy lessons of the 21st century must begin with the students, and they must be implemented both inside and outside the classroom.

KNOWLEDGE AS A CONSTRUCT

In order to provide a more student-centered approach to language and literacy development, we must first ask, What is *knowledge*? When, where, and how is knowledge (de)valued? Who are the producers and consumers of knowledge, and what types of knowledge do we produce and consume? What are the relationships between language, culture, reality, power, and knowledge? From the perspective of the Hip Hop Nation Speech Community (HHNSC), what does it mean to "know the ledge," or to "do the knowledge," to understand that "knowledge reigns supreme"? It is notable that the HHNSC's constructions of knowledge all beg the question, Knowledge for what, to what end, for what purpose? By interrogating the construct of knowledge, we are attempting to uncover and understand the educational ideologies of the present generation of Hip Hop youth.

A growing body of research on the relationship between Hip Hop Culture and language and literacy education indicates that scholars are beginning to investigate this area in new and exciting ways (Meacham & Anderson, 2003; Morrell, 2002).[1] As a teacher-researcher at the middle school and high school level, I have frequently drawn upon Hip Hop Culture in educational practice, but I have also developed ways of using Hip Hop Culture itself *as* educational practice. It is one thing to view the culture of our students as a resource for teaching about other subjects, and it is quite another to see our students as the *sources*, *investigators*, and *archivers* of varied and rich bodies of knowledge rooted in their cultural-linguistic reality.

KNOWLEDGE, REALITY, AND EDUCATION

It is essential for us to hear the voices of the Hip Hop Nation in order to understand Hip Hop Culture's educational ideologies. To that end, I'd like to share an excerpt of a conversation between me and the American C.R.E.A.M. Team's Bankie Santana, a Hip Hop artist comin up outta Harlem and protégé of the Wu-Tang Clan's Raekwon. In this conversation, Santana moves from his personal experiences with school and his desire to learn to a Marxist critique of American public education as a means of control exercised by the ruling class, to his vision of a school of his own—the *School of Reality*. We enter the dialogue at the point when Santana is describing himself as having an "old man's mind":

> *Bankie:* All my life. My grandfathers was telling me that. Everybody around me would say that, because I'm a deep thinker. As far as school go, I went through 12th grade and all of that. I understand the purpose of learning about George Washington and Abraham Lincoln. I understand that, because you cannot be in America and don't know how this country was founded and all that. You can't function right without knowing that. I understand that. But I knew that would be good for me academically. But when I walk out of the doors of the school that I was in, I knew that it was a whole nother world. The Whig Party don't exist in my hood, you know what I mean? So, I got to know. . . . The reason why a lot of minorities drop out of school, you know what I mean, because the board of education, they *plan* it that way.
>
> *Alim:* What do you mean by that?
>
> *Bankie:* They planned it that way because they statistically know that it's nothing there to keep your interest. And European Americans, let's just say that, they learn European history, you know what I mean? Other ethnic groups, they don't learn about themselves, you know what I mean? So, you learn about this other group of people so much and they don't give you nothing about yourself so you will stay in it and stay in it and stay in it, until you veer off from it, you know what I mean? And that's just how they know it. They know! Yeah, you know, it's like, with me, like I said, I was a street entrepreneur driving a 190 Benz to junior high school. And to come to school and pass my SATs and do all of that. So, I knew that it was a no-brainer. Academically, I probably was academically a genius, but I just never really focused in. I wanted to be a anthropologist. . . . But I just didn't continue the process of schooling to be that.
>
> *Alim:* You seem like the anthropologist type, too. You be thinkin about that shit.
>
> *Bankie:* C'mon, man, you know.
>
> *Alim:* Let's take it one step further and say if you had to design your own school so this type of shit wouldn't be the norm, how would you design your own school?

Bankie: What I would do, I think the world need to know one thing. I'ma give you something right here, and I *want* you to write this, man. I'ma give you something. And this for White people, this for Chinese, this for everybody to take this. And you can feel how you wanna feel. Alright. And I want you to quote Bankie on this. The reason why the forefathers of this country went to Africa and tricked the Africans into comin here, was because they seen the paradise that they built for theyselves in Africa. These people, the forefathers of this country, they went to so-called Africa . . . I know we Asiatic people. But they went to Africa, as the story is told, and they tricked people into believing that we would receive more gold for our labor in *this* country. They seen the palaces and the pyramids and they seen the technology that we had. They brung us back here. Captured us. Tricked us into gettin here. You wouldn't bring a uncivilized person to build a new country for you. You'd bring a person that you seen build a world for themselves to build you a new world. So, in these history books when they say that people were uncivilized, these people, *they biased to realities of life.* You can't get blinded. Look at the picture. And it worked. The forefathers of this country, they had a plan, and it worked. They said, "Let's get the scientists in Africa and have them build us a world in America." And through that, Louis Lattimere was the person who invented the filament inside the light bulb, you know what I mean? Charles Drew did open heart surgery *[sic]* Daniel Hale Williams, blood plasma. George Washington Carver invented the peanut to get plastic from, you know what I mean? Madame C. J. Walker did the straightening comb, you know. They reinvented a world for them. And this is what they planned on. So, my master school, my school would be—of course, you need European education. What the world need to respect is the Black Man that's trapped in America's education and history. That's what the *world* need to respect . . .

Alim: So, that's your academy.

Bankie: Basically.

Alim: What would you call it?

Bankie: I'll call it Reality. *School of Reality.* (unpublished interview, 2000)

What we witness in this conversation is a serious critique of the American public education system as being out of touch with both contemporary reality and the historical reality of Black Americans. Bankie's comments raise a critical point: As educators charged with educating the Hip Hop generation(s), it is essential that we have an accurate assessment of what our students *know*, as well as their attitudes toward what is required to be *known*. Examining the educational ideologies of our students is fundamental to an approach that *keeps it real* (Carter, 2005). As Bankie's comments demonstrate, the concepts of *knowledge* and *education* are often interpreted differently in many White and Black American communities, as they sometimes reflect strikingly different historical, cultural, and linguistic realities. So how can these differing ideologies be brought together into a single vision of education that takes into account the educational welfare of all students?

DA BOMB SQUAD COMPREHENSIVE LITERACY PROGRAM

Harnessing the pedagogical power of Hip Hop Culture in the classroom is not entirely new. It is merely the most recent manifestation of what language and education scholars have been advocating as good pedagogy for the past 2 decades. Hip Hop Culture has been used to develop a wide range of skills from general preschool learning (Hicks, 1987); reading (Morrow-Pretlow, 1994); writing and literary analysis (Milford, 1992); English grammar (Macklis, 1989); history, philosophy, politics and multiculturalism (Anderson, 1993; Brown 1995); Afrocentric curriculum (Honeman, 1990); and academic writing in college courses (Frisk, 1992; Strother, 1994). By encouraging the use of Hip Hop Culture in the classroom, I am advocating the need for educators to build upon the cultural-linguistic realities of Black students for academic success in the language arts classroom and beyond.

Da Bomb Squad Comprehensive Literacy Development Program employs the cultural-linguistic practices of contemporary Hip Hop Culture to motivate and assist students in developing their oral, written, and computer literacy skills. The program began in 1997 at Turner Middle School in Southwest Philly. Around that time, I had come to the realization that while academics had been studying the language of Black Americans for quite some time (more than 3 decades), their work had yielded small benefits for the speakers of BL, while yielding huge gains for the "experts" (Rickford, 1997). I felt it was time that scholars, educators, and linguists put this research to work for the communities and the youth, who had long been the objects of study but were still struggling.

During my studies at the University of Pennsylvania, I had the opportunity to collaborate with top scholars in urban education and linguistics, including William Labov and Ira Harkavy. It was our belief that decades of accumulated linguistic knowledge ought to be combined with a new and creative pedagogy in order to reverse the failure of our urban schools to properly educate Black Americans. One main question guided my thinking: How can we, as educators, linguists and scholars, use the cultural-linguistic practices and experiences of our students as the impetus for creative and effective educational praxis?

Upon entering Turner Middle School, I was told by more than one teacher that "these students can't write," and "you won't get them to write." And indeed, I soon recognized that many students were not motivated to learn. As is often the case, *curriculum* was disconnected from *community* and *culture*. From my own experience, I knew that Hip Hop Culture had a firm grasp on most Black American students. In fact, various studies (MME Productions, 1993) conclude that 97 to 98% of Black American students are influenced by Hip Hop Culture. Da Bomb Squad Comprehensive Literacy Development Program was therefore developed to use Hip Hop Culture in educational practice.

Da Bomb! (students chose the title) is a student magazine produced by the sixth graders at Turner Middle School. Some of the goals highlighted in the initial proposal for the magazine were the following:

- To develop skills in desktop publishing and computer literacy
- To develop skills in writing in several forms and styles: raps, poetry, letters, reviews, short stories, essays, fiction, editorials
- To encourage originality and creativity among students
- To expose students to multimedia and Internet resources with the aim of developing research skills
- To obtain formal skills in "standard English" writing, speaking, and communicating
- To use the culture and language of the students to learn various school and life skills

The students, of course, wanted to sell their magazines rather than distribute them for free. (These young kids was *straight paper-chasin*!) This exercise in magazine production also contributed to the development of reading skills, since student-produced magazines are an excellent way to motivate other students to read. In producing the magazine, students engaged in a wide range of literacy activities: hiphopological grammar lessons, oral interviews with peers and members of the Hip Hop community in Philly, polls of the student body about favorite topics in Hip Hop Culture, writing of raps and poems, comparative analysis and message analysis of Hip Hop song lyrics, and written autobiographies and biographies of their favorite Hip Hop artists. I'd like to focus on three classroom exercises in particular that highlight the relationship between knowledge, reality, and education in this discussion. These exercises build on Bankie's comments about the disconnect between the content of his schooling and the reality of his hood. The first exercise is *rappin*:

Rappin

WHY

Why, Why, Why?
Did they have to die?

Why did they have to die today?
I hope, I hope, I hope
They fly away.
Why did they become part of the ground?
All they wanted is to just be down.
Biggie, Biggie, Biggie, what did you do?
2pac, 2pac, 2pac, what's wrong with you?
People are crying
Cause we're all dying
Please stop violence Peace.

This rap was written by a sixth grader. Its subject—untimely death—is one that is all too familiar to young Bloods in Southwest Philly. The passion and the urgent seeking for an answer to life's unanswerable questions ("Why did they have to die today?") can be heard in the student's voice and frequent use of repetition ("Why, Why, Why?"). In the end, the tragic deaths of Biggie and 2pac, two rappers beloved by their community of fans, are related to the larger problem of violence in American society. The last line, "Please stop violence Peace," is deceptively simple. By juxtaposing "violence" and "Peace" in such a manner, the student rapper has illustrated the choice we must make as a society, lest we are forced to write more poems in the shapes of monuments to our young brothers and sisters.

On a literary level, the student is allowed to experiment with spoken language ("Cause" and "All they wanted is to just be down," for example) while creating a powerfully written rap. The next task for the student is to perform the rap in front of the class and to convey the same depth of feeling as in the written form. This is the bridge to oral literacy. The poem is then brought into a word-processing program and is formatted in the shape of a monument to the slain rappers, which promotes computer literacy.

Message Analysis

This exercise deals with a familiar topic for young females—notions of "prettiness" and "ugliness" in society. The student examines the message and the lyrics of TLC's song "Unpretty" and ends up giving advice to other young girls. (Rest in peace to young Lisa "Left Eye" Lopes of TLC, who was killed in a car crash in Honduras in April 2002.) The student's analysis follows

UNPRETTY

The song, "Unpretty" is saying that you should not do what you do not want to do. If you listen to this song you would know what it is about. And if you're insecure because of a man, you should get rid of him and "then get back to you." Just read this part of the song:

Never insecure until I met you
Now I'm in stupid
I used to be so cute to me
Just a little bit skinny
Why do I look to all these things
To keep me happy
Maybe get rid of you and then I'll get back to me

The song "Unpretty" was written as a poem by T-Boz while TLC was making their latest album, *Fanmail.* The song means to me that some people in reality are doing something they do not want to do, but they are doing it because they think it's right, or because their partners want them to do it. If you saw the video, Chili was getting breast implants because her boyfriend wanted her to get them. He thought her breasts were too small. When she got to the hospital she saw a lady getting her breast implants removed. She saw how the other lady was going through a lot of pain, and crying. Chili decided not to get the breast implants because she didn't feel like she needed them. She went home and kicked her boyfriend out, because he wanted her to do something that she did not want to do. If I were in that situation, I would have done the same thing. I hope you would do the same thing, too.

This type of message analysis deals with issues that are not well addressed by American society as a whole. While popular culture sometimes critiques society, Hip Hop Culture has the reputation of being uncompromisingly critical. These songs are an excellent way for students to begin analyzing and interpreting texts and to "put their writing to work" by sending out positive messages to the larger community. In this piece, the student analyzed not only the lyrics, but also the video for the song. Her conclusion is just as clear as her opening statement, in which she declares that "you should not do what you do not want to do."

In the course of this assignment, the student engaged in written literacy and computer literacy. Internet research was required, to dig up facts about the origin of the song. The student also gained valuable interpretive and analytical skills. By writing about a song she loves, she was motivated to do excellent work.

Review

The final example is an excerpt from a song review for Eve's "Love Is Blind." Eve, a rapper from Philly, was the most popular rapper at the time this review was written.

> When I hear the song "Love Is Blind," I think Eve's friend was really blinded by love. I think that Eve was trying to get her friend out of a bad relationship that really wasn't working out. It made me feel very upset that she would stay in an abusive relationship and Eve was being a great friend. And, NO, I wouldn't be in that relationship because I would never let any man put his hands on me.

This review, along with the message analysis above, allows students to make their own moral judgments. By doing this, the teacher is confronting issues with which these students—young as they are—are already familiar. Since these are songs that the students hear every day, we must take the approach that it is better to discuss them intelligently than to bemoan the situation or just hope that it will "go away." If our students come to class discussing issues that are pertinent to their realities, we gotta handle the situation. While we may not be comfortable introducing these topics, we must be prepared to deal with them when they arise.

HIPHOPOGRAPHY: THE ETHNOGRAPHY
OF HIP HOP CULTURE AND COMMUNICATION

When I began teaching high school, I wanted to go beyond using Hip Hop Culture as a motivational strategy for educating students in other subjects. I wanted to introduce Hip Hop Culture as the *subject* of scholarly investigation. This requires a shift in the way we view our students as learners. The present situation in most schools, despite volumes of educational research on the subject, is that teachers don't even recognize that their Black students *bring something* to class. Those who do recognize that fact move quickly towards an eradicationist philosophy, condemning and wiping out any signs of "Blackness" in the name of preparing their students for college and "the real world." Of course, what is cast as "the language of the real world" is the language of the dominating group—let's call it what it is—the variety of English that's consistent with the speech patterns and norms of use of educated, middle-class, White men. As scholars, sometimes we (myself included) allow ourselves to believe that the eradicationist view is a thing of the past and that the additive bidialectical view (adding "standard English" to the language variety that students possess) is the accepted norm. Judging from my own experience in schools, I must say that while the names have changed, the game has remained the same. As educators and scholars, we continue to view the language of Black students only in relation to that *other* variety (the one we call "standard"), rather than treating BL on its own terms. Thus we are reinforcing the same ideology that has stifled and suffocated the language and learning of our students since desegregation.

What would shock most teachers (and most Americans in general) is that when it comes to language, the most studied language variety in the sociolinguistic literature is BL, including its rich and diverse linguistic practices. From the work of sociolinguists, we know that Black discursive practices and modes of discourse are among the most inventive of all languages spoken in the United States (Mitchell-Kernan, 1972; Smitherman, 1977). My own writings examine how the language and linguistic practices of the HHNSC both build upon and expand the African American Oral Tradition. The discursive practices and cultural modes of discourse of the HHNSC—*call and response, multilayered totalizing expression, signifyin* and *bustin (bussin), tonal semantics* and *poetics, narrative sequencing* and *flow, battlin,* and *entering the cipher*—are as creative as they are complex (Alim, 2004a, 2006). With this in mind, I designed and taught a course called "Hiphopography: The Ethnography of Hip Hop Culture and Communication." The class trained students in ethnographic research methods so that they could actively participate in the study of their contemporary culture. Throughout the course, the students and I collected hundreds of hours of audiotaped and videotaped data in order to study the most recent instantiation of Black expressive culture. I'm talkin about Hip Hop Culture. Students cataloged their own lexical items, interviewed their peers and members of the local community, and produced a video documentary presenting a hiphopography of their school and community.

I'd like to share three examples of the students' research findings. These are part of a volume dedicated to the rich description of the language and linguistic practices of their localized HHNSC.

BATTLIN (NOUN)(VERB) AND FLOW (NOUN)(VERB)

Battlin involves more than one person. A **FREESTYLE** rapping contest when a group of people take turns rapping lyrics. They don't write the lyrics; they say them as they think of them off the top of their heads. As they take turns rapping back and forth, they're actually competing. In the end, the judges or the people watching the competition vote who won the competition and who had the better lyrics. Sometimes it is just obvious to the contenders who won by who **DISSED/CLOWNED** the other better.

*Also judged by who had the better meaning behind his/her words.

Example: JT and T-Reezy were battlin in the grass last week; they got on each other. JT got on T-Reezy's braids and face and T-Reezy got on JT about his height and women/girls.

The term comes from the idea of fighting with words. A battle is set up like a fight. One contender takes one side and the other takes the other. They rap at each other (in turn, though) until one *gives up* or a specific winner is announced. Usually done by males—those who tend to be street affiliated. Males talk about guns, women, and **SETS** (areas of affiliation) and other topics. Done at clubs, social events, on street corners, etc. Takes the place of actual fights at parties where people **FLOW**—to have a smooth current of rap lyrics. If a person messes up their rap lyrics while saying them, then they ain't flowin. Flowin does not necessarily have to rhyme, as long as your words go good together.

HUSH MODE AND SCRATCH THAT GREEN OFF YO NECK (PHRASE)

Hush mode is when you get **CLOWNED** (to get talked about rudely) and do not have a remark or comeback for that person. To be dumbfounded. Usually used when instigating or talking about a fight or argument.

Example 1:
AISHA: Shut up, Tee!
TEE: [doesn't say anything]
TEREESE: She got you on hush mode!

When somebody get **CAPPED ON**, and that person don't have anything to come back with, then the person who capped on them would say, "I got you on hush mode."

Example 2:
For example, say Shahira and Bibi are capping on each other and Shahira says to Bibi, "Yo mamma so old she used to gang bang with the Hebrews." If Bibi can't come back with something, then Shahira would say to her, "I got you on hush mode."
While we were defining the word, Jamal got on Tereese nerves and she said she was gon hit him . . .

Example 3:
TEREESE: I'mma bust you in yo mouth.
JAMAL: [silent]
AISHA: Oooh, Jamal, she got you on hush mode.
JAMAL: She ain't got me on hush mode.
TEREESE: I'mma hit you in yo mouth.
JAMAL: I WISH YOU WOULD.

Females use this phrase a lot because they tend to instigate more than males. Males sometimes use it when they want to start something. Someone might tell you to "scratch that green off yo neck" after you been hush moded.

Not sure of the origin of this phrase, but it's used after someone has been proven wrong.

Example 4:
For example, say two people are arguing and one of them got proven wrong, then someone would say to them, "Oooh, scratch that green off yo neck."

ROGUE (NOUN)

A word that people use as a substitute for another person's name. Originated in Sunnyside, California, and mainly used in Sunnyside. JT uses it a lot to say hi to people. "What's up rogue?"

Example 1: Waz up rogue?

Example 2: Dang, rogue, what you doing?!

See **DOGG, HOMIE, PATNA**

Males use it more, but females do often use it. Used by all races in Sunnyside. Used mainly with the younger generation.

Example 3:
Aisha was **CONVERSATIN** with Shahira on the phone and at the end she said, "alright, rogue." Then her mom asked her why they call each other rogue.

HIP HOP CULTURE AS EDUCATIONAL PRACTICE

As hiphopographers, the students create new categories of knowledge and original descriptions, which they gather from the field and from their own life experiences. None of these terms and descriptions have been fully described (most not even discussed) in the scholarly literature. The potential to make a real contribution to the study of Black culture and language lies in the production of new knowledge. Again, this type of learning experience requires that the curriculum be based in the cultural-linguistic reality of the students.

I would like to conclude by making an ideological distinction between a curriculum that is based in the cultural-linguistic reality of the students, and one that is *culturally appropriate, culturally responsive, culturally relevant,* or whatever other term we have produced to describe classroom practices that use the language and culture of the students to teach them part of the "acceptable" curricular canon. As education scholars of color, we often say that we value the linguistic and cultural resources our students bring to school, yet we are only willing to use that wealth of resources to fill them up with "standard English," literary interpretation of some acceptable canon, or some other prescribed academic skill (Jackson, 2006). We gotta go beyond that. Our students are bright enough to know when they bein played. The most state-of-the-art research on the education of linguistically and culturally diverse students may actually be sellin our students short. Why must their language and culture always be used to "take them somewhere else"? *Right here* look good to me. I challenge us to go beyond the clichéd "taking them from where they're at and leading them somewhere else" approach, lest we offer a strawberry-flavored, culturally sensitive pill for our children to swallow, the result of which would ultimately be the same sickness—the devaluation of their language and culture. Such a pill may be easier on the stomach, administered in language that is more palatable, but if real healing is to take place, we must shift the paradigm and turn to our students' abilities and experiences as the sources of knowledge and learning. Like Hip Hop pioneer KRS-One's Temple of Hiphop Kulture is doing with "Refinitions," and like Harvard's Hiphop Archive (now at Stanford) is doing with the Hiphop Community Activism and Education Roundtable, our students can shine as producers and preservers of their own cultural and linguistic knowledge.

An example of this type of linguistic knowledge is found in my analysis of Hip Hop poetics (Alim, 2003), which reveals that Hip Hop artists are not only using the conventional poetic constructions (feminine rhyme, masculine rhyme, end rhyme, and so on), but they are rhyme-travelin far beyond that, using innovative rhyming techniques such as *chain rhymes, back-to-back chain rhymes, compound internal rhymes, primary and secondary internal rhymes,* and polysyllabic rhyme strings of *octuple rhymes* and creating a *multirhyme matrix* unparalleled in American poetics. Rather than using Hip Hop Culture only as a means to cultivate an appreciation for poets such as Chaucer and Shakespeare (or even Amiri Baraka and Sonia Sanchez), why not turn our attention to the study of some of contemporary America's most innovative and inventive poets like Pharoahe Monch, Talib Kweli, Mos Def, Common, and Kanye West, among others? I am not suggesting that conventional bodies of knowledge be dropped from curricula in favor of these new approaches. What I am suggesting is that we need to take the language and culture of the HHNSC seriously enough to offer it as an area of knowledge that is worthy of study in schools. Further, we need to raise our expectations and provide opportunities for our students to be the producers of knowledge rooted in their cultural-linguistic realities.

NOTES

General Note: This chapter is dedicated to Bankie Santana, a good brother who was tryina do right, but like many young Black males, he fell victim to the streets. In 2000, Bankie was shot to death at 7:40 A.M. on the corner of 129th Street and Fifth Avenue in Harlem—only about two weeks after this interview was recorded. (Rest in peace, young homie.) Much respect to the American C.R.E.A.M. Team and the Mighty Wu-Tang Clan. Wu Forever. I'd like to acknowledge my students for their incredible work. Y'all have truly been an inspiration and are the driving force behind my research on teaching. Much respect to the young writers and hiphopographers. I am indebted to the Spencer Foundation for funding portions of this research. Also, thanks to Harvard University's W. E. B. Du Bois Institute for Afro-American Research and the Ford Foundation for sponsoring the historic Hiphop Community Activism and Education Roundtable. Thanks to Marcyliena Morgan, James Peterson, Josef Sorett, Dawn-Elissa Fischer Banks, Lauren Ferguson, Nicole Hodges, Dan McClure, and Kissie Morales.

1. Hip Hop Culture is sometimes defined as having four major elements: MC'ing (rappin), DJ'ing (spinnin records), breakdancing (sometimes known as "streetdancing"), and graffiti art (also known as "writing" or "tagging"). To these four elements, pioneering Hip Hop artist KRS-One adds a fifth—knowledge—and Afrika Bambaataa, founder of the Hip Hop Cultural Movement, would add a sixth, which he calls *overstanding*. Overstanding can be thought of as the ability to read between the lines and arrive at deeper, sometimes hidden meanings. It is a concept frequently used by Rastafarians. It is useful to distinguish between the terms *Hip Hop* and *rap*. Rappin, which is one aspect of Hip Hop Culture, consists of the aesthetic placement of verbal rhymes over musical beats. Hip Hop Culture refers not only to the various elements listed above, but also to the entire range of cultural activity and modes of being that encompass the Hip Hop Culture world. This is why Bloods be sayin, "Hip Hop ain't just music, it's a whole way of life!"

CHAPTER 2

The Ebonics Phenomenon, Language Planning, and the Hegemony of Standard English

Charles E. DeBose

Scholars engaged in the study of marginalized subjects often find themselves having to defend their work, if not their subject matter as a whole, as legitimate and worthy of academic attention. When the subject in question is a language, the work of scholars undertaken on its behalf may be viewed as a case of Language Planning (LP), the term used by linguists to describe deliberate efforts to encourage, discourage, or otherwise change the way language is used in a community. J. A. Fishman (1980) has defined LP as "the authoritative allocation of resources to language," in which the main "resources" at issue are recognition and legitimacy, and the relevant "authorities" include linguists, educators, and politicians. This is a particularly useful perspective for understanding the Ebonics phenomenon, by which I refer not only to the famous Ebonics Resolution of the Oakland School Board, but also to the academic scholarship on African American Language (AAL) out of which it grew (DeBose, 2005, pp. 56-57). Although scholars of AAL have acted with varying degrees of intention and consciousness as agents of language planning, their behavior nevertheless qualifies as LP, to the extent that they promote claims that are contrary to established social meaning.

Baugh (2000a) makes reference to the fact that "all human languages and dialects are equal in the eyes of science, even if they are not considered to be equal in the eyes of the law," and he cites his own personal need "to inform others" of that fact (p. 115). But the linguistic claim he invokes—that all language is systematic and rule governed—goes against the widely held pejorative view of varieties such as AAL, a view that much of society accepts as self-evident truth. To that extent, such a claim is *counterfactive*. Baugh is not alone in this regard, as we will see. In the ongoing debate on AAL, this is but one example we could cite of counterfactitive academic claims, and related efforts to defend and promote them, that fall under the rubric of LP.

One of the most important keys to understanding LP in education is the notion of the hegemony of standard English. Gramsci (1971) defines *hegemony* as a function of "civil society," and as one of two ways in which the dominant social group maintains its position—the other way being "direct domination." (p. 12) In other words, in addition to being carried out through the coercive means of state power employed by ruling groups to maintain control over society, hegemony is exercised through ideas, attitudes, myths, and values, and these are perpetuated through education and socialization. Hegemonic ideas and values therefore function to give legitimacy to the existing social order by providing justifications for inequalities in the distribution of social goods. In the realm of lifestyle and culture, the customs and practices of elite groups come to symbolize the benefits of membership in the elite and to serve as desirable attainments for persons striving toward elite status. When a particular language or way of speaking is associated with the elite, the ability to speak that language and speak it "correctly" may serve a legitimating function. That is, the superior position of the dominant group is justified by its "proper" speech. Similarly, the subordinate position of marginalized groups is legitimated by the characterization of their language in such pejorative terms as *poor, slovenly, broken, bastardized,* or *corrupt.*

Another variable relevant to the study of stigmatized/marginalized languages is the *social location* of the investigator vis-à-vis the subject matter under investigation (DeBose, 2005). African American linguistics emerged at a time when the nation was embroiled in monumental conflict over the civil and human rights of persons of African descent. The underrepresentation of African Americans in academia, and in linguistics in particular, produced common situations in which European American "experts" interacted with African American communities and individuals in asymmetrical relationships of Researcher-to-Informant, Principal Investigator-to-Research Assistant, and so forth. A good example of such collaboration is described by Labov (1972) in the introduction to *Language in the Inner City:*

> In our own group competence is divided between white researchers (Labov and Cohen) who are primarily linguists and outsiders to the vernacular culture, and Black researchers (Robins and Lewis) who know the culture of the inner city as full participants and share a deep understanding of it, but who remain relative outsiders to linguistic theory. (p. xiv)

Labov goes on to state his hope for a time when there will be more "linguists from the community" and the potential benefits to be derived from such a state of affairs.

As things turned out, and sooner than Labov may have expected, persons from the Black community did inject their voices into the rising debate on the nature of AAL and its implications for educational and public policy. A significant number of those voices were critical of existing AAL research. Some of those who began to speak out were linguists, but many hailed from other disciplines, such as psychology, education, speech communication, and Black studies. A pivotal event in the emergence of these critical African American voices was a caucus that occurred at a conference, "Cognitive and Language Development of the Black Child," held in St. Louis in January 1973—the same conference where the term *Ebonics* was first used. According to Robert L. Williams (1975):

> A significant incident occurred at the conference. The Black conferees were so critical of the work on the subject done by white researchers, many of whom happened to be present, that they decided to caucus among themselves and define Black language from a Black perspective. (p. ii)

The "white researchers" whose work was the target of criticism included linguists who made early contributions to the academic study of AAL. Such linguists might be regarded collectively for our purposes as *orthodox scholars*, while their counterparts—the "Black conferees" Williams mentions—could be termed *Ebonics scholars*. It is important to point out that the term *orthodox* is not used here as a synonym for *White*; I acknowledge the orthodox orientation of the work of a significant and growing number of scholars of African descent. Rather, these two categories should be understood as ideal types, representative of a tension in the field of AAL studies that affects different scholars in different ways. Nor are these types mutually exclusive. While there are important differences between what I call orthodox scholars, grouping them together provisionally as a school of thought is justified by their consensus on several important issues; and whatever differences exist between them are relatively minor compared with the various and divergent positions taken on those same important issues by Ebonics scholars.

Notwithstanding the idealized nature of these two camps, the theoretical disagreements that divide them are real and easily observed. One of the most fundamental disagreements is in how to define the primary object of study. For orthodox scholars, the conversation centers around a distinctively African American *linguistic system*. For Ebonicists, however, interest is focused on distinctively African American *ways of speaking*.

Some definitions may help illustrate this contrast. According to Stewart, a linguistic system is a "language-like [code]" with an appreciable amount of "structural stability, social spread, and consistency of usage." Under varying sociohistorical conditions, a linguistic system may occur as one of several distinct types, including *standard, vernacular, creole,* and *pidgin,* depending on the presence or absence of such attributes as "standardization," "autonomy," "historicity," and "vitality" (Stewart, 1968, pp. 533–537). The term *linguistic system* therefore facilitates discussion of a linguistic code at an abstract level, focusing on its grammatical structure, or *corpus*, independently of its sociohistorical *status*.

Contrast this with ways of speaking, which Gumperz and Hymes (1972) designate as a key concept of "the Ethnography of Communication." According to Hymes, "[R]ules of speaking are the ways in which speakers associate particular modes of speaking, topics or message forms with particular settings and activities" (p. 36). Hymes (1972) makes the following comment about incorporating such situational and social factors into the study of AAL:

> Recent work with Afro-American speech groups in the urban United States highlights the importance of these distinctions. Linguistically, urban Afro-American dialects . . . do not differ greatly from standard English. Yet Afro-American speakers differ radically from their white neighbors by the cultural emphasis they place on speech acts such as "signifying," "sounding," "toasts," etc. (pp. 36–37)

We have from the outset, therefore, two essentially different conceptions of the primary object of study: a language in the abstract, versus a language in its various social contexts. But the differences between orthodox and Ebonics scholars do not end there. Rather, their differing positions on this one issue inform how they perceive related issues, as reflected in their contrasting responses on what the language variety in question should be called and how it should be classified typologically. Their answers to these questions offer fundamental insights into the Ebonics phenomenon and how it relates to LP. Before going on, however, we should examine two important aspects of LP in AAL studies that are closely intertwined with the preceding notion of the hegemony of standard English: corpus planning and status planning.

CORPUS PLANNING

Most Americans perceive AAL as "bad English" and indicative of the failure or inability to produce "grammatical" language. Consequently, efforts to describe its grammatical structure qualify as LP to the extent that they claim that the object under study *has* grammatical structure. The mere assertion that AAL is a linguistics system of any type is counterfactitive and tends to be rejected by the linguistically uninformed, unless the case is stated effectively. Making that case is a form of *corpus planning*, the process of developing and codifying a language's resources so that it serves as a fully functional and acceptable mode of communication.

The most common strategy that linguists have employed for convincing lay audiences of AAL's grammatical structure has been to present detailed lists of features, grouped by level of analysis (Fasold & Wolfram, 1975). Such lists often include user-friendly ways of exemplifying the features, such as sets of words that AAL speakers pronounce as homonyms (Labov, 1972, pp. 3–20). In my own experience speaking before lay audiences, I have tried to demonstrate the systematicity of AAL by saying that "when we talk that way, we don't be messin up, we be followin rules." It usually gets a laugh, if nothing else. It also moves the discussion to a point where I can make a more substantive illustration of the novel idea for many persons that AAL "sho nuff do have a grammar." I often quote a line that children in the neighborhood where I grew up used when playing hide-and-seek to affirm that all were hid: "Ma mamma, yo mamma, hangin out clothes; ma mamma hit yo mamma in the nose. Did it hurt?"

I use the possessive pronouns /ma/ "my" and /yo/ "your" in the jingle to illustrate the entire paradigm of AAL possessive pronouns, shown in Table 2.1.

In the past few years contributions have begun to appear that describe AAL as a coherent system. Lisa Green's work (1993, 1995) is a case in point. Green uses a Government and Binding framework to describe how the aspect markers *be, done, bin* and *bin done* function in the AAL verb system. This represents a growing acceptance of formal methods of linguistic description that admit data derived from native speaker intuitions as well as empirical data.

The structural features of AAL, which are the central preoccupation of orthodox scholars, are of comparatively little interest in Ebonics scholarship, where the focus is on levels of culture and communication at which the finer points of grammar play only a minor part. When Ebonics scholars do call attention to structural details of AAL, it is often for the purpose of highlighting features that are claimed to be of African origin (e.g., DeBose & Faaraclas, 1993; Morgan, 1993; Smith, 1998; Williams, S., 1993). However, as we will see, the way in which we characterize the corpus or grammatical structure of a language has direct implications on how we characterize its relative status in comparison to other languages. A decision to describe AAL as a list of features that diverge from standard English is congruent with a decision to classify it as a nonautonomous variety of English (that is, a dialect or vernacular). Likewise, the use of an autonomous grammar (DeBose, 1992) to account for the same divergences is congruent with the claim that AAL is a separate linguistic system. And the identification of Africanisms in the present-day structure and use of AAL is congruent with efforts of Ebonics scholars to classify it genetically as an African language. The choices involved in conferring a recognized status on a language are part of the process known as *status planning*.

Table 2.1. AAL Possessive Pronouns

	Singular	*Plural*
First Person	my /ma/	our
Second Person	your /yo/	y'all
Third Person	his, her, its /is/	they

STATUS PLANNING

Given the prevalent popular conception of AAL as "bad English," the mere act of naming it is a form of recognition, and qualifies to that extent as status planning. The particular names chosen often imply decisions about the typological classification of AAL as either a dialect or a language. African American language studies began to coalesce as a field at a time when Black Americans were shifting in increasing numbers from a preference for being called "Negro" to a preference for the term *Black*. A reflection of this change can be seen in the use of terms such as *Negro Dialect* and *Nonstandard Negro English* in earlier works on AAL, terms that have since lost currency.

A variety of terms have been used that include the word *Black*, together with *dialect, English, vernacular*, or *language*, in one combination or another. The inclusion of *English* in the name has profound symbolic meaning in the context of the struggle of African Americans for liberation from the subordinate status imposed on them by American society (DeBose, 2005, pp. 78–79). The term *Ebonics* emerged in response to the need for an Afrocentric term that avoids the undesirable connotations of *English*, while at the same time implying the status of a separate language. Note the definition of Ebonics that emerged from the 1973 caucus:

> Ebonics may be defined as the linguistic and paralinguistic features which on a concentric continuum represent the communicative competence of the West African, Caribbean, and United States slave descendants of African origin. It includes the various idioms, patois, argots, ideolects, and social dialects of Black people. (Williams, 1975, p. vi)

The term *U.S. Ebonics* (Smitherman, 2000) refers specifically to the variety of Ebonics spoken by persons of African descent in the United States. Although not explicitly stated in the official definition, *U.S. Ebonics* implies a language variety that combines surface features of Anglo English with deep-structural influences of West African languages. Smitherman (2000) makes this African influence explicit:

U.S. Ebonics refers to those language patterns and communication styles that

1. are derived from Niger-Congo (African) languages; and/or
2. are derived from Creole languages of the Caribbean; and/or
3. are derived from the linguistic interaction of English and African languages, creating a language related to but not directly the same as either English or West African languages. (p. 20)

The term *African American Language* (AAL) also avoids the symbolic sense of subordination to English, and is preferred by some scholars. A resolution approved by the Committee of Linguists of African Descent (CLAD) in the wake of the Ebonics Resolution expressed the consensus of the group on a number of points regarding the nature, history, and educational implications of AAL, but the group was unable to reach a consensus on what it should be called. Elsewhere, I have used *Variety X* as a neutral term for AAL, in recognition of the continuing variation in the preferred scholarly terminology (DeBose, 2001b, 2005).

The tendency of orthodox scholars to choose a name for AAL that includes the word *English* reflects a preference for classifying it typologically as a dialect of English, rather than as a separate language. To justify this preference, orthodox scholars often cite several generally accepted linguistic criteria that have long been used for determining whether a variety is a language or dialect (namely, speakers' attitudes, mutual intelligibility, a language having "its own army and navy").

Smitherman (2000) reflects an awareness of the role of hegemony in this issue when she asserts that the question of whether Ebonics "is a language or a dialect is not one that can be definitively answered by linguistics. Ultimately, this is a political, not a linguistic question." Smitherman further comments on how she "started using the term 'language' rather than 'dialect' . . . [s]omewhere around the mid-1970s." She explains her reasoning by noting that although the term *dialect* "is perfectly respectable among linguists . . . it has gotten a bad rap among the public and is almost always used in a pejorative sense." She further explains, "Because of this negative public view of anything called a 'dialect,' many linguists started using the term 'variety'" (2000, p. 14). Smitherman's observation provides an occasion to comment on the socially constructed nature of reality. Statements such as "A language is a dialect with an army and navy," and "Norwegian and Danish are different languages because the speakers say so," are informal ways of saying that the concepts *dialect* and *language* are social constructs themselves; they are the product of politics, education, socialization, advertising, and public relations. So, one could add, are the concepts of *standard* and *nonstandard* English.

LANGUAGE IN EDUCATION PLANNING

On the subject of language in education planning (Wiley, 1996, p. 130), the contrasting approaches of AAL scholars are reflected in a threefold typology of policy options: *suppression, limited recognition,* and *full recognition* (DeBose, 2005, p. 40; Van Keulen, Weddington, & DeBose, 1998, pp. xvi–vxiii). The traditional policy of suppression consists of ideas and values that are part of the established hegemonic system and therefore embedded in the everyday experiences that society takes for granted. As such, suppression represents the status quo, whereas the other two options represent counterfactitive claims of academics and visionaries.

The proposal of the Oakland School Board to recognize Ebonics as a language in its own right flew in the face of the traditional view of Ebonics as substandard English, a characterization supported by the educational establishment but challenged by linguistic theory. At the height of the Ebonics controversy, voices could be heard vigorously advocating all three of the above-mentioned policy options through their answers to the question, Should Ebonics be allowed in the classroom? A *yes* answer indicated support for full recognition of AAL. The majority of those answering *no* favored suppression, based on what was for them the self-evident truth—namely, that "bad," "incorrect," "ungrammatical," "substandard," or "slang" English *ain got no business in nobody's classroom.* Some of those who answered *no,* however, did so from an informed perspective—recognizing that AAL is valid, according to linguistic theory, but hesitating to support anything more than limited recognition.

The policy of limited recognition differs from the policy of suppression in that it rejects the traditional pejorative characterization of AAL and insists on recognizing it as a systematic and rule-governed variety of English, albeit subordinate to standard English. A good example of this position is a statement made by Robbins Burling in his book *English in Black and White.* Burling (1973) explains why he cannot support the option of "full acceptance":

> The policy of full acceptance of the dialect should appeal to our sense of democracy. We may feel that each man should be allowed to speak in his own way and that no child should be handicapped by having to divert his attention from other subjects while coping with a new spoken style. But the dangers of this policy are obvious. It is doubtful that even the most splendidly educated young man or woman will find employment if he [or she] continues to speak the language of the Black ghetto, and many educators argue that the practical if unjust world demands the standard dialect. (p. 132)

The option for which Burling settles is to "encourage bidialectalism." This is the same policy preference of many practicing linguists, and while I lack hard data, my sense as a participant in the field is that it represents the consensus of orthodox scholars. An underlying premise of the policy is that the inability to express oneself in anything but AAL is tantamount to a handicap, limiting one's capacity for effective communication. The remedy for such a handicap, according to advocates of this view, is the acquisition of standard English as a medium of wider communication, while maintaining AAL for in-group use.

Burling's reference to "the practical if unjust world" is an informal acquiescence to the hegemony of standard English (DeBose, 2005, pp. 20, 41). In other words, while all dialects are equal in theory, some dialects are more equal than others. The policy of limited recognition may be rightly criticized for the manner in which it uses the notion of a "less equal dialect" to legitimate the hegemony of standard English. The terms *dialect* and *vernacular* used in this way are nothing more than euphemisms for *nonstandard*. Limited recognition differs from suppression mainly in that it recognizes AAL for the limited purpose of training teachers to teach standard English in a manner that reflects the current state of linguistic knowledge.

Modifying current practices in standard English instruction to accommodate AAL speakers is one of the most pervasive orthodox approaches to language in education planning. A great deal of work in this area has involved the development of materials, workshops, and seminars for teacher training. Teachers are given information about AAL with the aim of facilitating a change of attitude from devaluing it to recognizing it as just different.

A legal precedent for limited recognition exists in the landmark court case known as the *King v. Ann Arbor* Black English decision (Chambers, 1983), which recognized Black English as a "home and community language," while designating standard English as the language of "the school, the commercial world, the arts, the sciences, and the professions." *King* explicitly affirmed the responsibility of teachers to teach in a manner that is informed by linguistic knowledge, citing "The failure of the defendant Board to provide leadership and help for its teachers in learning about the existence of 'Black English' . . . and to suggest to those same teachers ways and means of using that knowledge" (Bailey, 1983, p. 2).

Two interesting projects proposed by orthodox scholars during the 1960s combined elements of both limited recognition and full recognition. The first of these was a proposal to adapt foreign-language teaching methods to the teaching of standard English as a second dialect to AAL speakers (Stewart, 1967). The second proposal recommended the use of texts written in AAL (so-called dialect readers) to teach initial reading skills to AAL speakers (Baratz & Shuy, 1969; Rickford & Rickford, 1995). In their efforts to promote bidialectalism, both projects conform to the policy of limited recognition. But in their acceptance of AAL as a modern, functional language of instruction, they come close to full recognition.

The policy of full recognition is marked by its logical consistency. Given the tendency among linguists to reject the pejorative status imposed upon AAL by society, the most consistent response to the question of what to do about it is expressed in the folk adage "If it ain't broke, don't fix it."(DeBose, 2005, p. 40) In my own advocacy of a policy of full recognition, I sometimes break it down to the colloquial imperative "Don't mess wit my language, cause it ain nothin wrong wit it." After stating my position, I am quick to clarify that while I favor such a policy, I realize that there are serious political obstacles to its implementation.

I readily support the goal of standard English literacy for all students, although not for the same reasons as those advanced by advocates of suppression. I do not believe in the superiority of standard English. I do believe that AAL speakers have the option of using standard English as a tool of survival, if they so choose, and I continue to insist, "Ain nothing wrong wit my language." The question we should be asking, I believe, is whether oral proficiency in standard English is a prerequisite to written proficiency. And related to that, what degree of mastery of standard English should be expected of students for specific purposes such as grade promotion, graduation, and admission to college?

As an advocate of full recognition, I prefer to characterize AAL as a language in its own right, and I support its use not only in the Black community and the performing arts, but in the classroom as well. The above-mentioned projects for teaching standard English as a second language to AAL speakers imply a status in the classroom for AAL equal to that of recognized minority languages such as Spanish or Vietnamese. Be that as it may, a frequently cited reason for the failure of such projects to catch on is the unenthusiastic support they have received from the Black community.

Although none of the articles in Williams's *Ebonics* (1975) explicitly advocates a policy of full recognition of AAL, several are highly critical of specific features of the policy of limited recognition. Sims (1975) offers a candid Black perspective on the dialect readers proposal. She cites a passage from what she describes as "a set of experimental readers designed to teach beginning reading to speakers of Black dialect" and notes how the text is laden with stereotypes about "disadvantaged" Black families. She notes how the family in one story "has seven children—no father—and is headed by two women." She further observes that "Ollie and Leroy and their friends play in the city streets. Neither Big Momma nor their mothers ever refer to the boys as anything other than 'Boy.' Big Sister La Verne is afraid of water bugs, but 'La Verne she ain't scared of no roach'" (p. 22).

Sims takes issue not only with the proposal of using dialect readers, but also with the underlying idea that oral proficiency in standard English is a prerequisite to school achievement. She calls attention to the difference between "*receptive* and *productive* language processes" and to the ability to use both successfully. "Since reading is a receptive process," Sims argues, "a reader does not need to be able to speak a dialect in order to read it. That is, a speaker of Black dialect can learn to read standard English without becoming a speaker of standard English" (p. 24).

Orlando Taylor (1975) departs from the usual view of AAL as nonstandard English by defining Black English as "the totality of language used in the Black community" (p. 34). According to this definition, both standard and nonstandard varieties are included in the "totality," and "there is no longer a choice to be made between Black and Standard English" (p. 35). Taylor's model is consistent with the linguistic principle of the equality of dialects. Speakers of any dialect of American English have the option of stylistically varying their speech to a more or less formal, more or less intimate register, including a standard register. It follows that both nonstandard and standard features may occur in the speech of any dialect.

Another noteworthy aspect of Taylor's article is its use of empirical data to describe the social reality of language as experienced by members of the Black community. One trend that emerges clearly is a conservative attitude among Black parents regarding the role of AAL in the classroom. Taylor's data show that the hegemony of standard English has much the same effect on the Black community as it does on other segments of society. Another important finding in Taylor's work is the high degree of bidialectalism already prevalent among Black students, as suggested by a 76% positive response rate to the question "Can you switch dialects easily?" (Taylor, 1975, p. 36).

Ernie Smith (1975) provides an intimately personal account of being treated in school as though he had a cultural or verbal deficit. Recalling his early elementary school experiences, Smith reports, "I was confronted with the fact that my language was different and that this difference was perceived as a 'deficiency' which needed to be corrected." Smith describes the way school officials demeaned his language ability in his presence:

> Often during Parent-Teacher Conferences or at Open House Conferences, my teachers were not hesitant to suggest to my parents, and to parents of other children, that we should be assigned to the school speech clinic for speech therapy or to the school psychologist for a diagnostic examination, and treatment for possible congenital mental disorders. (p. 77)

Smith goes on to describe how he developed street knowledge of such traditional Black ways of speaking as "jeffin" and "game whoopin." (p. 80) He also recounts how, encouraged by mentors in the Nation of Islam, he eventually became adept at public speaking and worked as a political activist before earning a graduate degree in linguistics and becoming a contributor to Ebonics scholarship.

Smith's account illustrates well how most inequalities are not the result of coercive state power so much as the effect of hegemonic ideas. Many of the racist laws and rationales that once served to justify the subordination of Black Americans have since been overturned and discredited. Moreover, African Americans themselves have debunked hegemonic ideas through personal achievement, financial success, religious piety, scholarship, and artistic greatness. And yet one idea that Americans still hold dear, and that many Black people still buy into, is the superiority of standard English over other varieties.

The amazing public reaction to the Oakland Ebonics resolution was a sobering reminder of the power of this one hegemonic idea. It is a power that linguists understand almost instinctively, powerful enough to intimidate all but the most foolhardy into giving quiescent lip service to the equality of dialects tempered by the double-talk that some dialects are more equal than others. Only those who have nothing to lose are likely to find ways of mounting a sustained challenge to the hegemony of standard English.

The Ebonics scholarship discussed above represents unusually clear and critical thinking on the subject. In the years since these ideas first began appearing in print, models of classroom teaching have emerged based on philosophical principles and pedagogical approaches developed by Ebonics scholars and true to the wording of the original Ebonics resolution. These models explicitly recognize Ebonics as a language in its own right, with "West and Niger Congo African" roots (Baugh, 2000a, p. 39). What is most distinctive about Ebonics-based instruction, however, is that Ebonics is just one component of a comprehensive curriculum designed to connect the experiences students bring from home with aspects of African and African American history and culture. This Afrocentric curriculum may be seen as part of a larger goal of Ebonics scholarship: to contribute to the struggle for African American liberation in a way that promotes a counterhegemonic system of meaning that is embedded in African American culture (Baer & Singer, 1992). Such a system invokes solidarity between African Americans and persons of African descent throughout the Diaspora, calling attention to cultural and linguistic commonalities that symbolize the ideal of unity.

UNRESOLVED ISSUES: WHERE DO WE GO FROM HERE?

The different and often conflicting positions scholars have taken in the study of AAL, and in promoting educational success for its speakers, highlights an important fact: Certain fundamental issues must be resolved before any degree of societal recognition for AAL can be achieved. At the level of corpus planning, what Labov (1972) said more than 30 years ago still holds true: "The definitive grammar of BEV [Black English Vernacular] has not been written" (p. xiv). There is little hope of getting the general public to accept the claim of linguists that AAL speakers "be followin rules" if linguists themselves can't agree what the rules are. At the level of status planning, the issue of whether AAL is an autonomous system or a variety of English remains unresolved. Moreover, any resolution must acknowledge that terms such as *nonstandard, dialect,* and *vernacular,* which are value neutral in technical linguistic usage, have pejorative connotations in everyday usage. A small step in the right direction might be to follow Smitherman in opting for the more neutral term *variety,* allowing for critical discourse to continue regardless of whether we consider it English or not.

In the area of language in education planning, we need to reconsider the idea of pushing "bidialectalism" as a palliative for the education of Black students. We are sending mixed messages by saying that there is nothing wrong with AAL, while at the same time implying that it is not good enough for the academy or the world of work. When we affirm the utilitarian value of speaking standard English, and when we advocate access to standard English proficiency for all, we should also be sure to affirm the rights of speakers of all language varieties to speak them with pride and assurance.

CHAPTER 3

Developing Academic English for Standard English Learners

Noma LeMoine and Sharroky Hollie

In 1977, the year that I (Noma LeMoine) completed my master's degree in language and speech pathology, I was in my 3rd year with the Los Angeles Unified School District (LAUSD) as an itinerant speech and language specialist and had served one year as a diagnostic specialist identifying students with speech and language pathologies. The students I encountered in my work and my experiences in special education classrooms had caused me to reflect on the role of language in placement decisions. I screened hundreds of students who clearly had no language pathology yet had referrals from teachers and psychologists. They were speakers of African American Language (AAL). I began to wonder whether educators were confusing language difference with language pathology, and to what degree language difference might be affecting scores on IQ tests and other standardized examinations.

That same year, Geneva Smitherman's *Talkin and Testifyin: The Language of Black America* hit the streets. Who was this woman whose words flowed like honey, sweet and thick with cultural essence? Smitherman had the gift of framing the most complex linguistic concepts with ease, and in the next sentence transposing the conversation to a *"Whats up, girl, you gittin this?"* discourse style that reminded me of all that was good in my world. This book, and the many that Smitherman wrote afterward, were key in laying the foundation for our work in the LAUSD with students for whom Standard American English (SAE) is not native.

When I completed a second master's degree, this one in education, the work of Smitherman again inspired my thesis, "The Design and Development of an Instructional Model for Facilitating Standard English Mastery in African American Speakers of Non-Standard Language." I had no idea that several years later I would have the opportunity to revisit this design and develop a program to address the language and literacy needs of more than 94,000 African American students in the LAUSD. That program would come to be known as the Academic English Mastery Program (AEMP).

ACADEMIC ENGLISH MASTERY PROGRAM

AEMP is a response to the 1988 LAUSD study titled *The Children Can No Longer Wait: An Action Plan to End Low Achievement and Establish Educational Excellence*. This study called for instruction appropriate to the specific language needs of students with limited proficiency in SAE and for staff development on topics that "come directly from the needs of students [and] teachers, which address both the content (what) and the process (how) of teaching." AEMP currently serves more than 50 schools, thousands of teachers, and tens of thousands of students—including African Americans, Mexican Americans, Hawaiian Americans, and Native Americans—referred to in the program as Standard English Learners (SELs).

The AEMP program is designed to infuse curricula with research-based strategies that facilitate the acquisition of SAE in its oral and written forms, while concomitantly validating the home language and culture of the students. The primary goal is for students to use SAE proficiently and, in the process, experience increased, enriching literacy opportunities and greater academic achievement (LeMoine & LAUSD, 1999). AEMP's rationale is that too many minority students are failing in American schools, interned in classrooms where their language is devalued and where teachers' low expectations and limited understanding of their language and culture hamper their achievement. Many minority students arrive at school speaking a language different from the language of instruction. How teachers respond to this linguistic diversity in the classroom has significant implications for students' academic success.

PROFESSIONAL DEVELOPMENT

The professional development component of the AEMP involves a weeklong summer institute, an educational seminar series, intersession courses, demonstration lessons, and a weekend professional development conference. Each of these activities is intended to increase teachers' knowledge about linguistic research and effective instructional strategies that have been shown to help SELs achieve positive outcomes. More positive outcomes, in turn, create more positive attitudes toward nonstandard languages (NSLs).

During the summer institute, teachers receive in-depth knowledge about linguistic research, culturally responsive pedagogy, and the best literacy practices. Teachers work in small groups to develop lessons and observe demonstration lessons in language development and literacy acquisition.

During the school year, the AEMP Educational Seminar Series is aimed at new teachers, paraeducators, and parents. Similar to the summer institute, the seminars focus on using appropriate methodologies for fostering language, literacy, and learning in students who speak NSLs. There are four seminar topics. The first provides information on the historical development and linguistic features of AAL, Chicano English, Hawaiian Pidgin English, and Native American dialects, as important links to facilitating mastery of SAE. The second seminar introduces teachers to six research-based approaches to the acquisition of school-based literacy. The third seminar provides information on the culture, learning styles, and strengths of students for whom SAE is not native, emphasizing the development of critical thinking skills and mastery of subject matter content. Finally, the last seminar focuses on the infusion of the history and culture of SELs into the curriculum. Teachers learn how to use culturally responsive pedagogy to incorporate knowledge about the civilizations and cultural contributions of Africa, Mexico, Hawaii, and the precolonial United States into their work.

The culminating event for AEMP's professional development component is the annual weekend conference for K–12 educators, administrators, and parents. Attendees have the opportunity to participate in workshops led by the best classroom practitioners in AEMP. Conference participants attend seminars featuring nationally recognized experts in language, literacy, and learning. The conference also offers opportunities to preview and purchase instructional resources and materials, including culturally relevant literature for children, educational software, videos, cultural art and artifacts, posters, and games. These professional development efforts translate into increased knowledge and instructional improvement.

VALIDATED KNOWLEDGE: SIX CRITICAL INSTRUCTIONAL APPROACHES

Each part of AEMP's professional development component revolves around one of six well-developed, research-based instructional approaches: (1) building teachers' knowledge and linguistic awareness about NSLs; (2) using second-language acquisition methodology to facilitate acquisition of the language of school; (3) infusing linguistic information into daily instruction; (4) incorporating a balanced approach to literacy, cultural awareness, and infusion; (5) building on learning styles and strengths of SELs to support learning; and (6) encouraging culturally responsive pedagogy and the infusion of students' history and culture into the curriculum. AEMP teachers develop their instruction around these six approaches as they focus on the cultural and linguistic needs of SELs.

Of the six approaches listed above, linguistic awareness and infusion is the most crucial (Adger, Christian, & Taylor, 1999). NSL speakers must come to understand that their home language and the language of school are not the same. As students learn to recognize the sometimes subtle differences between standard and NSL forms, they become better able to edit their writing for differences in grammar, syntax, and vocabulary and to use SAE structure proficiently in its oral and written forms.

Second-language acquisition methodologies speak to the fallacy that the structure of NSLs directly mirrors that of SAE (Peitzman & Gadda, 1991). Teachers must recognize that the existence of vocabulary common to both NSLs and SAE often veils the complex phonological, syntactical, and pragmatic differences between the languages and masks the difficulties that SELs have with SAE forms. These "language differences" call for the use of second-language acquisition methods or specially designed academic instruction to support SELs' access to academic content.

A balanced approach to literacy (Au, Carroll, & Scheu, 1997) involves the provision and use of instructional strategies geared toward SELs. In some instances this may mean emphasizing phonemic awareness and phonological principles, while in other cases it might involve using a meaning-construction approach. The important thing is to view "balanced" in terms of what is skill-level appropriate and needed by the learner. For example, phonics must be taught in the context of the child's language (the sound system that he or she hears ordinarily and uses every day) as well as in the context of the target language. Consider how, for some speakers of AAL, the interdental fricative *-th* in words such as *birthday* is pronounced as the labiodental fricative *–f,* as in *birfday*. Some speakers of AAL, like many speakers of West African languages, do not possess the interdental fricative *–th*.

Teachers of SELs should become familiar with the learning styles and strengths that these students bring to the classroom. Hilliard (1999) has empirically defined the learning styles of African and African American students. He found that African American students view their environment as a whole rather than in isolated parts; prefer intuitive rather than deductive or inductive reasoning; approximate concepts of number, time, and space; attend to people stimuli rather than object stimuli; and rely on nonverbal as well as verbal communication. However, African American students, he contends, are asked to function in a European-centered cultural style. The differences between the learning and behavioral styles of SELs and the style preferred by teachers often contribute to lowered expectations on the part of educators, resulting in lowered academic performance by the students.

Cultural awareness and infusion is defined as a pedagogy that empowers students intellectually, socially, emotionally, and politically by using cultural and historical referents to convey knowledge, impart skills, and change attitudes (Ladson-Billings, 1994). Ladson-Billings reports that teachers practicing culturally relevant teaching know how to support learning by consciously creating social interactions to help them meet the criteria of academic success, cultural competence, and critical consciousness. Teachers must develop culturally consistent ways of interacting with students from cultures different from their own, and they must learn to adapt instruction so that SELs are accepted and accommodated in the classroom.

A final and often forgotten area of importance is the classroom learning environment. Understanding the environment-behavior relationship enables teachers to organize and equip the classroom so that successful literacy behaviors are likely to occur. All arranged environments influence learning behavior. The placement of furniture, the selection of learning materials, and even the arrangement of those materials can all send strong messages that encourage students to act in particular ways. SELs thrive in environments that stimulate verbal conversations and language acquisition. The practice of surrounding students with an environment rife with language-rich symbols and print is well founded. In summary of AEMP, Smitherman (1999) wrote:

> By far the most concentrated and comprehensive classroom practices embracing a philosophy of multilingualism are those in . . . [AEMP]. Since 1991, [AEMP], designed for grades K–8, has used a historical, linguistic, cultural approach, and a philosophy of additive bilingualism to teach language and literacy skills to students whose primary language is Ebonics. (p. 12)

Smitherman's work has also greatly influenced AEMP's efforts in two other areas: teachers' attitudes toward SELs, and writing instruction in the AEMP classroom.

TEACHER ATTITUDES

According to Smitherman (2000), "Language is the foundation stone of education and the medium of instruction in all subjects and disciplines throughout schooling. It is critical that teachers have an understanding of and appreciation for the language students bring to school" (p. 119). In other words, a teacher's attitude determines his or her altitude and the level of success students achieve in the classroom. Smitherman, like many others, recognizes that inadequate language and literacy instruction for African American students is pervasive throughout the entire educational system. Most English teachers working with SELs, particularly those working with African American students, fail to acknowledge AAL as legitimate and harbor negative attitudes toward the students' language. This attitude in turn leads to negative expectations and negative outcomes for the students. Smitherman (2000) maintains, "Negative language attitudes are directed toward the 'Blackness' of Black English: The attitudes and the language itself are the consequences of the historical operations of racism in the United States." (p. 143). Negative societal attitudes toward AAL have been widely documented (Baugh, 1999b; Bowie & Bond, 1994, Bronstein, Dubner, Lee, & Raphael, 1970; Guskin, 1970; Meier, 1999; Smitherman, 1977; H. Taylor, 1991; Wolfram, 1999). Baugh (1999b) confirms the persistence of negative attitudes toward AAL when he reports that many of the student teachers at Stanford University harbor linguistic and racial stereotypes about low-income and minority students. The most pronounced evidence of this negative attitude, Baugh reports, comes in the form of student teacher comments about African American students as "incapable and linguistically incoherent" (p. 89).

Cummins (1989) speaks to the impact of negative teacher attitudes on student performance. He maintains that the educational experience of minority students is a direct consequence of how teachers define themselves in relation to minority communities. Teachers who devalue the language, culture, and experiences of minority students convey messages that hurt the students' classroom performance. Likewise, Fairchild and Edwards-Evans (1990) write that "teachers who expect failure, typically demand less, provide less information and feedback, and generally engage in conscious and unconscious behaviors that produce failure" (p. 78).

Janet Taylor (1983) found that speakers of AAL were rated lower in reading comprehension than SAE speakers with equivalent reading skills when teachers held negative attitudes toward AAL. Her data revealed a 95% probability that teachers with negative attitudes will evaluate readers differently on the basis of the speech variety used during oral reading. Hanni Taylor (1991) reports a similar finding, following a study of college English teachers interacting with African American students:

> The dialect of Black students often interferes with the standard English expectation of the other writing teachers on campus. . . . [T]he student's use of grammatical, lexical, or phonological forms that although habitually used in Black English and perceived as correct by the speaker . . . when used in standard English may be judged as "sloppy or wrong" by the standard English speaker, or worse yet as linguistic distortions. (p. 6)

Low expectations on the part of teachers set in motion a self-fulfilling prophecy that results in students with lowered aspirations and achievement levels, students who are increasingly disadvantaged by the educational system as they move through it. The damaging impact of these negative attitudes on student outcomes is the reason why teacher education is critically important.

The question of how best to foster positive attitudes among teachers toward students for whom SAE is not native has been minimally investigated and is rarely considered in the development of teacher-preparation programs. Smitherman (1983) asserts that these "negative linguistic attitudes are reflected in institutional policies and practices that become educationally dysfunctional for African American students" (p. 141). Fairchild and Edwards-Evans (1990) report that "the expectation of lower academic achievement potential for African Americans is so pervasive it might be considered an axiom of American Education" (p. 79). As African American SELs read themselves in their teachers' eyes and acts, their own behaviors are modified in ways that result in increased failure. In response to the ways students react to perceptions of denigration, Adger, Wolfram, and Detwyler (1993) suggest that students be given the tools—through sociolinguistic education—to identify language contrasts and to counteract negative attitudes toward NSLs.

Specific research on identifying factors that form the basis of negative attitudes toward AAL and those who speak it has largely been overlooked by scholars interested in NSLs. Bowie and Bond's (1994) study attempted to determine the effect that exposure to information on AAL had in teacher-preparation programs. They compared the attitudes of teachers who had some exposure to AAL research in at least one course to those who had no exposure to the topic at all. Using a survey designed to measure attitudes toward the structure and usefulness of AAL and the consequences of using it in the educational setting, Bowie and Bond found that exposure to the topic of AAL, even to a limited degree, appeared to have some relationship with attitudes toward it. A greater percentage of those presented with AAL research in at least one of their courses disagreed with the following statements:

- Black English is an inferior language system.
- One of the goals of the American school should be the standardization of the English Language.
- Black English should be discouraged.
- The sooner we eliminate Black English, the better.

Seventy-six percent of the teachers felt that AAL did not sound as good as SAE, and 61% believed that AAL "operated under a faulty grammar system."

An interesting finding of the study was that while 63% of survey respondents felt that a teacher's rejection of the native language of a student can be harmful, just 39 percent believed that attempts to eliminate AAL could be psychologically damaging to African American students.

Smitherman (2000) notes, "What students need (and here I would say both Black and White students) is not models of correctness—they have their own anyway—but broader understanding of the intricate connection between one's language and his cultural experience, combined with insight into the political nature and social stratification of American dialects" (p. 128). She further relates that "English teachers frequently are not trained in linguistics, but inservice programs and workshops could be one way of providing such vitally needed knowledge" (p. 129).

LeMoine's (2003) investigation of teacher attitudes toward AAL confirmed that this problem can be addressed through well-designed teacher-training programs that include courses, seminars, and workshops on AAL, language variation, and linguistics, such as those used by AEMP. Questionnaires completed by teachers completing the AEMP training reveal substantial attitude shifts and further validate the positive effect of knowledge building in this area. Typical comments from teachers participating in the AEMP seminars include the following:

> "I really learned and gained clarity on the influence linguistic ability has on student learning. I think these types of seminars should be given at every school. All teachers should be aware of the importance of language in student achievement."

> "An extremely valuable seminar. I recently relocated to LA from New York City [and] it is most unfortunate that they do not have such training. Clearly it changes negative attitudes due mostly to misinformation to better understanding of these students and better classroom instruction."

> "I thought the seminar was excellent. I learned a lot about language development. I actually didn't know all the variables involved in the way Africans in America acquired their language and I was totally unaware of the different language features."

Most linguists would agree with Finegan (1980) that "the correctness of 'grammar' or 'English usage' is relative," meaning that the appropriateness of the language used in a given exchange depends on the audience, setting, topic, and speaker (p. 9). However, AAL is not viewed as an appropriate school language, and students who use it in school environments often experience rejection and other negative ramifications. AEMP attempts to reshape the beliefs and attitudes of both teachers and students in ways that enhance their roles as educators and learners.

WRITING

Smitherman's 20-year study of African American students writing on the National Assessment of Educational Progress (NAEP) provided an opportunity to examine the voices of thousands of students. "My goal was to develop a profile of written literacy accomplishments of African American youth, at the school-leaving age, over the span of a generation," Smitherman noted (2000, p. 163). The findings from this study provide a foreground of how the teachers in the AEMP approach the writing process in their literacy instruction.

Smitherman and her associates analyzed 2,764 essays written by 17-year-old African American students in 1969, 1979, 1984, and 1988–1999. An NAEP-trained teacher-rater scored each essay in two ways, focusing on (1) specific writing tasks and (2) overall writing competency. The researchers examined the use of AAL in these essays based on the presence or absence of certain linguistic variables. The data was statistically analyzed using analysis of variance, Pearson correlation for the determination of covariation of rater scores, and AAL significance level. There were four major findings in the study:

1. The frequency of AAL usage in all essays for all years was generally low, and certain prevalent AAL linguistic features (such as habitual be) occurred infrequently. Linguistic variables, such as copula, -ed morpheme, -s morpheme, and it-expletive, declined from 1984 to 1988.
2. There was a correlation between essay modality and the production of AAL. Smitherman and her team theorized that when the writer is familiar with the form, he or she produces less "Black English." Further analysis using different comparisons proved inconclusive.
3. A negative correlation was found in the results of rater evaluation and AAL distribution and frequency. In other words, the more AAL that was present, the lower the overall writing competency.
4. Writing scores of African American students did not exhibit any dramatic improvements over the decade from 1979 to 1988–1989.

Smitherman (2000) and her associates concluded that AAL did not affect rater's scores around specific writing tasks and the use of AAL had significantly declined since 1969.

The fact that writers are not penalized for BEV [Black English Vernacular] in terms of their accomplishments of specific writing tasks is a testimony to the various educational and social forces that have served to sensitize teachers about dialects. All of these forces and events have had an impact on the linguistic liberation of African American students in the nation's schools and classrooms.

> The clear implication is that teachers now seem comfortable with and demon-
> strate the competence to divorce success in writing modality from attention to
> features of grammar. (p. 175)

This conclusion serves as the springboard for "forces" such as the AEMP. What
the researchers found in regard to teachers becoming more sensitized toward home
language use in speaking and writing matches with what AEMP provides through
professional development and demonstrates through classroom instruction.

However, despite declines in AAL use on the NAEP essays and improved
teacher attitudes, an achievement gap remains in literacy for African American
students when compared with other ethnic groups. Major methodological concerns remain as well in regard to literacy instruction for SELs. In particular, how
are teachers affirming and accommodating the language SELs bring to the classroom? And to what extent are any writing improvements based on the eradica-
tion mode of instruction, versus an additive model espoused by AEMP?

Smitherman directly addresses these questions and instructional issues in
"The Blacker the Berry, the Sweeter the Juice" (1994b). While much of the focus of the study was on African American discourse patterns and AAL grammar
patterns, the connection to the AEMP and writing instruction is found in the
implication-and-conclusion section. Smitherman offers four suggestions for writing instruction:

1. Capitalize on the strengths of African American cultural discourse.
2. Encourage students toward the field dependency style, which enables
   them to produce a more powerful, meaningful, and highly rated essay.
3. Design strategies for incorporating the Black imaginative, storytelling
   style into student production of other essay modalities.
4. Deemphasize the students' concerns about AAL grammar. Overconcen-
   tration on these forms frequently suppresses the production of African
   American discourse and its rich, expressive style. (p. 90)

AEMP instructors not only teach in many of the ways that Smitherman
suggests, but they also deepen the issues and concepts from a practitioner's
standpoint. AEMP teachers are trained to have their students write on a daily
basis with the use of journal writing, reader response, or both. Writing on a
daily basis is a major tenet of the AEMP pedagogy. Teachers are shown how to
incorporate the multiple stages of the writing process where they fit into daily
instruction, rather than using writing as an isolated, periodic event. Teachers
also introduce contrastive analysis, a second-language-learning technique that
points out predictable contrasts between SAE and AAL features. Pointing out
such contrasts so that students can identify and negotiate the differences be-

tween different languages has been advocated for more than 30 years (Rickford, 1999). Hanni Taylor (1991) studied the use of contrastive analysis with community college students in Chicago. With the experimental group, Taylor used contrastive analysis, specifically drawing attention to points on which Ebonics and SAE were different. Taylor's findings revealed a 59% reduction in the use of nonstandard language structures in students' writing when contrastive analysis was used regularly. Her conclusion was that this process of comparing the two varieties seems to lead to a greater metalinguistic awareness.

RESULTS

Of course, what goes on in professional development and what goes on in the classroom can be completely different. In 1999, AEMP instructional specialists observed nearly 1,000 classrooms to look at how well the goals of the AEMP professional development matched reality. The results were encouraging. What they discovered was the use of writing instructional strategies and activities that capitalized on African American discourse patterns and encouraged students to write powerfully and meaningfully. These strategies and activities included the following:

- Activating and using student background knowledge
- Emphasizing naturalistic language experiences
- Acknowledging and respecting cultural and linguistic diversity
- Using visuals, realia, manipulatives, graphic organizers, multimedia, and other sources to explain concepts, accommodating the student's culture and language
- Infusing student's history and culture into daily instruction
- Encouraging other students to recognize, respect, and appreciate their language and culture.

As it applies to writing instruction, the AEMP instructional specialists found that the AEMP teachers were:

- Providing students with written communication models consistently
- Providing opportunities for students to share their writing with peers in small and whole groups
- Providing opportunities for students to write daily
- Using language experience to write down student talk
- Using some aspects of the writing process on a daily basis
- Using technology to develop written language.

A few AEMP teachers have had some success with emphasizing the specific linguistic variables using a variety of strategies and instructional foci. The following particular contrastive analysis strategies were being employed:

- Using contrastive analysis conceptually
- Using linguistic contrastive analysis
- Using contextual and situational contrastive analysis to edit oral and written language for SAE structure
- Demonstrating knowledge of NSLs, their system of rules, sounds, and meaning and their impact on learning
- Analyzing linguistic differences in oral and written form
- Modeling SAE in oral and written form
- Providing opportunities for students to differentiate the linguistic features of NSLs forms from those of standard languages.

A district study (Maddahian & Sandamela, 2000) conducted by the evaluation branch examined the effectiveness of these strategies. The specific purpose of the evaluation was to determine the effectiveness of AEMP in increasing students' general and academic use of SAE. A pre-/posttest control design was applied to examine the impact of AEMP over time with experimental and control groups. The district study sample comprised 20 classrooms—16 experimental and 4 control. Pretests and posttests in writing and speaking were administered to each classroom.

The researchers used a formal, criterion-referenced test called the Language Assessment Measure (LAM). The pre-/posttest was specifically designed to determine the level of use of SAE with AAL speakers. The LAM is an individually administered test with two forms, A and B. Both have three elements: a short word-repetition pretest, a sentence-repetition task, and four stories that the administrator reads to the child. The test emphasizes the student's ability to answer/speak in SAE. For its study, the evaluation branch randomly chose 10 African American students from each participating teacher's classroom as the student sample. In the fall of 1998, Form A pretests were administered to both groups. In the spring of 1999, Form B posttests were conducted.

In Table 3.1, mean pre-/posttest scores on the writing test are compared, along with overall gains. Two pertinent findings emerged from this study. The first finding was that a statistically significant difference between the experimental and control groups occurred for posttest scores, with AEMP students outperforming the control students. The average posttest score for the AEMP group was 13.3 on a 20-point scale, compared with 10.8 for the control group.

The second but equally important finding was a statistically significant difference on writing gain scores for the AEMP students. The average gain was

Table 3.1. T-Test Comparisons of AEMP Students and Non-AEMP Students on Language Assessment Measure: Writing

Group Test	Pretest Mean	Posttest Mean	Gain
AEMP Students	10.8	13.3	2.5*
Non-AEMP Students	9.1	10.7	1.7*

*$p \leq .01$

2.5 points on a 20-point scale, compared with 1.7 for the control group. A significant score for the control group also appeared, but the posttest mean for the AEMP group was higher than that of the control group.

In a complementary study, Hollie (2000) examined the instructional implementation levels of the AEMP teachers who participated in the district's study. The intent was to pinpoint specific strategies that the successful AEMP teachers were using on a consistent basis and to determine to what extent there was a correlation between the high-implementing teachers and student outcomes. Hollie's study begins to explore how teacher programs such as AEMP vary instruction, particularly around the issues of language learning and culturally responsive teaching for SELs.

In almost all instances, the high-implementing teachers used the instructional strategies at consistent levels. These teachers were particularly strong in modeling SAE in oral and written forms and in analyzing linguistic differences (oral-contrastive analysis). Students in these classrooms had greater outcomes than students from other classrooms with less implementation. In short, the highest-implementing teachers had the greatest gains, offering further evidence of the effectiveness of AEMP in its attempts at ensuring all students equal access to the core educational curriculum in the LAUSD, particularly children of color.

The work of AEMP is an important charge that targets the elimination of disparities in educational outcomes for underachieving students. AEMP's primary goal is for SELs to acquire proficiency in Standard academic English as a prerequisite tool for accessing rigorous core curricula. This goal is achieved by building teachers' knowledge, understanding, and appreciation of the language and literacy experiences of SELs and through the identification of research-based best practices that build on these experiences to promote the acquisition of school language, literacy, and learning.

CHAPTER 4

The Art and Science of Teaching Narrative Reading Comprehension

An Innovative Approach

Angela Rickford

The current educational climate of standardized tests, state standards, student benchmarks, teacher accountability, and student achievement has put the spotlight on K–12 teachers and their performance in the classroom. Simultaneously, the call for a "back to basics" approach in public schools has revitalized an emphasis on the three Rs, with reading receiving the greatest attention. According to the National Assessment of Educational Progress 1998 Report Card for the Nation and the States, an average of only 17% of 4th-grade students scored in the "proficient" range in national reading tests. On January 8, 2002, President George W. Bush signed into law an education bill aimed at improving reading, backed by a pledge of $900 million a year for the following 6 years. However, like many educational issues, the reading problem is complex and nuanced.

The challenge is particularly great in California, where ethnically diverse students now comprise the majority in public schools. Many of these students enter school speaking myriad languages and dialects, and while they must learn to read English, it is often not their mother tongue. In addition, the number of children identified as reading disabled has increased, with a significant portion coming from the ranks of ethnic-minority students. Statistics show that more than 7% of the national school-age population has learning disabilities, which often translates to reading difficulties (U.S. Department of Education, 1999). But this percentage can be higher in a typical ethnic-minority school in California. The need to teach reading so that these children will learn further compounds the problem.

Teachers often feel unprepared to meet this challenge because of the level of expertise they bring to the task of teaching reading. As a reading-teacher educator in the oldest teacher education institution in Northern California, I work with a selection of K–12 classroom teachers in that part of the state. These teachers realize the gravity of their responsibility, and they are anxious to equip themselves with the requisite knowledge and skills for the job.

At the beginning of my methods course in the teaching of reading, I usually conduct a brief "getting to know you" survey of my students. One of the questions I ask is "What would you like to get out of this class in terms of your interests and needs?" The following responses, gathered from the reading courses I taught in spring and fall 2001, are typical:

> "Helping children/students improve their decoding and their reading comprehension [so that they could] read on their own and enjoy it." (Spring 2001)

> "My biggest challenge is assisting my students in comprehending what they read. . . . I'm also nervous about making sure my EL [English Learner] students understand/comprehend what they read." (Fall 2001)

> "I would like instruction on more concrete tools to take back to my classroom, especially tips on modifying lessons for varying degrees of reading ability among students, . . . specific strategies to help with decoding and comprehension, and more tools for the toolbox." (Fall 2001)

> "Helping students enjoy books and reading as much as I do . . . and combining core curriculum [reading comprehension, math, and so on] with reading difficulties." (Spring 2001)

These responses show that reading teachers strive to make their students engaged learners. More specifically, they want them to be able to (1) decode properly, and (2) comprehend what they read.

The ability to decode is important, but the ability to comprehend is paramount, because it represents the ultimate purpose of reading. The focus of this chapter will therefore be on reading comprehension, paying special attention to narrative text, which can account for as much as 92% of the text read by elementary-age children (Trabasso, 1993). In what follows, we will examine two powerful strategies that teachers can use to improve their students' understanding of the narratives they read: (1) attention to narrative structure and (2) strategy in question design.

LITERATURE REVIEW

Research has demonstrated the importance of text structure in written communication and the application of cognitive strategies to enhance textual understanding (Boyle, 1996; Calfee, Chambliss, & Beretz, 1991). Focusing on textual structure can orient students toward an awareness of the "building blocks" that writers use in creating texts. This conceptual approach to teaching reading comprehension can be applied to both narrative and expository texts, but it lends itself particularly well to narrative, because of the commonality and predictability of elements that authors frequently use in designing a good story (Lukens, 1999).

Ever since the concept of "story grammar" evolved out of Noam Chomsky's (1957) tree diagrams depicting relationships between grammatical functions in a sentence, research on story structure has offered valuable insights into the complex processes involved in reading comprehension. Traditionally, this kind of research has operated on the "micro" level of textual understanding, examining idea units, propositions, and hierarchies, concepts largely confined to the narrowly circumscribed domains of linguistics and psychology (Van den Broek & Trabasso, 1986). But the same principles have since been applied in the field of education to the study of textual structure on the "macro" level, specifically in the study of narrative.

Pearson and Camperell (1994) have shown, for example, that any violations in the integrity of story structure can cause a decrease in reading comprehension. Approaching the matter from another angle, Anderson's (1985) research on schema theory highlights the fact that there is often more than one possible interpretation of text, depending on a variety of factors that intrude from the reader's background. These kinds of insights should inform the way reading and language arts teachers are trained in reading education and help guide them when they return to their K–12 classrooms. Sadly, however, the most prevalent methods of teaching reading comprehension are not grounded in a solid foundation of pedagogical research, but rather proceed from a simplistic "reading to learn" perspective (Fisher, Fox, & Paille, 1996, p. 410).

In an effort to rectify the piecemeal approach to teaching literature practiced in many classrooms, and the weak pedagogy exercised by poorly trained teachers (Darling-Hammond, 2000; Rickford 2002), the California State Department of Education produced a blueprint for teaching reading comprehension that endorsed research-based approaches. The California Language Arts Framework (California State Department of Education, 1999) cites "text structure" (p. 20) as a key component in teaching narratives and reading comprehension. It further states that it is important for students to understand "the structural features of narrative text" (p. 25) and the "commonalities in narrative text" (p. 25) when studying stories. Similarly, the English-Language Arts Content Standards for 1st through 8th grade (a subsection of the California Language Arts Framework) recommends attention to "structural features" or "literary elements," and promotes "narrative analysis of grade-level appropriate text" (California State Department of Education, 1999, p. 78) at every step from kindergarten through 12th grade.

The document also asserts that "the elements of 'story grammar'" can be used as a framework for teaching higher-level comprehension skills (p. 34).

Promoting the structural analysis of narratives as a means of teaching comprehension is a move in the right direction. As Bruner (1960) observed almost a half century ago, "Knowledge one has acquired without sufficient structure to tie it together is knowledge that is likely to be forgotten. . . . [A]n unconnected set of facts has a pitiably short half-life in memory" (p. 31). And as Wiggins and McTighe (1998) point out, understanding must necessarily take place "by design." In other words, by paying explicit attention to the concrete structural components of narratives, and to the ways in which authors manipulate them, teachers can build an effective scaffolding that will aid their children's understanding of narrative text.

Calfee and Patrick (1995) offer the following critique of questioning techniques currently used in our schools:

> What is a real question? Real questions connect. School questions are often artificial. The teacher asks the question, the student's job is to answer, but the teacher knows the right answer. It's a game. A real question is one where the questioner is genuinely interested in learning something from someone else. . . . The essence of real discourse is unpredictability and authenticity. (p. 62)

In a guide designed to help teachers improve classroom questions, Chuska (1995) makes the following pronouncement:

> Questions are one of the major instructional strategies teachers use throughout the year. . . . [T]eachers ask 50 questions per period, or 350 per day. However, that frequency in questions indicates that the questions are fact-based and allow little opportunity for higher-level thinking or application. (p. 14)

These two excerpts point to a dilemma: Questioning is a critical element in the teaching/learning process, but the questions that teachers ask often tend to be cognitively unstimulating. Indeed, skillful questioning techniques are often what set excellent teachers apart. Ruddell (1999) proposes classifying teachers as "influential" or "uninfluential," based on their ability to facilitate critical thinking in their classrooms by asking good questions. What makes some questions better than others? Heath (1983) distinguishes between contextualized and decontextualized questions, with the former (questions situated within the contextual parameters of the text) identified as more thought provoking than the latter (questions lifted superficially from the text). Similarly, Rosenblatt (1991) promotes the value of "aesthetic" questioning, which grants children the opportunity to experience text in a meaningful and personal way, as opposed to "efferent" questioning, which teaches them only to extract factual, surface-level information.

Education critics complain that the mode of questioning typically found in elementary schools today is rigid, uninspired, and based on an outdated factory-model style. Tierney and Pearson (1981) contend that children's interactions with narrative text are often "sabotaged by an excessive use of poorly fitting questions, e.g., detail questions dealing with trivial information under the guise of skill objectives" (p. 866). Darling-Hammond (1985) decries the minimal skills and literal comprehension that students are continually required to demonstrate instead of higher levels of thinking. And Calfee and Patrick (1995) call for the kind of comprehension questions that "help provoke students' thought and not merely force them to recall data" (p. 150).

Ironically, as an instructional technique, questioning has received significant attention in the research literature on reading comprehension. Bloom's *Taxonomy of Educational Objectives* (1956), the seminal work on critical thinking, spawned various analyses and conceptions of questioning. His proposed taxonomy made a distinction between inferential thinking, problem solving, elaboration, representation, application, synthesis, analysis, and evaluation at the higher end of the questioning hierarchy, and basic recall and recognition at the lower end. In recent years, teaching students to generate their own questions during reading has emerged as a sound approach to teaching reading comprehension. Strategies such as "questioning-the-author" (Beck, McKeown, Hamilton, & Kucan, 1997), "reciprocal teaching" (Palinscar & Brown, 1984), "transactional strategies instruction" (Brown, Pressley, Van Meter, & Schuder, 1996), and other self-questioning techniques (Paris, Wixson, & Palinscar, 1986) all include this important component. Unfortunately, many of these techniques are formulated specifically for content area reading, while narrative questioning has remained largely relegated to questions generated in the teacher's head following the reading of a story, or to those prescribed by the conventional elementary school basal reader text.

Such questions, and others that teachers devise to accompany stories, are often of the lower-order memory and recall variety, rather than the more complex, interpretive, evaluative, and critical-thinking questions that Bloom proposed (Rickford, 1999, 2001). Of course, coming up with critical-thinking questions also requires some critical thinking on the part of the teacher. This is where a familiarity with the strategies and techniques of narrative structural analysis can prove most helpful.

STUDY DESIGN AND METHODS

Teaching Narrative Appreciation, Analysis, and Comprehension

Most of the materials used in this study were gleaned from the work done by teacher trainees who took my reading-methods course during the spring and fall of 2001, and from the class projects done by their own K–12 students. The course is designed to address the teaching of reading from a broad perspective, examining both content and pedagogy. In terms of content, we look at the teaching of decoding (phonemic awareness and phonics, vocabulary development, spelling, and narratives and exposition), content area reading, and writing. In terms of pedagogy, I emphasize the importance of paying attention to the cultural propensities of students; examining how children learn; understanding the importance of discussion, collaboration, and group work; generating activities that promote engagement and participation; and supporting project-based learning. The course upholds these principles of teaching not only in a theoretical way, but also concretely, as I incorporate the techniques we discuss into my own teaching. By practicing what I preach, I hope to model the performance I expect from teachers when they return to their own classrooms. The following summary of the "teaching narrative reading" component of the course is intended to demonstrate the principles and strategies of narrative structural analysis at work.

To begin with, teacher trainees engaged with carefully selected preparatory readings on children and stories (Applebee, 1979) and critiques of children's literature (Lukens, 1999). I encouraged them to reflect on their own past and present interactions with stories and to consider what elements of those stories seemed to make them particularly enjoyable or not enjoyable. This Socratic approach generated enthusiasm and led the class to self-identify some of the important structural narrative features that we would soon draw upon in our analyses of stories. These structural components can be divided into two categories: the primary elements of character, theme, plot, and setting; and the more ancillary (yet important) subelements of problems, solutions, actions, and emotions.

Following this, we discussed my own research on teaching narrative reading comprehension through structural analysis and strategic questioning (Rickford, 1999), as well as techniques for communicating to their own students the importance of structure. We also considered the importance of organizational structures as a strategy for enhancing cognition in struggling readers (Boyle, 1996) and how this relates to outlining "story grammar" elements as a means of facilitating reading comprehension.

As the culminating activity, class members worked on a baseline project involving graphic and semantic organizers designed to illustrate the essential elements of narrative comprehension. The narrative structures they used (see Figure 4.1) were adapted from Calfee and Wolf (1988) and Calfee and Patrick (1995). We used the same language labels to identify the graphics that would represent the structural framework of narratives: Character Weave, Story Graph, Episode Analysis Chart, and Conceptual Map. I stressed that it would be important to coach their students to recognize the structural similarities across stories. I then read a short story out loud, either an African folk tale titled "The Woman and the Tree Children" (spring 2001) or a Mexican folk tale titled "The Woman Who Outshone the Sun" (fall 2001). These stories were chosen to reinforce the importance of selecting stories that were culturally congruent (Ladson-Billings, 1995) with their K–12 students' backgrounds. I then asked the class to work in small groups on one of the following four narrative analysis exercises:

> *Assignment 1*: Construct a Character Weave. You may use the same catego-
> ries as the ones that appear in the sample (character's physical appear-
> ance, behavior, feelings about self, and feelings about others), but you
> may also create new ones.
>
> *Assignment 2*: Draw a Story Graph. Be sure your graph represents the be-
> ginning, progression, and end of the story, that it reflects the various
> levels of emotional intensity that the characters display, and that you
> indicate what events precipitate the rise and fall of their emotions.
>
> *Assignment 3*: Design an Episodic Analysis Chart. First, decide how many
> episodes there are and where they occur. Fill in the "Challenge, Emo-
> tion, Action, and Outcome" cells for each episode of your figure with
> real text, in order to demonstrate that a narrative episode is a conceptual
> unit incorporating these four chunks.
>
> *Assignment 4*: Create a Conceptual Map of the story using the narrative ele-
> ments of Character, Theme, Plot, and Setting. Fill in as much detail as
> you can in each subsection of the graphic in order to make the meaning
> of the various components clear to your students.

The structure of the Character Weave (see Figure 4.1b) reflects the horizontal and vertical interlacing pattern of the loom and serves as a metaphor for analyzing characters and laying out their characteristics in a matrix. The Story Graph (see Figure 4.1c) uses undulating lines to represent the levels of action and emotion found in a story from the beginning to the resolution. The Episodic Analysis Chart (see Figure 4.1d) reflects the concept that each episode in a story has its own internal integrity, consisting of a challenge met by the response of an emotion, followed by an action and a final outcome, only to begin the cycle all over again. Finally, the Conceptual Map (see Figure 4.1a) represents the gestalt of narrative text structure in that it highlights the primary "design" elements of narratives: character, theme, plot, and setting, with accompanying details.

The teachers worked on big sheets of butcher paper, which I had brought to class for that purpose, and used their markers and crayons with the same excitement

Figure 4.1. Sample Framework of Organizational Structures for Analyzing Narratives

(a) Conceptual Map

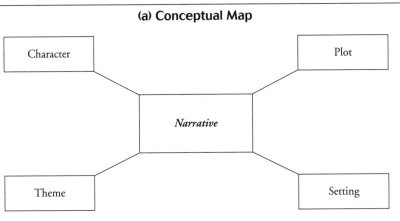

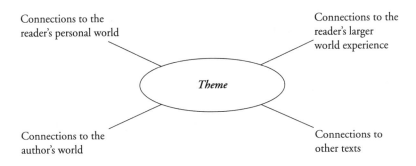

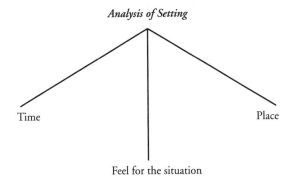

Figure 4.1. *(continued)*

(b) Character Weave

Character	Physical Appearance	Behavior	Feelings
A			
B			
C			

(c) Story Graph

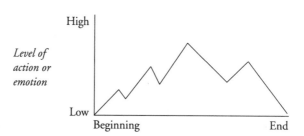

(d) Episode Analysis Chart

	Problem	Emotional Response	Action	Outcome
1				
2				
3				

Source: Adapted from Calfee & Wolf (1988) and Calfee & Patrick (1995).

they hoped to generate with their youngsters back at school. Indeed, they seemed to grasp that teaching their students to use narrative structures as a scaffold for reading comprehension could translate into a powerful metacognitive strategy for them, and even forestall problems for their struggling readers. As one teacher put it:

> Hands-on, visual aids to add to my classes is a wonderful asset. I like putting theory into practice, and doing the kinds of things we should be doing with our students.

Teaching Narrative Question Design

We then proceeded to the issue of narrative questioning. We discussed the work of Oakes (1985) on how schools foster inequality by offering access to higher forms of knowledge (including selective kinds of questions) to students in advanced classes. We also discussed Heath's (1982b) comparative study on the kinds of inauthentic questions asked at school versus the more real-world questions asked at home. Teacher trainees also read a chapter from Rouch and Birr's (1984) guide on activities for teaching reading, which sensitized them to different levels of questioning—literal versus critical and interpretive. Then I introduced them to the technique of categorizing and labeling questions as a practical device, as recommended in my own work on teaching narratives and reading comprehension (Rickford, 1999).

Finally, in response to the readings and instruction, the class generated a list of three guidelines for designing questions based on the stories:

1. Questions should include in their scope both higher-order, critical thinking and lower-order, memory types with an emphasis on higher-order questions as "real-world" and "workplace" prototypes.
2. Questions should be labeled where possible to ensure focus, purposefulness, and clarity.
3. Questions should be integrated with the structure of the text to facilitate interconnection with its narrative elements and continuity of knowledge in teaching narrative reading comprehension.

We operationalized the first guideline with the plan to generate questions under four categories: General, Recall, Interpretive, and Creative. General Questions are those that ask students to give a "gut" reaction to a story—to say whether they liked it and why, an important first step in trying to understand the story. Recall Questions refer to the conventional closed question, the answer to which could be lifted superficially from the text. Interpretive Questions and Creative Questions are flexible and open ended, and they generate the kind of critical thinking that is the hallmark of higher-order skills.

As for the second guideline, teachers agreed to construct labels that readily identified the kinds of questions they were asking. For example, under the umbrella of Interpretive Questions would fall all questions requiring thought, inference, deduction, or reasoning. Such questions might be labeled for students as Inference Questions, Problem-Solving Questions, Deductive Reasoning Questions, Creative Reading Questions, and so on.

Regarding the third guideline, teachers realized that finding a seamless connection between narrative structural analysis and question construction was essential for helping their students understand stories. Revisiting the framework of their narrative structures, they devised a strategy for interconnecting narrative text structure and question design.

Their strategy was multilayered. They would ask General and Recall questions based on every story they read. They were used to these questions and felt confident in their ability to construct them. However, some of the Interpretive and Creative questions seemed to "fit" naturally in one or another of the four narrative structures they were working with. For example, teachers felt that the Character Weave would be a natural source for a "Favorite Character Question" or "Character Qualities Question." Similarly, they felt that the information gleaned from building a Story Graph could be harnessed to question students about a constellation of narrative features, ranging from plot development, to the sequence of events, to the change in the emotional status of an individual. Based on this structure, they might ask a "Plot Development Question," an "Inference Question," or an "Inductive Reasoning Question," such as "Why did X feel that way (sad, happy, and so on) after Y did or said that? Give reasons for your answer." We discussed how important it was to teach students to articulate reasons for their thinking.

Teachers decided that the Episode Analysis Chart contained so many "ministories" that there were opportunities here for a wide range of questions, including more "Interpretive Questions" or "Problem-Solving Questions" of the kind defined above, or "Creative Reading Questions" that in some way asked students to relate the story to their own world or circumstances. Finally, like the Episodic Analysis Chart, the Conceptual Map was comprehensive enough to justify a question from any of the four categories above. Since the theme or main idea of the story was identified here and was often a moral or good lesson in popular and didactic narratives, teachers felt that this would be the right source for a question about the moral makeup of story characters. The Conceptual Map structure could therefore be devoted to a "Moral Judgment Question."

FINDINGS

Toward the end of the course, the teachers shared their experiences using the questioning strategy we had devised together. They also shared examples of the project work their students had done in studying various narratives, using the element of structure as an entrée. Figure 4.2 summarizes these examples, giving story titles and identifying the narrative structures the children used as their means of analysis, as well as the kinds of questions the teachers designed. In this section, we will look at some of their results in detail.

Character Weave

Teachers reported that they used the Character Weave model to show their students how characters, as vehicles for developing theme, are one of the enduring facets of good narratives. They reported that they were able to vary the difficulty of this assignment to match their students' abilities. Sometimes they provided students with the categories for sketching characteristics (located on the horizontal axis of the weave), as in the case of the first four columns in Figure 4.3, and then had their students fill in the cells based on their own reading of the story. Sometimes they also allowed students to come up with their own categories, as in the case of the fifth column, "Symbolism." Teachers reported that their students enjoyed the process of creating character portraits using the weave structure as an instructional aid. They also learned to investigate characters more closely than they had done before and to reflect on their depth and complexity. Figure 4.3 displays a character weave created by middle schoolers built from the legendary Mexican folk tale "La Mujer que

Figure 4.2. Summary of Samples of K–12 Narrative Analysis Structures and Teachers' Strategically Designed Comprehension Questions

Grade Level	Story Title	Narrative Structure	Question Types
Lower Elementary	"The Velveteen Rabbit," by Margery Williams	Conceptual Map	General and Creative Reading Questions
Upper Elementary	"The Woman Who Outshone the Sun" and "The Legend of Lucia Zenteno," by Alejandro Cruz Martinez	Character Weave	Character Qualities, Moral Judgment, Creative Reading, and Problem Solving Questions
Middle School	"Follow the Drinking Gourd," by Jeanette Winter	Episodic Analysis Chart	Creative Reading, Problem Solving, and Interpretive Reading Questions
Upper Elementary or Middle School	"Bush Medicine," by Faustin Charles	Story Graph	Basic Recall, Inductive Reasoning, and Plot Development Questions

Figure 4.3. "The Woman Who Outshone the Sun": Character Weave

Character	Physical Appearance	Feelings for Others	Behavior	Symbolism
Lucia	long glorious hair, radiant, impressive	compassionate, kind, loyal, tolerant, forgiving	dignified, gentle, accepting, long-suffering	goodness, bounty
River	beautiful, full of life, cool	loved Lucia, accepted all	nurturing, especially loyal to Lucia, inclusive	life
Elders	old	honored diversity, humble, concerned	at first ambivalent, wise, spoke truth	wisdom, teaching
Townspeople	young and old	selfish, fearful of unknown, bigoted, spiteful	hurtful to Lucia, stubborn, traditional, fearful	ignorance, human frailty, prejudice

Selection of Comprehension Questions:

1. Compare the qualities of Lucia Zenteno with those of the townspeople as shown by their behavior in the story. (Character Qualities Question)
2. Why did the townspeople ignore the elder's advice to treat Lucia with respect? Were they right or wrong to ignore them? (Moral Judgment Question)

brillaba aun mas que El Sol" ("The Woman Who Outshone the Sun"). The matrix reflects the depth of interaction students experienced with the text and shows their understanding of the multiple roles and functions of the characters in the story.

Story Graph

Teachers used the Story Graph to help their students track plot development and ultimately to remember the importance of this feature as they created their own stories. Using Story Graphs, teachers were able to demonstrate the buildup to a climactic peak and the subsequent denouement that are the hallmarks of successful narratives. The upper elementary students who constructed the Story Graph based on the "Bush Medicine" story (Figure 4.4) used the angular outline and sharp lines to denote change in action and emotion. Following the Story Graph project, the teachers helped their students coin such terms as *peaks, valleys, up the mountainside,* and *down the hill,* which they were then able to use when talking about story structure. Other teachers said that for K–3 students they used a piece of woolen yarn to trace the actions of stories, for visual and tactile reinforcement.

Figure 4.4. "Bush Medicine": Story Graph

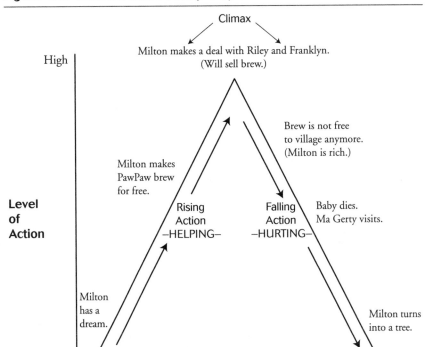

Climax

Milton makes a deal with Riley and Franklyn.
(Will sell brew.)

High

Milton makes
PawPaw brew
for free.

Brew is not free
to village anymore.
(Milton is rich.)

Level
of
Action

Rising
Action
—HELPING—

Falling
Action
—HURTING—

Baby dies.
Ma Gerty visits.

Milton
has a
dream.

Milton turns
into a tree.

Low

Exposition

Resolution

Selection of Comprehension Questions:

1. Why did Milton go to the pawpaw tree in his backyard? (Basic Recall Question)
2. How does the role that Ma Gerty plays in "Bush Medicine" (Milton's conscience) help the story unfold? (Plot Development Question; Inductive Reasoning Question)

Episode Analysis Chart

Teachers used the Episode Analysis Chart as a heuristic for helping their students understand that the narrative episode is a conceptual chunk, a series of events that occur as part of a larger sequence between the "initiating problem" and final "resolution" of a story. Figure 4.5 provides an example of an Episode Analysis of the "Follow the Drinking Gourd" story created by eighth graders. In this story, as in others, teachers noted that they helped their students understand that the episode acts as the receptacle for dramatic action and character

Figure 4.5. "Follow the Drinking Gourd": Episode Analysis Chart

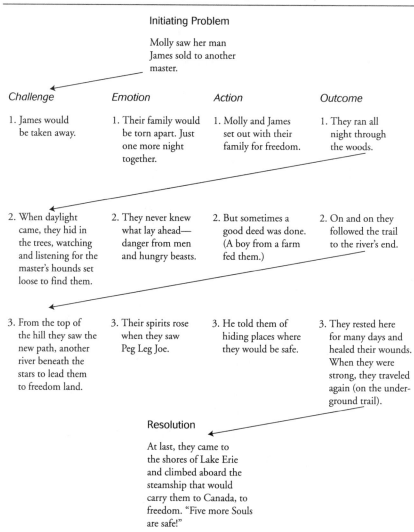

Initiating Problem

Molly saw her man
James sold to another
master.

Challenge	Emotion	Action	Outcome
1. James would be taken away.	1. Their family would be torn apart. Just one more night together.	1. Molly and James set out with their family for freedom.	1. They ran all night through the woods.
2. When daylight came, they hid in the trees, watching and listening for the master's hounds set loose to find them.	2. They never knew what lay ahead—danger from men and hungry beasts.	2. But sometimes a good deed was done. (A boy from a farm fed them.)	2. On and on they followed the trail to the river's end.
3. From the top of the hill they saw the new path, another river beneath the stars to lead them to freedom land.	3. Their spirits rose when they saw Peg Leg Joe.	3. He told them of hiding places where they would be safe.	3. They rested here for many days and healed their wounds. When they were strong, they traveled again (on the underground trail).

Resolution

At last, they came to
the shores of Lake Erie
and climbed aboard the
steamship that would
carry them to Canada, to
freedom. "Five more Souls
are safe!"

Selection of Comprehension Questions:

1. Why do you think White people like those on the Quaker Farm helped the runaway slaves? Would you have done the same if you were in their place? Give reasons for your answer. (Problem-Solving Question; Creative Reading Question)

2. Why do you think the runaway family had to hide in the trees in the woods during the daytime? (Interpretive Reading Question)

involvement in a story. This was an important discovery that they hoped would later feed into their students' own creative writing. Teachers understood, and were able to pass on to their students, that there is no fixed number of episodes in any given story. For example, in the "La mujer" story, some groups identified three episodes, some six. Teachers encouraged students to decide, based on the latter's intuitions and growing knowledge of story structure, where episodes began and ended and to articulate and defend such decisions. Teachers reported that students felt empowered by this approach and that it helped them understand how stories were structured from the inside out.

Conceptual Map

Teachers reported that they used the Conceptual Map to introduce their students to the fundamentals of narrative structure. Students were reportedly comfortable using it as a tool because of its simplicity and comprehensiveness, and teachers were able to adapt this strategy to the ability level of their students. For beginning readers, the character bubble could involve a straightforward listing of narrative characters, as in the example of "The Velveteen Rabbit" (Figure 4.6). However, with a more advanced story such as O. Henry's "Gift of the Magi" (see Rickford, 2002), more-mature students could be expected to provide a deeper, more thorough exploration. Similarly, *theme* could be defined very broadly to include almost all student suggestions, or it could be restricted to focus on a few specific issues, depending on the teacher's purpose. More-advanced students were encouraged to connect the story theme to their personal worlds, to the reader's larger world experience, to other texts, to the author's world, and even to history (as the section labeled "theme" in Figure 4.1. suggests). According to the same principle, plot could involve a cursory listing of story events (as the first graders provided in Figure 4.6) or a more comprehensive summary. When asked to state the setting, children could simply offer "the boy's house" or "Bunnyland," or else give answers that are more informative and sophisticated, depending on grade level and ability.

The structural-analysis projects that the students produced under the guidance of their teachers demonstrated a growing understanding of narratives on the part of both teacher and student. Their work validates the principle that "if teachers want students to 'get the author's message,' they are well advised to model for students how to figure out what the author's general framework or structure is, and then allow students to practice discovering it on their own" (Pearson & Camperell, 1994, p. 338).

It should be noted also that teachers used the question design matrix as it was intended, as a heuristic in the service of better-constructed questions, not as a

Figure 4.6. "The Velveteen Rabbit": Conceptual Map

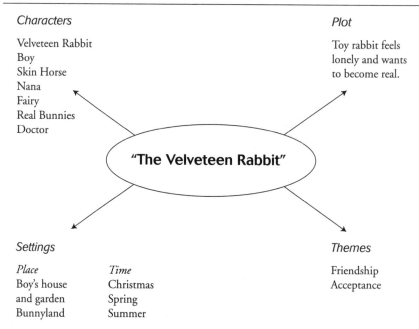

Characters

Velveteen Rabbit
Boy
Skin Horse
Nana
Fairy
Real Bunnies
Doctor

Plot

Toy rabbit feels
lonely and wants
to become real.

"The Velveteen Rabbit"

Settings

Place	*Time*
Boy's house	Christmas
and garden	Spring
Bunnyland	Summer

Themes

Friendship
Acceptance

Selection of Comprehension Questions:

1. Did you enjoy the story "The Velveteen Rabbit"? Explain why or why not. (General Question)
2. If a fairy granted you a wish like the fairy granted the Velveteen Rabbit, what would it be? Give reasons for your answer. (Creative Reading Question)

crutch. They were able to use it creatively to serve their particular purposes, without conforming rigidly to any predetermined plan. This flexibility was shown by the way they were able to manipulate the types of questions they chose to connect with specific structural analysis exercises.

By the end of the course, teachers had the opportunity to reflect on their own growth and learning. They reviewed the questions they constructed to reinforce story grammar concepts, and experienced metacognitive insights into the processes they had explored. For example, they realized that many of the exciting "higher order" thinking questions that they constructed were garnered from critical points within the structure of the stories. Such questions tended to be derived from points of maximum interaction between characters (as in the "La mujer" story when the river in the person of Lucia Zenteno felt betrayed by the townspeople) or episodes showing high levels of emotional intensity (as in the "Bush Medicine" story, when Milton stops giving the pawpaw medicine for free). These "ah ha" moments were significant, since they indicated a sustained level of engagement and understanding on the teachers' part, the kind of engagement that their students would undoubtedly benefit from in turn. As one teacher explained: "I have started to utilize this questioning technique and framework in my RSP [Resource Specialist Program] and regular English classes and have found the results to be favorable."

IMPLICATIONS AND CONCLUSION

> At the very least, educators should help children to fulfill their expectations about stories. We can do this by giving children stories that have sufficient structure for them to grasp. . . . We can help children achieve their expectations by questioning them appropriately. Questions drawn haphazardly from facts in the story are of course misleading to children. Comprehension of a story is not comprehension of haphazard facts . . . but it is comprehension of the structure
> —J. T. Guthrie, "Story Comprehension and Fables"

The preceding quote underscores the importance of paying attention to narrative structure and designing strategic questions in teaching narrative reading comprehension. If we want teachers to perform effectively and children to learn well, we must equip teachers with the knowledge and expertise they need to stimulate the cognitive processes that are vital to their children's success. Teacher modeling, direct explanation, peer collaboration, scaffolded instruction, project learning, and metacognitive strategies must become not only the source of workplace buzzwords, but functional tools that support real communication, learning, and understanding.

It is a truism of education that students learn better and become more engaged when they feel competent to handle the assignments and tasks set before them. In this chapter we have explored simple but powerful ways to help teachers achieve this goal when they are teaching narrative reading and comprehension. The strategies and techniques presented here are not intended as a panacea, nor do they encompass everything students need to know about narratives. But they can equip students with the requisite tools to engage meaningfully with narrative texts and achieve a measure of conceptual clarity, whether they're reading for pleasure or for school. When curriculum and instruction combine to promote the kind of metacognitive development demonstrated by teachers and students in this study, perhaps teacher accountability and student achievement can become achievable goals—and standardized tests, state standards, and student benchmarks meaningful realities.

Part II

CULTURE, COMMUNICATION, AND CONSCIOUSNESS

CHAPTER 5

The Power of the Rap

The Black Idiom
and the New Black Poetry

Geneva Smitherman

What Do It Mean to Be a Word Warrior? *by Haki Madhubuti*

it is not in her to run
or look the other way
in the face of white shadows
casting their blood-ties over the
tired feet, quick speech & dream talk
of Black people.

Love opened her heart early & often
giving her the spirit and soul to travel
into the submerged metaphors of the
languages of her nation.
while talkin a free talk
the common became actual as in
memory be language and
language be memory only
if it be ours.

Black Arts Literature—of which the New Black Poetry is the most important manifestation—emerged during the past decade as the appropriate artistic counterpart to Black Power. Rhetoric and shouting aside, this new thrust was, on a very basic level, simply a call to Black folks to redefine Blackness and reevaluate the Black Experience. For the writer, this reassessment has culminated in a redefinition of the role of the artist and a new perspective on what constitutes Art. The creator of Black Arts Literature envisions himself as a Necromancer,[1]

a skillful manipulator of the Art of Black Magic, whose job it is to "heal" Black folks through the evocative power of Art and transform their suffering into constructive political action. Black Art, then, must of necessity, be functional and relevant to the lives and daily struggles of Black people. Yet it must be *Art,* for the heroic Word-Magician of this new era insists on products that are within the boundaries of formal literary expression.

It should be noted in passing, however, that the contemporary rediscovery and legitimizing of the Black Cultural Heritage is not new in this century. Nor is the political protest stance of the Black writer. Poets like Claude McKay and Countee Cullen, of the Harlem Renaissance Movement of the 1920s, wove both themes of protest and beauty-in-Blackness into their works. But the current Black Art Revival differs from that of the Renaissance in two major respects. First, today's Black artist is not content to be simply a *writer,* sounding his protest only through his art. He sees himself as a Black *man* first, and thus as an active participant in the struggle for Black Liberation. Second, rejecting the elitist tendencies of the Renaissance literati, the new Black writer is making Herculean efforts to create a literature that will reach and reflect common Black folks. The objective is to prevent today's Cultural Consciousness Movement from becoming like that of the Harlem Renaissance, which, according to Langston Hughes (1940), ordinary Harlemites had not even heard of, and if they had, "it hadn't raised their wages any" (p. 228).

The grass roots, lacking the Black Bourgeoisie's White middle-class aspirations, have been the bearers and sustainers of Black culture through the centuries. In representing the masses, the new Art will be expressive of the uniqueness of Afro-American culture. Hence the quest among Black Arts writers for a style rooted in this cultural sensibility, a style that is emerging as an identifiable Black Aesthetic. Nowhere is this Aesthetic more strikingly revealed than in the *language* of the New Black Poetry, for in creating this new linguistic form, the poets are not only tapping the reservoir of the Black Cultural Universe but doing so in the Black Idiom (which is what makes much of this poetry difficult reading for Whites, and also lends credence to the frequent claim of Black writers that the critics of Black literature should be Black). Within the limitations of written form, today's poets are attempting to capture the flavor of Black American speech—its rhythms and sounds, both its dialect and style. Through their artistic efforts, the poets seem to be saying: If the message is new, the medium must be new also. (Other genres of Black Arts Literature that reflect attempts to synthesize medium and message are, for instance, John Oliver Killens's novel, *Cotillion* [1971], rendered in what Killens labels "Afro-Americanese," and the plays of Ed Bullins, especially the published version of his *Duplex* [1971]. However, poetry continues to be the dominant literary expression of the New Black Writers, for reasons that should become apparent shortly.)

The necessity for this new poetic medium can be best explained within the context of the interrelationship between language and cultural values, especially as it relates to the experience of Afro-Americans. It is a well-founded concept of linguistic anthropology that language is a key to understanding culture. The idiomatic structure and nuances of a language can give us insight into the thought patterns and value structure of another culture. For instance, in linguist Benjamin Whorf's (1956) study of the North American Hopi Indians, he demonstrated the correlation between the non-European Hopi language and the concomitant non-European way the Hopi perceives the world and subsequently organizes his culture. On a psychological level, language is intricately bound up with the individual's sense of identity and group consciousness. In the history of man's inhumanity to man, it is clearly understandable why the conqueror forces his victims to learn his language, for there is truth to the axiom: As you speak, so you think. Certainly this principle has been operative in the history of colonized people where the colonizer's language and culture occupy a position superior to that of the colonized, even among the oppressed persons themselves. (The fact that America was once a colony of England goes a long way toward explaining why British English still commands such great prestige in this country—despite the real communication barrier it poses for most Americans.)

Black psychiatrist Frantz Fanon (1967) has brilliantly analyzed the colonized African mind, explaining its tragically sick identification with the European culture that oppressed it. The denigration of the African's native language was a basic manifestation of the cultural rejection of Africa by both Europeans and Africans. Speaking of the "Negro and language" in the French West Indies, Fanon characterized the situation thus:

> Every dialect is a way of thinking. . . . And the fact that the newly returned [i.e., from European schools] Negro adopts a language different from that of the group into which he was born is evidence of a dislocation, a separation. (p. 25)

In showing why the "Negro adopts such a position . . . with respect to European languages," Fanon argued:

> It is because he wants to emphasize the rupture that has now occurred. He is incarnating a new type of man that he imposes on his associates and his family. And so his old mother can no longer understand him when he talks to her about his *duds*, the family's *crummy joint*, the *dump* . . . all of it, of course, tricked out with the appropriate accent. (p. 36)

In the American context, the negative attitude toward Black speech—shared by Blacks and Whites alike—is but a variation on this same theme. Historically, Black

English was the usage pattern of Uncle Remus and Uncle Tom. Contemporaneously, it is the dialect heavily concentrated in America's urban Black ghettos. Consistently, it has been labeled "poor English." Yet it is a speech pattern that adheres to systematic and regularized grammatical rules (hence "pattern"). More important, it continues to be the language of the Group, the Folk, the Black masses to whom the New Poets have committed their talents. Revitalizing the Black Cultural Sensibility dictates that the old pejorative associations be replaced with new positive ones. And so, like the Antilles Negro, who "goes home from France expressing himself in the dialect if he wants to make it plain that nothing has changed," American Black poets are articulating the new consciousness in the lingo of the Folk. For the people's lingo is the poet's lingo too. No longer is the Black writer to be set apart from his ghetto brethren by using the "standard" dialect (known as "talkin proper," or "tryin to talk White" in the Black community.) The father of the Black Arts Movement, Imamu Amiri Baraka (1966)—also known as LeRoi Jones–attests to the political and cultural oneness triggered by Black English:

> I heard an old Negro street singer last week, Reverend Pearly Brown, singing, "God don't never change!" This is a precise thing he is singing. He does not mean "God does not ever change!" He means "God don't never change!" The difference is in the final human reference . . . the form of passage through the world. A man who is rich and famous who sings, "God don't never change," is confirming his hegemony and good fortune . . . or merely calling the bank. A blind hopeless Black American is saying something very different. Being told to "speak proper," meaning that you become fluent with the jargon of power, is also a part of not "speaking proper." That is, the culture which desperately understands that it does not "speak proper," or is not fluent with the terms of social strength, also understands somewhere that its desire to gain such fluency is done at a terrifying risk. The bourgeois Negro accepts such risk as profit. But does *close-ter* (in the context of "jes a close-ter, walk wi-thee") mean the same thing as *closer?* Close-ter, in the term of its user is, believe me, exact. It means a quality of existence, of actual physical disposition perhaps . . . in its manifestation as a *tone* and *rhythm* by which people live, most often in response to common modes of thought best enforced by some factor of environmental emotion that is exact and specific. Even the picture it summons is different, and certainly the "Thee" that is used to connect the implied "Me" with, is different. The God of the damned cannot know the God of the damner, that is, cannot know he is God. As no Blues person can really believe emotionally in Pascal's God, or Wittgenstein's question, "Can the concept of God exist in a perfectly logical language?" Answer: "God don't never change." (pp. 171–172)

Equally significant in the poets' use of the Black Idiom is their keen awareness of the highly oral nature of Black culture. To get the written word to the

Black nonreading, still essentially pre-literate community, the New Black Writer, must, as Don Lee (1969b) says,

> move into the small volume direction . . . small Black works that can be put into the back pockets and purses, volumes that can be conveniently read during the 15 minute coffee break or during the lunch hour . . . we as Black poets and writers are aware of the fact that the masses (and I do not use the word lightly for I am part of the masses) of Black people *do not read books.* (pp. 53–57)

In these "small volumes" the poets have capitalized on the fact that though Black folks don't *read,* they highly value verbal skills expressed *orally.* Emphasis is on the ability to rap, and Black culture abounds with verbal rituals and rhetorical devices through which this oral linguistic competence can be expressed.

I am accounting here for a tradition in the Black Experience in which verbal performance becomes both a means of establishing one's reputation and a teaching/socializing force. Black talk is never simple cocktail chitchat, but a functional dynamic that is simultaneously a mechanism for learning about life and the world and a vehicle for achieving group recognition. Even in what appears to be only casual conversation, whoever speaks is aware that his personality is on exhibit and his status at stake. He must have some knowledge to contribute to the group, and his contribution must be presented in a dazzling, entertaining manner. Black speakers are greatly flamboyant, flashy, and exaggerative; Black raps are highly stylized, dramatic, and spectacular; speakers and raps are conveyors of information. But Black communicative performance is a two-way street, and so the "audience" becomes both observers and participants in the speech event. With its responses, the listeners can influence the direction of a given rap and at the same time acknowledge (or withhold) their approval, depending on the linguistic skill of the speaker. No preacher can succeed if he's not a good talker. One of the culture heroes of the barbershop, poolhall, or street corner is bound to be the cat who captures everybody's attention with dashing displays of verbal ingenuity. H. Rap Brown was dubbed "Rap" because of his rapping ability, and the continuing success of Chicago's Rev. Jesse Jackson is due in large measure to his ability to "win friends and influence people" with his rap. I mean like in the church or on a street corner, a Brother is only as bad as his rap bees.

I move now to a consideration of the specific rhetorical devices and linguistic patterns inherent in Black verbal style and the artistry involved in the poets' use of this vehicle for the conveyance of Black Consciousness. Most of my examples will come from Don Lee, the dynamic young writer, who, of all the new Black poets, has most effectively capitalized on the Black Idiom for maximum power and poetic effect.

LINGUISTIC FEATURES IN THE NEW BLACK POETRY

From a strictly linguistic view, Black speech can be characterized in terms of lexicon (vocabulary), syntax (grammar), and phonology (pronunciation). Without delving into the technical controversy over whether these patterns are derived from a West African or an Anglo-Saxon language base (Dillard, 1972; McDavid, 1951, 1967), we can apply the term *Black English* on the grounds of statistical validity, since the dialect is used by an overwhelmingly greater percentage of Blacks than Whites.

The phonological items employed represent the poets' attempts to spell according to Black America's pronunciation. Due to the vagaries of the English spelling system, this is a difficult task and the poets here meet with uneven success. It makes sense for Ernie Mkalimoto (1969) to title his poem "Energy for a New Thang," since Black folk say *thang*, not *thing*. Similarly, Don Lee (1968, 1969j, 1970b) will write *mo* for *more* and *befo* for *before* because characteristically Blacks delete intervocalic arid final *r*'s. Sonia Sanchez (1970b) renders the loss of participial endings with such forms as *hitten, tryin*, etc. Even some rather extreme instances come off all right, as in Baraka's (1969) attempt to capture Black America's pronunciation of *head* with *haid*. However, such substitutions as *u* for *you*, *wd.* and *cd.* for *would* and *could*, respectively, and *yr.* for *your* (as in *yr. head*—why not *yo head?*) do not fit any Black scheme of things, and often such alterations do nothing more than make for difficult reading. Nonetheless, we should be apprised of what the poets are trying to do and can certainly applaud their successes in oral performance, for here is where the full range of Black intonation patterns, tonal qualities, and other aspects of Black phonology in the poetry spring to life.

Syntax is much more easily rendered orthographically than phonology, and in their employment of grammatical usage, the poets are quite successful in reproducing the dialect. They reveal a fine and accurate artistic ear for the systematic features of Black English syntax and thus skillfully enhance the conversational flavor of the poetry. The most pronounced and distinctive feature of Black English syntax (also the most often cited in the current literature on Black speech), is the use of *be* as finite verb. Characteristically *be* (also *bees* and *bes)* indicates a repeated state of affairs (i.e., durative aspect). *Be* is omitted when the statement applies only to the present or when it has the effect of communicating an all-time truth (i.e., no habitual occurrence is conveyed.) For example, *the coffee be cold* means the coffee is repeatedly, daily, cold; *the coffee cold* means the coffee is cold now. Some examples from Lee: "u bes hitten the man hard all day long" (1969i, p. 57) and "why she be doing the things she don't do" (1970a, p. 22). Due to its obvious difference from "White English," then, *be* is a favorite of the poets, often employed to the point of overuse, and occasionally not in strict conformity with the rules for its application. For example, Sonia Sanchez's (1970a) "we bes the culture bearers," for *we the culture bearers*—i.e., as a simple statement of an all-time fact.

The lexical items in the New Black Poetry are those generally labeled Afro-American slang—words like *cool, hip, up-tight, dig,* etc.—ordinary terms with two levels of meaning. This attribution of double meanings to common English words has its origin in the use of a coded language among slaves. Lacking a really different language in which to camouflage their feelings and thoughts from the slave master—now the Man—Black folks simply took the Anglo-Saxon vocabulary and made it work for them by imposing upon English words a Black semantic slant. On the Black English level, "stealing away to Jesus" really indicated stealing away from the slave master, and today every Black person knows that your "main nigger" is your best friend. While many terms from the Black Lexicon now enjoy mainstream currency, there are still some expressions that remain insulated in Black America because they are so firmly rooted in the Black Experience and cannot properly be understood outside the context of that Experience (*doo-rag* and *pimp*, discussed below, are two such examples). These terms, along with those borrowed by and popularized in White America, have become the conceptual tools of the New Black Poets.

Artistically, the use of Black lexical items gives the poets greater powers of metaphorical condensation within a political-cultural framework that their audience is hip to. Consider, for example, Don Lee's (1969g) description of Malcolm X as being from a "long line of super-cools, doo-rag lovers, and revolutionary pimps" (p. 33). *Super-cools* and *pimps*, living outside the bounds of the White man's law and customs, are culture heroes, dashing, flamboyant men, who don't work and manage to survive by their cunning, wits, and unfortunately, exploitation of other (usually Black) people. A *pimp* lives off the earnings of Black prostitutes; a *super-cool* is a hustler who may have a variety of *games*, i.e., devious schemes for obtaining what he wants, as confidence ("con") game. *Doo-rag* refers to the scarves Black men wear around their heads to hold their pressed (artificially straightened and curled) hair in place. This process is commonly referred to as a "do." (I am talking about a time Pre-Naturals when such coiffured hair was believed to enhance the beauty and sex appeal of Black men.) What Lee is alluding to, of course, is Malcolm X's early life as a criminal, dope pusher, and pimp. However, the fact that Lee calls him a "revolutionary" pimp suggests that the leadership and Black political consciousness Malcolm later exhibited lay within him all the time. By extension, Lee is also implying that the same revolutionary potential lies in other Black pimps. With this phrasing, then, the poet has used a cultural image and message familiar to his (Black) audience and with a great stroke of brevity has allowed a line to reveal a complete story. (Such, of course, is the way any good poet operates; what is unique here is the effective execution of the operation in a Black way.)

STYLISTIC FEATURES IN THE NEW BLACK POETRY

As the preceding discussion of Afro-American lexicon suggested, it is in style, rather than language per se, that the cultural distinctiveness of the Black Idiom can be located. That is to say that it is not so much the words themselves (which are, after all, English), but the way in which the words are used—the way in which the various patterns of Black communication combine with Black verbal rituals to produce a style that reflects the collective sensibility of Afro-Americans. There is a Black style of speaking/rapping, quite apart from patterns of dialect, and while, as I said earlier, debate ensues over the *linguistic* origins of Black speech, there is general consensus that the stylistic patterns are the sole property of Black folks. It is in style, rather than in strict dialect usage, that the power of the rap is made most manifest, and while not all the New Black Poets liberally use the dialect, they *do* heavily exploit Black verbal style, making this the unifying focal point in the form of the New Black Poetry.

The style of the Black Idiom consists of a Sacred and a Secular component, with both dimensions sharing certain rhetorical commonalities. Elsewhere I have delineated Sacred and Secular styles in greater detail (Smitherman, 1973). Suffice it here to say that while the Secular style is the primary domain of the street corner rapper, and the Sacred that of the preacher, no sharp dichotomy exists. The Black preacher's rap and Black church service abound in secularisms and there is very often a sacred quality surrounding the verbal rituals of the Secular style. (The Sacred-Secular continuum in Black culture is exhibited most strikingly in Black music where Gospel and Blues are often indistinguishable—only by digging on the lyrics can you tell). The stylistic features in the New Black Poetry are the Dozens, the Toast, Call-Response, Signification, and Rhythmic Pattern. The first two exist in the Secular Tradition only. The last three appear in both the Sacred and Secular Traditions, but for reasons too complicated to go into here (the decline of religion in contemporary times being a prime one), the poets rely on secular variations of these three devices.

The Dozens

This is a verbal game played by talking disparagingly about someone's mother. The game can extend, by analogy, to include other relatives and even ancestors (although, like Langston Hughes's Jesse B. Semple, most Black folks don't "play the Dozens that far back") (Hughes, 1961, p. 3). The objective is to better one's opponent with more-caustic and usually more-humorous insults. Played for fun or viciousness—and it can be either—the Dozens is a competitive oral test of linguistic ingenuity and verbal fluency in which the winner, determined by the audience's responses, becomes a culture hero.

Lee (1969f) uses the Dozens to speak satirically of the nonsensical attempts of Blacks to "outBlack" one another:

> into the sixties
> a word was born . . . . . . BLACK
> & with Black came poets
> & from the poet's ball points came:
> Black doubleBlack purpleBlack blueBlack beenBlack was
> Black daybeforeyesterday Blackerthan ultraBlack super
> Black BlackBlack yellowBlack niggerBlack Blackwhi-te-man
> Blackerthanyoueverbes 1/4 Black unBlack coldBlack clear
> Black my momma's Blackerthanyourmomma . . . . . . (pp. 22–23)

In his short "tribute" to George Wallace, he again uses this ritual to great effect:

> wallace for president
> his momma for vice-president
>   was scribbled
>   on the men's room wall
>   on
>   over
>   the toilet
> where
> it's
> supposed to be. (Lee, 1969e, p. 34)

Maya Angelou (of *I Know Why the Caged Bird Sings* fame) plays not the Dozens, but the "Thirteens," with separate but stylistically parallel versions denouncing the untogetha actions of both Blacks and Whites:

THE THIRTEENS (BLACK)

Your Momma took to shouting
Your Poppa's gone to war,
Your sister's in the streets
Your brother's in the bar,
The thirteens. Right On.

. . . .

And you, you make me sorry
You out here by yourself,
I'd call you something dirty,
But there just ain't nothing left,
Cept
The thirteens. Right On.

THE THIRTEENS (WHITE)

Your Momma kissed the chauffeur,
Your Poppa balled the cook,
Your sister did the dirty,
in the middle of the book,
The thirteens. Right On.

. . . .

Your money thinks you're something
But if I'd learned to curse,
I'd tell you what your name is
But there just ain't nothing worse
than
The thirteens. Right On.
       (Angelou, 1971, pp. 46–47)

The Toast

The Toast is a narrative tale, complete with rhymed lines and poetic imagery—gutsy and sexual. The hero is usually a fearless, defiant Black man (what Black folks approvingly call a "bad nigguh"), who overcomes seemingly insurmountable odds. Like Stag-O-Lee who was so bad even White folks feared him and only God was able to kill him—even then it took "3,412 angels 14 days, 11 hours, and 32 minutes to carry the giant death thunderbolt to the Lord" (Lester, 1969, p. 129). The hero might be symbolized in animal form, like the Signifying Monkey, who, though the underdog, outdoes the big, bad Lion (symbolizing the White man).

Black prison poet Etheridge Knight (1968) "toasts" two such bad nigguhs. One is the Black prisoner Hard Rock, who "was 'known not to take no shit / From nobody,' and he had the scars to prove it" (p. 11). I mean Hard Rock was so bad he "had once bit / A screw on the thumb and poisoned him with syphilitic spit" (p. 12). Knight's other superbad underdog is Shine, the protagonist in the old Black folk Toast "Shine and the Sinking of the Titanic." In his poeticized and effectively condensed version, Knight (1971) gives formal literary expression to Shine's heroic deeds with such lines as

> And, yeah, brothers,
> while white/america sings about the unsink
> able molly brown
> (who was hustling the titanic
> when it went down)
> I sing to thee of Shine
> the stoker who was hip
> enough to flee the fucking ship
> and let the white folks drown
> with screams on their lips
> yeah, I sing of Shine
> and how the millionaire banker stood on the deck
> and pulled from his pocket a million dollar check
> saying Shine Shine save poor me
> and I'll give you all the money a Black boy needs—
> how Shine looked at the money and then at the sea
> and said jump in muthafucka and swim like me—
> (pp. 209–210)

The Toast-Teller narrates in first person and embellishes the tale according to his own verbal whims; hence no two versions are ever alike, not even when related by the same person. Told in epic fashion, the movement of the Toast proceeds episodically with the overriding theme being the omnipotence of Black folks as symbolized in the lone figure of the Black hero. Full of braggadocio, he is always talkin bout how bad he bees, and his boasting consumes a good portion of the Toast's content. This aspect of the Toast is given a refreshing and innovative poetic twist in Nikki Giovanni's (1970) "Ego Tripping":

> I was born in the congo
> I walked to the fertile crescent and built
> the sphinx
> I designed a pyramid so tough that a star
> that only glows every one hundred years falls
> into the center giving divine perfect light
> I am bad
> . . . .
> I sowed diamonds in my back yard
> My bowels deliver uranium
> the filings from my fingernails are
> semi-precious jewels
> On a trip north
> I caught a cold and blew
> My nose giving oil to the arab world
> I am so hip even my errors are correct
> I sailed west to reach east and had to round off
> the earth as I went
> The hair from my head thinned and gold was laid
> across three continents
>
> I am so perfect so divine so ethereal so surreal
> I cannot be comprehended
> except by my permission
> I mean . . . I . . . can fly
> like a bird in the sky . . . (pp. 37–38)

Call-Response

Call-Response is a basic ritual in the Black Idiom. It is what one hears in Black churches where the preacher's rap is punctuated by *Amen's, Tell it Reb's, Yes, Lord's,* etc. It is what Richard Wright describes in the opening scene of "Big Boy Leaves Home" (1936) and again in the street corner scene in *Black Boy* (1937). It is a pattern in which the speaker's solo voice alternates or is intermingled with the audience's response. This can take the form of a back-and-forth banter between the rapper and various members of the audience in which, for instance, they will raise points to see how skillfully he deals with them. Or the audience will spur the speaker on to greater heights of verbal accomplishment by their expressions of approval, such as laughter, or with phrases like "Oh, you mean, nigger," "Get back, baby," or "Get down man," etc. When the New Black Poet performs, responses such as these and frequent *Teach Brother's* may interrupt him, but he is not unsettled by this; rather he thrives on audience involvement. Of course the poetry on the printed page obviously cannot reflect the Call-Response Pattern, but in a reading, the poet demonstrates his awareness of this ritual and its essential function as a pattern of Black communication. He wants to, indeed *needs* to, know that his audience is moved by his rap and gauges its power by the degree and extent of their vocal responses.

Signification

This is a ritualized insult, a verbal put-down, in which the speaker needles (i.e., *signifies)* his audience or some member of the audience either to initiate verbal "war" or to make a point hit home. Also synonymous with the Black term *Capping,* effective Signification is characterized by exploitation of the unexpected and quick verbal surprises. Like the Dozens, Signification is accepted within a game context, with both opponent and audience expecting the speaker to launch this offensive to achieve his desired effect. Many of Don Lee's titles are excellent examples of Signification, e.g.: "Nigerian Unity / or little niggers killing little niggers"; "Reflections on a Lost Love (for my brothers who think they are lovers and my sisters who are the real-lovers)"; "A Poem for Negro intellectuals (if there bes such a thing)"; "A Message All Blackpeople Can Dig (+ a few Negroes too)"; "On Seeing Diana go Madddddd (on the very special occasion of the death of her two dogs—Tiffany & Li'l Bit—when she cried her eyelashes off)" (1969c, 1970b).

Lee's (1969a) "But he was cool or: he even stopped for green lights" is one of the best poetic uses of this device. Here he employs the Signification of the title as a unifying image throughout the poem. Using the metaphor of *cool* ironically, Lee proceeds to castigate the typical self-styled Black revolutionary, caught up in rhetoric and appearance; all talk and no action. "Super-cool" thinks he is "ultra-hip"; yet he is doing nothing constructive to aid the cause of Black Liberation beyond "greeting u in Swahili, saying good-by in Yoruba, and wearing a double natural that wd. put the sisters to shame." (I mean, like, can you dig a cat being so cool that he even stops for GREEN lights?) Lee gets excellent poetic and political mileage out of the color imagery in the poem, juxtaposing green-cool with red-hot. To be Black is not to be calm, cool, and collected. To be Black is to be angrily aware of, heated, and moved by Black oppression. "To be Black is to be very-hot."

Rhythmic Pattern

Here I refer to the Black Idiom's emphasis on rhyme and sound. The speaker's voice tone assumes a sonorous, musical quality. The sound of what he is saying is often more important than sense, in any sheer semantic way, hence there is a good deal of repetition and rhyming for effect. The idea is to mesmerize his audience with the magical sounds of his message. It is this device that links Black verbal style with Black musical style. In using it, the poets are capturing not only the flavor of the Black Idiom, but approximating the sound and soul of Black music, which is believed to be the most important dynamic of Black Cultural Reality. Lyrics or phrases from Black music are interspersed within the poetry, to be sung when the poem is read aloud, as in Lee's title poem, "Don't Cry, Scream (for John Coltrane / from a Black poet / in a basement apt. crying dry tears of 'you ain't gone.')" (1969d). At the end of the following stanza, Lee sings the Ray Charles/Temptations version of "Yesterday" for full effect:

> swung on a faggot who politely
> scratched his ass in my presence.
> he smiled broken teeth stained from
> his over-used tongue, fisted-face.
> teeth dropped in tune with ray
> charles singing "yesterday."

In addition, the marginalia of this poem contains such instructions as "sing loud & high with feeling" and "sing loud & high with feeling letting yr / voice break."

In a similarly effective fashion, Baraka (1970) draws upon James Brown's first hit recording, "Please, Please, Please." The poem is "The Nation Is Like Ourselves." In it, Baraka pleads for the return of middle-class Blacks back to the community fold. Having employed the entreaty "please" in several stanzas ("please mister liberated nigger," "please mr ethnic meditations professor," "doctor nigger, please," etc.), Baraka concludes with

> yes the sweet lost nigger
>   you are our nation sick ass assimilado
>   please come back
>   like james brown say
>   please please please (p. 11)

Black poetic raps, like their secular counterparts in the Black Oral Tradition, achieve a fluidity and flowingness due to this Rhythmic Pattern. The poets' breathless, unpunctuated, rap-rap-rap-rap-rap-rap bombards the audience with words, working a kind of hypnotic Black magic on their souls, and hitting the mind and heart in fresh, unexpected ways like good poetry does. Lee's (1969h) "Poem to Complement Other poems," combining musical effects and repetition, excellently exemplifies the totality of this Rhythmic Pattern. Exhorting Black folks to enter into a new state of consciousness, the Poet details the types of changes required and the necessity for change. Each statement begins and/or ends with the word *change*. Some examples:

> change. from the last drop to the first, maxwellhouse did. change.
>   change.
> Colored is something written on southern outhouses. change.
> greyhound did, i mean they got rest rooms on buses. change.
> change, stop being an instant yes machine. change. (p. 36)

The poem continues like this for several lines, building to the climax of the last stanza, where the word *change* is repeated 23 times in near succession. With the final lines of repetition, Lee plays off on the phonological similarity between *change* and *chain* and gives us something reminiscent of Aretha Franklin singing about the "chains of love." (It's obvious, of course, what kind of "chains" Lee is singing about.)

> realenemy change your enemy change your change change change
>   your enemy change change change change your change change
>   change. (p. 38)

By this point, the audience is completely, nearly mystically engrossed in the evocative call of the poem and prepared for its message, contained in the hard-hitting impact of the concluding line: "change your mind nigger."

Traditionally, poetry was recited and/or sung such that its creator was a kind of performing bard. Couple this with Black Culture's emphasis on orality, music, and verbal performance. It then becomes clear why the poetic genre strikes at the heart of the Black Cultural Sensibility, and also why it is only through oral delivery that the audience can fully appreciate the artistic import and meaning of the New Black Poetry. The linguistic/stylistic machinery of this Poetry is firmly located in the Black Oral Tradition, and the Black Poet of today is forging a new art form steeped in the uniqueness of Black Expressive Style. When used skillfully, by, for example, a Don Lee, who is able to synthesize the emotional and the cerebral, this Style becomes an excellent poetic strategy to deliver a political message and to move Black folks to constructive political action. This, then, is the "Power of the Rap."

NOTE

1.   I borrow this term from Black fictionist Ishmael Reed (see also his Introduction to *19 Necromancers From Now* [New York: Doubleday, 1970]), who says:

Sometimes I feel that the condition of the Afro-American writer in this country is so strange that one has to go to the supernatural for an analogy. Manipulation of the word has always been related in the mind to manipulation of nature. One utters a few words and stones roll aside, the dead are raised and the river beds emptied of their content.

The Afro-American artist is similar to the Necromancer (a word whose etymology is revealing in itself!). He is a conjuror who works JuJu upon his oppressors; a witch doctor who frees his fellow victims from the psychic attack launched by demons of the outer and inner world.

CHAPTER 6

Sounds Bouncin Off Paper

Black Language Memories and Meditations

Sonia Sanchez

When I was at San Francisco State University in 1967, I taught a course on Black English. I used poetry books, anthologies. Most of the things we did at the time were mimeographed. This was before Xerox copies. This was the mimeomachine era and we got blue and purple on our hands. The Sistas in the Black Student Union would type up all the poems I needed and most of them were written in Urban Black English. Young people who came into our class spoke in this fashion. They felt drawn to this poetry because it reflected them. They felt themselves in the language that was spoken in this poetry, that was written in this poetry. When people see themselves and hear themselves, they recognize themselves. As a consequence of hearing themselves in the language, they say, "Indeed I am." It is possible to see oneself in a poem, you know.

When the students in my course began writing, they did so in their language. I accepted it in class. I encouraged it. I saw that they were nervous about writing. It seemed to me that what was important was to get them to write what they spoke. I told people to get tape recorders, have someone write down what they said. So when they brought their papers in, here was this magical writing with all this language. And it was like, Black English, you know. It had all the lyricism. It had all the beat. And I said, "Read it out loud." And they read it out loud. And they heard the music. They heard the beauty. And I said, "The terrible thing we have to do now is translate this. It's just like translating Spanish to English. When you translate Nicolas Guillén to English you lose something. Keep the one written in Black English and now let's translate it and see what it becomes, and see what it loses." And then they learned how to do that. They didn't mind doing it. They had success with their own language first, and then we said, "Let us now go from 'I be' to 'I am.'"

In the course, I let them write just what they felt. They spelled just as they wanted to spell. Black English was acceptable in the classroom because many of these people had been told they couldn't write. We released them and said, "It's okay." I remember a student who was having a terrible time writing. I let him tape his stuff and we got it transcribed. I showed it to him and said, "See, you can write." He looked up and said, "Ohhhhhhhhhhhhhhhhhh!" Sometimes you think that you can't do something because it's not done in the usual way, in the way that you are accustomed to seeing it.

My classroom was an extension of the community. I had people sitting on the floor, sitting out in the hallways. When I was doing the lecture on Black Literature, people would come from all over the community. They weren't registered but I would let them come and listen. My students went to help Joe Goncalves produce his *Journal of Black Poetry*. The point was that you wrote but you also made a contribution to the community. You learned how to put out a magazine. From the very beginning, we always said there must be a connection between your courses and the community. Some of these same students would come out and do readings with me.

Others would help with the Saturday Freedom School where the children would come and learn things about Blackness, about Black History. They were held off campus in the Black community. We also had a lot of readings on campus. We invited Baraka out to San Francisco to do the cultural part of the Black Studies Program. He was brought out to be the Cultural Director in a sense. That's how we started doing things at the Black House. The Black House was a house where Eldridge Cleaver moved to—in the heart of San Francisco where Black Arts Movement people came together. It was Baraka, Ed Bullins, Marvin X, and myself. We did readings. We cooked and sold food. People would be lined up around the block to get in. We read poetry. We planned the programs. Baraka and Bullins did some of their plays. Theater troupes would come and perform.

When we got out there, we were to teach Black Studies and the president of San Francisco State said he hadn't agreed to have a Black Studies program. So we were all out there with no money and no jobs. In order to combat what the president had done, we gave our courses anyway. We taught for free, at night. The students came out in spite of what the university said. People piled in. Of course, one semester later Black Studies became a reality and we taught our classes and got paid for it.

I taught in a high school out there in San Francisco. There were men at risk in the high school where I taught. They were all high school age. Maybe some older than high school. I taught them English. Every course that I did I used Black poetry. Black literature. I was doing both classes at the same time. Since I wasn't getting paid to teach at San Francisco, I had to find a job. I was teaching high school during the day and university classes at night, which was unusual. Students had their other classes during the day and our classes at night. See, we were proving that the president had lied when he said, "No, I didn't promise this." So what we did was just give courses at night to show that we were committed to Black Studies.

MALCOLM X AND THE USE OF BLACK LANGUAGE

Prior to going out to San Francisco State I'd never taught Black Language. We used to go out in the streets in California. We used to go out with Ed Bullins, Amiri Baraka, Marvin X, and Sarah Fabio and do our poetry and our plays in the streets of Oakland. In Oakland! In Oakland! And you know, we'd go out and we'd beat the drum and bring people outside. And they'd bring their little chairs out. In that Black House in San Francisco we were replicating what happened in the Black Arts Repertory Theatre in Harlem, in that brownstone on 131st Street.

San Francisco was the turning point for me because by the time I got out there my writing had begun to change. It changed in 1965 with the death of Malcolm. There was the anger at what had happened, that this country could just kill someone as important and powerful as he was. And progressive as he was, too. Do you know what I'm saying? My writing was picked up by Baraka and published in the journal *Liberation* that came out of Paris and Algeria. That was one of the reasons that they asked me to come out to California.

I think Malcolm authenticated the use of Black Language, although he doesn't get credit for it. He said things using really Black English. I did a program, "Malcolm: The Poet." That's what I called him. I took his speeches and arranged them so it was indeed poetry. In some of his speeches he'd use "Wrong English" to emphasize something. He brought the cadence and rhythm of Black English, the rise and fall, the control of an audience. His poetry engaged his audience in such a fashion that they couldn't move. He mesmerized people. His style of delivery was distinctly Black. It was also humorous. We fell out laughing. He'd make us get angry, then he'd bring us back down to reality. He also would use phrases that were distinctly Black. We would look up and recognize. That's why I say poetry is subconscious. It is as much work for those who listen and say "Amen" as it is for those who recite it. Malcolm brought to us a consciousness we knew already. And he was up on current events. He would mention someone's name in a speech that perhaps we didn't know. I would rush out to the Schomburg to find out who that was. He would bring in Africa and what was going on in the world. He brought the world's stage to us.

Shortly after Malcolm's death, Dudley Randall put out a call around the country that he was doing an anthology of poems for Malcolm. I had done this poem almost right after his death:

MALCOLM *by Sonia Sanchez*

do not speak to me of martyrdom
of men who die to be remembered
on some parish day
i don't believe in dying
though I too shall die
and voices like castaments
will echo me
yet this man
this dreamer,
thick-lipped with words
will never speak again
and in each winter
when the cold air cracks
with frost, I'll breathe

his breath and mourn
my gun-filled nights
he was the sun that tagged
the western sky and
melted tiger-scholars
while they searched for stripes,
he said, 'fuck you white
man,' we have been
curled too long, nothing
is sacred now, not your
white face nor any

land that separates
until some voices
squat with spasms.

do not speak to me of living
life is obscene with crowds
of white on Black
death is my pulse
what might have been
is not for him/or me

but what could have been
floods the womb until I drown.

(Reprinted with permission from D. Randall & M. G. Burroughs [Eds.], *For Malcolm: Poems on the Life and Death of Malcolm X* [Detroit: Broadside Press, 1969])

I wanted that poem to be beautiful for him because he was a beautiful man. I wanted that poem to show some of the anger that he felt, too. And then I wanted that poem to end in such a way that he would be eternal, that he would be viable, current. Every time you read it you would see him. He would be always on our tongues. What Malcolm did is that he gave us the power to speak in our own tongue, our own Black Language. It was my duty to continue the message of this man called Malcolm. It was my duty to educate, to say out loud what people were too afraid to say. From Malcolm I learned to think critically about everything. I had to start thinking critically about Africa, about the movies I saw, about the television I watched. Everything. When you are conscious, you are conscious. When you are unconscious, people can say anything to you and either you will not respond or you will agree. When you are conscious you will say, "Let me examine that before I respond to it."

CELEBRATING THE PEOPLE WHO SPEAK BLACK ENGLISH

When there was a debate around the issue of Black English as a language, Jimmy Baldwin said, "Of course it is a language." He said you get upset when we go ahead and use it and make something of it. You don't teach us properly. Then when we do what we do and do it well, you gon come and say, "Ah, ah, is this right?" Of course it is. What caused me to use Black English? It came from some place deep inside. It came from reading Sterling Brown. It came from reading Langston Hughes. It came from reading Miss Margaret Walker. It came from reading people who were using Black English and celebrating the people who spoke Black English and saying out loud, "These are authentic people. These are people who deserve to be heard. We will celebrate them and give them life and beauty." I realized that there was some herstory and history for us to do that.

LANGUAGE IS A WOMAN

I have a theory that language is a woman. I've always thought it. When you finally bring that beauty out of it, you cry, you scream. You have the same feeling as if you were having sex. Language does that. Language is the reason that we are humans. It distinguishes us from the lower animals. When we speak this Black Language we are bringing forth the beauty of our souls. We are saying that there is herstory here. Look how we made our own language. When they didn't allow us to speak "proper English" or didn't teach us. Look at this language that came out of our womb. Look at this language that we gave birth to. That is why, to me, Black English is a woman. It came out of our loins in order to say we existed, we are, we be; we threw it out and said, "Here it is, are that!"

Today, Urban Black English is the smart repartee. The back and forth kinda thing. Quick retort. The cloaked response. Moving to New York, a lot of our poems were about being smart and urban, like Malcolm was smart and urban/urbane. There was always a quick repartee going on. There is something, too, that makes it really deep and connected. Real Black English is connected to what is going on in the lifestyles of people, what is going on in the poverty, what is going on in not having, what is going on in saying out loud, "Hey, this is really what's happening to me and my people." It's like the poem I did about the woman who left her child in the crack house. The language that woman used is real, that real hard language. She said, "I'm here to tell you how I be. I'm this Black woman. I'm this woman with a child and I wanna tell you how hard it is for me to be." When the guy in the crack house turns to her, he says, "I want her. I need a virgin. Your pussy is too loose. You had so much traffic up yo pussy you could pull a truck up there and still have room for something else. . . ." I'm not just saying that for shock. I'm saying that anybody who would look at a little girl as a sexual partner would look at this woman, who is a crack addict, and say that. Be true to the language. Some people took the stuff that we said as vulgar. But when you live in some communities you hear that. You hear that language. You hear people thinking these thoughts. So what are you gonna say? Are you gonna go and censor it and say, "Let me put it a nicer way"?

The great thing about being a Mother/Woman is that you can sometimes use language that is very hard and people feel offended by it. Then you can turn right around and write a beautiful poem celebrating all of us. You have to admit that in our community we have all of these contradictions that go on.

WE BE WORD SORCERERS

In the introduction to *We Be Word Sorcerers*, I said, "Each one of us represented in this collection was born Negro in America with no knowledge of himself or history. Each one of us was the finished product of an American dream, nightmarish in concept and execution. Each one of us has survived to begin our journey toward Blackness." I was talking about several things. I was saying that we are the people who pick up the language and reformulate it, reconfigure what it means to be Black, what it means to be poor, what it means to be surviving, what it means to be beautiful in a country that says everything that is exaggerated or large is not beautiful. That's what I'm saying when I say we be word sorcerers. We come with the magic of words. We come with these magical words that can turn you into human beings.

BLACKS TRANSFORMED ENGLISH
LIKE COLTRANE DID "MY FAVORITE THINGS"

I always called it Black English. It wasn't called Black Dialect. Like Coltrane took the standard composition "My Favorite Things" and transformed it, we took English and transformed it. I used to hear the old "My Favorite Things" on the radio and I would turn it off. When Trane did "My Favorite Things," I understood that he and his music and the space that he opened up to me were my favorite things. That's what he did. He transformed it. And that's what we did. I imagine us as slaves trying to speak this English, and we asked them to repeat it. And when they didn't repeat it so we could hear it, we repeated it in our own way. We repeated it with our own beat, with our own African sensibility. That African sensibility made us say words that were quite different. They had a different style, a different sound, a different beat. And a different meaning, or at least a dual meaning. We had to do that in order to survive.

What I remember about reading to an audience the first time is that I was stricken at how the words stayed on the page. And how at the same time I remembered the language of my grandmother and my father and jazz musicians, how their sounds bounced off paper, went into some sacred space of broken tongues, reentered the atmosphere at such a pace that their reentry burned the edges of our souls and our ears.

Sometimes when people hear me read from *We A BaddDDD People*, they say to me, "I didn't read it that way." And I say, that's okay. Poetry works on many levels. One level is to hear the poet read her/his work. Another level is to take that poem home and read it to yourself silently. And then at other times you read it aloud. It doesn't really matter what it's all about. I always hear the music when I write. The difficulty before was that I did nothing with it. I might have made a notation, such as "to be sung," or I might have searched out words, or I might have written things in a choppy manner that would give a sense of musicality or nonmusicality. But I always heard some distant music someplace.

One of the first poems where I actually wrote, "to be sung," was in *We A BaddDDD People*. It was "a coltrane poem," but I never read it aloud. I would read it at home. Some people did not understand *We A BaddDDD People*. They liked *Homecoming*, but they didn't understand what I was trying to do with *We A BaddDDD People*. I was experimenting a lot with language and that book was necessary for me. They didn't understand the satirical point and Black humor of the "Suicide Poem." They didn't understand the "coltrane poem" and the "Poem for My Father," or the necessary hard-hitting words of "Revolution."

When I first heard the rappers I said out loud, "They gon get in trouble, because that's what we did." We got in trouble because we told the truth. We are an extension of each other. Or we are a continuation of each other. We continue the tradition and we bring an innovation to it each time. I say the Hip Hop Movement came out of the Black Arts Movement. And it was a natural progression, just as we really came out of the Harlem Renaissance. The Depression and The War, and then, here we came! The Civil Rights Movement, and there was a lull again, and then the country took everything that it could away from these young men and women in school. But the most important thing is that we are inventive. We invent and reinvent ourselves.

THE BLACKNESS OF SOUND IN HIP HOP POETICS

These new poets, the Hip Hop poets, heard the sound and picked it up. And they did the same thing we did with poetry and sound. They did the sound, the pace of sound, the swiftness of sound, the discordant way of looking at the world of sound, the Blackness of sound, the color of sound, the beat of sound, but above all was that fast beat. It is what I call the *New Bebopic Beat*. Because when the BeBop people started to play, nobody could keep up with them. It was so fast that you couldn't hear. I would always say to my kids when I first heard Hip Hop, "I can't hear it. I don't understand it." It was the same thing when Dizzy and Max were playing. Nobody could play it except them, and nobody could hear it. You had to have a fast ear to hear it. Otherwise they would play it and done been gone. Same thing happened with rap. It came at a fast pace and if you turned your head, you missed it. It was gone. The BeBop, the Bam and the Hip Hop.

I love our language. Once you understand what language can do, I tell you there is a reaaaaallllllll love affair that is going on there. Do you know what I am saying? And it is something that will last for a lifetime. My grandmother spoke Black English. She wasn't "an educated woman." It was her language and I used to imitate that language. They thought for a while that I was laughing at her, but I was doing it because it was so pretty. I heard the beauty of her language. So whatever she would say, I would say it. I would repeat it right behind her, just falling out on the floor, laughing, humming her words, because it was so pretty. She would say it and she would smile. It was like all the ordinary things you know that are beautiful. I didn't have the knowledge to appreciate it at that particular time but I knew I was in the midst of beauty.

NOTE

This chapter is based on numerous conversations with James G. Spady, editor of *360 Degreez of Sonia Sanchez: Hip Hop, Narrativity, Iqhawe, and Public Spaces of Being*. (*B.Ma*, 6.1 [Fall, 2001]).

CHAPTER 7

African American Communicative Practices

Improvisation, Semantic License, and Augmentation

Arthur K. Spears

The radical difference between the discursive tool kit of African Americans and other Americans, Whites in particular, is revealed by an observation I have made numerous times. Often at social gatherings of Blacks and Whites (or other non-Blacks), everyone begins the evening talking together. The talk is effortless, natural, and unmonitored. There arrives, however, a point late in the evening when many of the Black guests in integrated conversation groups begin shifting into Black ways of speaking. As this continues, the Whites (and other non-Blacks) increasingly fall silent, no longer able to fully understand or participate in the conversation that the Blacks are carrying on. Their confusion must result from listening to remarks made in English, the common language, whose meaning, intent, and relevance cannot be interpreted, for the simple reason that those remarks require a different communicative competence. These occurrences are instructive for highlighting the difference between linguistic (grammatical) competence and communicative (discourse) competence. They also reinforce the idea that the principal differences between Black ways of speaking and other forms of American speech lie in communicative practices. This is one of several reasons why African American communicative practices require more attention.

African Americans live out their lives in the context of two norm sets, the Eurocentric and the African Diasporic. These norm sets are frequently in conflict, as Du Bois (1961) and other scholars have noted. Often African Americans covertly value African Diasporic norms and behaviors while paying lip service to Eurocentric norms. But increasingly, especially during the past 40 years, there has been more sentiment in the Black community in favor of Black people being themselves, following the standards and norms of Black culture rather than worrying about how European Americans see us. Indeed, how Black people are seen by the outside community is determined primarily by the requirements of institutional White supremacy in the extraction of wealth from people of color and non-elite Whites. The sentiment against self-censure is notable in Hip Hop Culture and its products, and in the refusal of many Black artists appearing on television and film to modify their speech and nonverbal communication in deference to White (middle-class) norms. Increasingly, Black standards and norms are also infiltrating general American and, to a lesser extent, global popular culture, so that norm conflicts that were once severe have been significantly attenuated, where not erased.

These remarks are part of my continuing project to describe and theorize Black American communicative practices in macro and micro terms. Some of the most interesting and distinctive features of African American Language (AAL) grammar are to be uncovered in the kinds of African American discourses considered unsuitable for drawing rooms where hegemonic, Eurocentric norms prevail, but accepted without comment (even with satisfaction) by those who have been entertained and enlivened by Black talk. Readers who do not wish to be exposed to uncensored language (i.e., so-called obscenity) should read no further.

It has also been noted by a number of AAL scholars (notably Rickford, 1977) that U.S. Black ways of speaking probably connect us more to Caribbean creole languages than does AAL grammar. It also appears that Black ways of speaking, more so than any other aspect of language study, will help us understand the nature of African American culture, above and beyond its relationship to other cultures of the African Diaspora. This is because ways of speaking best illustrate elements of style and, more broadly, dispositions in self-presentation. For example, we note the remarkable use of *improvisation* in Black ways of speaking, a quality often noted in writing on Black music, in cuisine, and in playing sports.

The term *semantic license* is relatively straightforward. It refers to the freedom AAL speakers exercise in creating *neologisms*, or new words.[1] The invention of a word or larger constituent—for example, a phrase or clause—may involve the following:

- *resemanticized words:* attaching new meanings to preexisting morphs (e.g., *butter* and *phat*, general terms of positive evaluation)
- *nonce expressions:* new morphs and new meanings to go with them (e.g., *emusculation;* see below). These are created for the moment, not used repeatedly. Some resemanticized words start out as nonce expressions and go on to become established, at least for a while, in a community. For example, *edumacation* ("education") has been around at least during the 20th century. Constituents such as these are of interest because they

have been adopted into the AAL lexicon, becoming established new expressions. They may be part of the transient lexicon (i.e., slang), or they may become permanent for all practical purposes, as has *edumacation.*[2]

Augmentation refers to the expansion of words by means of adding segments or syllables in the process of inventing new words. But augmentation can also refer to the expansion of phrases and clauses through the addition of entire words. In cases where a phrase or clause has been augmented, an augmentation of individual words within those constituents may also occur.

Obviously, the augmentation of words involves semantic license; the two notions are interconnected. Semantic license, though, does not necessarily involve augmentation, since an existing form may be given a new meaning. The augmentation of constituents larger than the word may also involve semantic license, because novel forms are being created to express meanings that could be expressed using "plain" morphological and syntactic strategies. I oppose "plain" strategies to creative strategies that stretch and play with the morphological and syntactic rules of the language. Syntactic augmentation can be thought of as the process of taking a constituent with plain syntax and applying creativity to augment it. The following examples illustrate the difference:

- Get out of bed.
- Get your lazy behind[3] out of bed.

The second example incorporates a pseudoreflexive phrase, *lazy behind,* which fills in for an understood reflexive *yourself,* as in "Get yourself out of bed."

It could be argued that plain and creative aspects of morphology and syntax should not be distinguished except for discussions of poetics; or perhaps the distinction should be thought of as one that involves a continuum, rather than an opposition, allowing that performance-related creativity is present to varying degrees in most speech.

The example that follows illustrates semantic license with which a new meaning is attached to a preexisting morph:

Parent: It's time for you guys to go to bed.
Child: Aw, we don't want to go to bed now, we're watching . . .
Parent: I'm going to watch your behind with this pan if you don't turn off that TV and . . .

In this example, *watch* is used to signify *whip, beat,* or any number of other verbs that might express punitive action resulting from the child's questioning parental orders. The verbal routine exemplified occurs in the United States in non-AAL contexts with other ethnic groups, but semantic license is most extensive in AAL communities. Another example is useful. I recall watching the "Magic Air Show," the name given by several friends to a basketball game featuring Michael "Air" Jordan, the most celebrated basketball player of all time, and "Magic" Johnson. At one point in the game, one of the men present said something about "they got that emusculation." It is ironic that the nonce word is so close to *emasculation*, which was clearly not what the speaker meant. He referred instead to the feats of physical wizardry the players were able to perform on the court, thanks to their amazing musculature. The speaker sought emphasis: He wanted a special word to mark the special occasion and the special, unusual actions he was witnessing. That he laughed along with the others at his comment indicated his awareness of taking semantic license.[4]

Often, the use of semantic license is functionally similar to the use of *phonetically altered words*. This includes augmented words such as *edumacation* and *yoogly* ("ugly"), which have phonetic segments augmented by extra syllables or more phonetically salient vowels. Phonetically altered words may also involve *diminution*, whereby, for example, a diphthong becomes a monophthong, producing [hwIt] *whit* ("White"); or, where the initial glide and diphthong following it are changed, producing [çit][5] *ooh-eet* ("White"). These examples are usually used when Whites are around, when speakers dramatize their mock fear of Whites overhearing them, or both. Phonetically altered words are similar to words and phrases used with *semantic license,* in that phonetic alteration is a performative feature of speech.

Black style, the *Black aesthetic, Black performativity*—these are three terms, among others, that have been used to capture the most significant, interconnecting themes found throughout African American culture. The study of Black ways of speaking can illuminate the broad area these three terms attempt to capture, and what we may also refer to as Black culture generally, outside of language. Various forms of Black music—jazz, gospel, rhythm and blues—in their original forms made great use of basic Black cultural strands, such as improvisation and call-response, in expressing deep cultural attitudes and stylistic constants.[6]

Indeed, recent writings have extended our understanding of Black cultural strands to sport, especially in regard to the currently preeminent Black sport, basketball. Black players have dominated the game not only numerically, but also stylistically, by injecting general Black cultural constants into it, so much so that these features have become identified with the game and in some cases incorporated into the rules. Writers on basketball seem to agree that the injection of the Black aesthetic into basketball has helped it to replace baseball as the quintessentially American sport. After all, any quintessentially American activity is significantly Black in its cultural traits. These cultural strands are all connected in such a way that to mention one of them is to mention several more at the same time.

Performativity, for example, is equally evident in basketball, Black ways of speaking, and musical genres. By *performativity*, I mean the stylistic dramatization of the self that individuals infuse into their behaviors. Members of other ethnic groups (e.g., American White groups) often see these behaviors as inappropriate forms of attention-grabbing self-expression.

Boyd (1997) gets at the connections between various areas of African American culture in discussing a "truly disadvantaged Black male aesthetic" in gangsta rap, as well as other African American cultural forms:

> [Basketball is] . . . in its present form . . . an extension of Black popular culture, similar to jazz in an earlier era. . . . Detroit Pistons teams of the late 1980s and early 1990s became highly successful by playing in a *style* that had clearly evolved from the *depths of Black culture.* . . . With a style similar to that of gangsta rap, the Pistons [Detroit's professional basketball team] brought a menacing and aggressive, hard-nosed, no-bend, defense that many criticized for being too violent. (pp. 106–110, emphasis added)

This style of basketball recalls the ethic-aesthetic of the gangsta life as it is lived in lower-income Black neighborhoods and celebrated in gangsta rap. (See also Dyson's [1993] remarks on basketball and the Black aesthetic.)

Mentioning gangsta-ism is not to glorify this particular subpattern of Black culture, but to note that its performativity, among other features (sartorial emphasis, for example) ties it to Black culture in general. Boyd's description of basketball could just as well apply to crap and poker games in Black neighborhoods during the 1950s and 1960s.

DIRECTNESS:
A PRINCIPLE OF AFRICAN AMERICAN LANGUAGE USE

The project that Smitherman (1977, 2000) has implicitly undertaken in her work on AAL use is a search for widespread features that give AAL its distinctiveness. I used the term *principle* (Spears, 2001) to refer to behavior that characterizes much, but not all, of AAL use. Smitherman (1977) establishes four AAL speech principles: *signification* (also *signifying*), *narrative sequencing, call-response,* and *tonal semantics.* All these are interconnected. For example, in narrative sequencing, one may witness call-response, tonal semantics, and signification. The speech principle that I have discussed (Spears, 2001), *directness*,[7] is related to Smitherman's four principles. Thus, tonal semantics may be used in directness, and directness frequently characterizes narrative sequencing and call-response. Signification, like other African American speech genres (e.g., reading a person and playing the dozens) is direct by its very nature (Spears, 2001).

Direct speech is identified on the basis of form (sounds, words, etc.); content (literal meaning as well as intended function and actual function, i.e., its perlocutionary force); subject matter; and context of utterance, which is necessary to determine whether directness occurs and, if so, what it means. *Directness* is characterized by some combination of candor, aggressiveness, negative criticism, dysphemism, abuse, conflict, and obscenity, all often used consciously in the creation of interpersonal drama. The use of directness frequently involves a performance, with an audience and with nonverbal gesticulations often associated with performance. It is important to note that it is practically impossible to speak of directness without using culturally loaded, biased language, which may impart a negative cast to directness. Directness can actually have number of functions, ranging from positive (e.g., compliments) to negative (e.g., upbraiding and insults).

Smitherman (1977) and other AAL scholars (e.g., Mitchell-Kernan 1971; Morgan, 1998) have discussed what is referred to as *indirection*, which should not be taken as the opposite of directness. Indirection occurs when a speaker makes comments that require knowledge of audience and social setting for their interpretation, comments that may seem ambiguous on a superficial level but that are practically unambiguous given the knowledge that participants in the speech event have. Indirect speech may be direct if its interpretation is linked, for example, to insult. (See Spears, 2001, and Morgan, 1998, for a discussion of these and related terms.)

Directness can involve performance when remarks are made in a creative way, instead of stated plainly. In augmentation, syntax is complicated by adding words and circumlocutions that in many instances involve so-called obscenity. I write "so-called obscenity," because obscenity is a product of community norms. What is considered obscene in some communities is not necessarily obscene in others. For example, the word *bloody*, considered a swear word in Britain, is not an obscenity in the United States. Discussions of obscenity typically assume that hegemonic language norms reign across many social contexts in which they are actually not in effect.

The real issue is how we deal with different language norms within different communities, even within the same society. Related to this is the issue of power: How do we classify types of language that are censured by mainstream society as controversial or obscene, but that are not seen that way by people who speak those types and others outside the mainstream? Whose norms prevail? The position that I have taken is that we have to consider context and interlocutors before labeling expressions as obscene. Thus, if someone uses *bitch* as a perfectly neutral, unremarkable term for "female," or as a term of address for close relatives and friends (as happens in many if not most African American youth speech contexts), then it is pointless to consider *bitch* obscene. In such a case, the word has been *neutralized*: It no longer carries any negative traits associated with obscenity. Once neutralized in one context, some so-called obscene expressions may become neutralized in most or all other contexts in which members of certain social groups find themselves. In other words, they carry such expressions with them virtually everywhere they go, using them indifferently and attaching no special significance to them. In these cases, such expressions have been *normalized*. This is what has happened with *nigga*,[8] which has always been neutralized in some speech situations in African American communities.

The normalization of uncensored expressions is hardly unique to the Black community. It occurs with more and more frequency throughout the United States, Europe, and other areas of the world. It is part of the general postmodern phenomenon whereby language and other behaviors once restricted to a limited set of social settings today may be found across a wide range of social contexts.[9] In our newer buildings we see stylistic eclecticism, with remembrances and borrowings from the past mixed with signs of the new. Nudity, once restricted to the bedroom, the locker room, and X-rated films, today occurs in a wide range of social contexts. One important feature of postmodernism is choice—a wider range of possible choices, leading to the dismantling of boundaries.

We see this process of boundary breaking, fragmentation, and displacement in communicative practices as well, as language that was once kept strictly out of the drawing room is now welcomed in—and into the classroom, too. We are seeing "a new way of talkin'," as the traditional African American gospel song puts it. As once restricted expressions travel to a broader range of social settings, these expressions lose their capacity to shock and become ordinary, unremarkable terms. They become *normalized*.

TOWARD A GRAMMAR OF AUGMENTATION

Much of the directness in African American discourse is communicated through grammatical strategies making use of augmentation. In this section, we will examine some of the mechanisms through which directness is expressed, with the aim of outlining what a grammar of augmentation might look like.

The word most frequently employed in augments is *ass* and its equivalents, such as *booty, behind,* and metonyms such as *asshole* and *butthole*. There are three basic types of augments: those containing (1) pseudo reflexives; (2) pseudo (nonreflexive) pronouns; and (3) compound *ass*; or discourse *ass* (the term used in Spears, 1998).

1. *Pseudo reflexives*: Normally, a body part word substitutes for a reflexive pronoun.

> 1. Get your lazy ass out of bed.
> Cf. Get out of bed, Get yourself out of bed

The body-part word used in such expressions depends on the discourse context and must be relevant in some way to the situation. Thus,

> 2. Get your frog eyes out of here—what are you looking at?
> Cf. Get (yourself) out of here . . .

In the second example above, the issue is someone's looking where he/she shouldn't, so it is appropriate to use *eyes* in this sentence.

2. *Pseudo (nonrelexive) pronouns*: These substitute for a noun or pronoun.

> 3. His ass gon be sorry.
> Cf. *He gon be sorry.*

> 4. I saw her ass yesterday.
> Cf. *I saw her yesterday.*

> 5. I saw her give it to her ass.
> Cf. *I saw her give it to her.*

> 6. Sheila saw him give her ass that ring.
> Cf. *Sheila saw him give her that ring.*

> 7. He'll do anything for her ass.
> Cf. *He'll do anything for her.*

> 8. I peeped ("saw") her going in the club with his ass.
> Cf. *I peeped her going in the club with him.*

3. *Ass* compounds have a semantically bleached *ass* in them. The *ass* in these expressions does not refer to the anatomy; its meaning is grammatical rather than lexical. It is a discourse marker, an expressive element explicitly marking a discourse as direct or heightening the poetic and performance character of what is said or both. Unlike pseudo reflexives and pseudo pronouns, *ass* compounds (1) allow only the word *ass*, (2) may have inanimate referents, and (3) must be followed by a noun (including *self/selves*). The following examples illustrate these points:

9. Get all that ugly-ass junk out of here.
Cf. *Get all that ugly junk out of here.*

10. a. *Get all that ugly-butt junk out of here.
    b. *Get all that ugly-asshole junk out of here.
    c. *Get all that ugly-behind junk out of here.
    d. *Get all that ugly-eyed junk out of here.

Compound *ass* is semantically abstract and no longer references the body in any literal way. Indeed, that is one reason why it can be used in referring to inanimate objects. It can also be used in cases where the morpheme(s) with which it is compounded cannot refer to buttocks, e.g.,

11. Look at that smart-ass nigga.

Smart is an adjective that cannot refer to buttocks. However, in the case of adjectives that could refer to anatomical *ass*, there can be ambiguity:

12. Look at that fat ass idiot.

In the example above, I have not inserted a hyphen, which would indicate the use of compound *ass*. If compound *ass* were employed, the sentence could indicate that the individual in question is fat, while expressing nothing concerning his or her posterior specifically. Alternatively, the sentence could also explicitly refer to the individual's buttocks (with anatomical *ass*). The ambiguity, of course, stems from the fact that *fat* can describe the whole body or the body part alone.

The past tense suffix *-ed* provides another way (in my vernacular) of disambiguating the two senses of *ass*. Compound *ass* cannot occur with the suffix while anatomical *ass* can:

13. Look at that smart-ass idiot.

14. *Look at that smart-assed idiot.

but,

15. Look at that fat-ass idiot.

16. *Look at that fat-assed idiot.

17. Look at that fat assed idiot.

In my vernacular, Example 16 would have to be interpreted as anatomical. Notice that other anatomical expressions usually require the *-ed* suffix:

18. a. Look at that cross eyed fool.
    b. *Look at that cross eye fool.
    c. Look at that pigeon toed fool.
    d. *Look at that pigeon toe fool.

This is not always the case, however. There is some variation among speakers as to which body part words require the *-ed* suffix.

19. a. Look at that big headed fool.
    b. Look at that big head fool.

Ass compounds must be followed by a noun, as illustrated below:

20. a. *John is trifling-ass.
    b. *John is bitch-ass.
    c. *John is jive-ass ("insincere").

21. a. *John is a trifling-ass
    b. *John is a bitch-ass
    c. *John is a jive-ass.

Note that an *ass* compound cannot be grammatical whether it is construed as an adjective without any determiners (as in Example 20) or as a noun with a determiner (as in Example 21). These examples have an actual adjective in the *ass* compound, but note that in the following examples, *ass* is compounded with a noun, *bitch*. Therefore, the syntactic category (part of speech) of the word in the compound does not affect its grammaticality in cases where no noun follows the compound. Ungrammaticality without a following noun is quite independent of the part(s) of speech appearing in the compound.

22. a. John is a trifling-ass idiot.
    b. John is a bitch-ass idiot.
    c. John is a jive-ass idiot.

23. a. *Look at that trifling-ass.
    b. *Look at that bitch-ass.
    c. *Look at that jive-ass.

24. a. Look at that trifling-ass idiot.
    b. Look at that bitch-ass idiot.
    c. Look at that jive-ass idiot.

All three of the augment types may be self-referential. This is expected because they may be used in making positive remarks or in presenting a referent positively (whether the overall remark is positive or not):

25. You know, I am one fine-ass ("good-looking") muthafucka. (ass compound)

26. You know they gon pick his ass because he's got the qualifications. (pseudo pronoun)

27. You need to get your fine ass out of this hole ("dive"). (pseudo reflexive)

CONCLUSION

As with some other African American communicative practices, augmentation is found in the speech of other communities, but not to the same extent nor with the full range of grammatical strategies found in AAL. It is well known that style involves not only words and expressions, but also morphology and syntax. Some morphemes and syntactic constructions are restricted to certain styles of speech, as illustrated in the following sentence using the second subjunctive *were*, where the verb in the hypostasis is inverted with that clause's subject:

28. Were I you, I would leave immediately.
Cf. If I was you, I would leave immediately.

We cannot say that augmentation is restricted to directness, although the two are closely associated. Augmentation provides the perfect vehicle for expressing direct content and for displaying creativity, both in the grammatical sense and in the performative, improvisatory sense.

NOTES

1. *Neologism* is used in practically the sense as Morgan's (2001) *new word*, which she illustrates with new words of rap artists, (e.g., those of the artist Aceyalone [1995], *All Balls Don't Bounce* [Capitol. 30023], cited in Morgan, 2001) such as *arhythamaticulas*

and *arhythamatic* (Morgan, 2001). The term *neologism* is elaborated slightly differently here.

2. *Edumacation* often occurs in utterances such as *I didn't know you had all that edumacation*, in response to the speaker's learning that an interlocutor has a PhD or some other terminal degree. Years ago, before it was common to encounter Blacks with college degrees, it might easily be used by someone without a college education speaking of someone in college or with a college degree. This was the same period during which the expression *college man* was used, indicating that a man had graduated from college. (It's interesting that there was no corresponding term *college woman* that was used with any regularity. No doubt this ties into gender relations at the time: *College man* signaled marriageability based on class status and earning ability, the latter not normally the major factor in a woman's marriageability. Said of a married man, it indicated the social acceptability of the man and his family; a college-educated woman married to a noncollegeman could not confer the corresponding social acceptability on her family.) The use of *edumacation* conveys great admiration, envy, an effort at social equalizing—i.e., bringing down a notch or two the person with the education in that it gently mocks that education, or humbling oneself before assumed great accomplishment, or both.

3. In the community in which I was raised, and in the typical African American community, *behind* and its equivalents are frequently used in strong directives from adult to children notably and in a range of other settings as well.

4. However, he was probably not aware of the close-sounding *emasculation*'s existence as a word. Since its meaning is so different from what he intended, practically the opposite, had he been aware of it, he probably would have steered clear of anything sounding like it.

5. IPA symbols are used.

6. Sometimes, once these cultural forms are formally institutionalized, e.g., jazz music in university music programs, they may loose some of the traits that tie them into Black general culture because they have been divorced from the sociocultural contexts that produced them. They cease to have an organic, dialectic relationship with the society and culture in which they originated.

7. I have been using the term for some time. However, I should note that Wolfram and Schilling-Estes (1998) use the term in referring basically to the same phenomenon, though in a somewhat different sense.

8. I spell it *n-i-g-g-a* to distinguish it from *n-i-g-g-e-r*, which is associated with Whites and has a different meaning, and, as of late, a different referent also, since *nigga* is nowadays used by some American English speakers to refer to non-Blacks.

9. For an excellent discussion of postmodernism and poststructuralism, see Sarup (1989).

Part III

TOWARD LINGUISTIC EMANCIPATION

CHAPTER 8

Linguistic Emancipation in Global Perspective

John Baugh and Geneva Smitherman

We are ever mindful of linguistic oppression and the social dislocation that feeds it. While the remarks in this chapter and those of other contributors to this volume echo the voices of our enslaved African ancestors, we seek to affirm and exceed the linguistic legacy born of the African slave trade. Our focus will be primarily on African American Language (AAL), concentrating on the period since the ruling in *King v. Ann Arbor,* the so-called Black English case of 1979 that resounded throughout the United States like a revolutionary "shot heard round the world." From the time of *King* up to the present, there has been a voluminous body of linguistic research on the speech of Africans in the United States. We summarize some of the most critical research conducted during this period and conclude with a call for scholarly responsibility on language matters within and beyond the African Diaspora.

Recognizing that the past informs the present, and that, as the late James Baldwin said, we carry our history with us, we will first take a brief look at the earliest work on AAL. Work from the 19th century focused on the language's "exotic" and "pathological" character, its lingering Old English archaicisms and its "baby talk" quality. James Harrison's study, published in 1884, is, as far as we know, the first scholarly treatise on the subject. Although linguistically unsophisticated by today's standards, Harrison's "outline of Negro language-usage" is akin to a grammar, with verb paradigms, pronunciation lists, and several pages of "specimen Negroisms" ("to make yo'se'f skace = to run away") (pp. 261–278). Harrison contended that much of "Negro English," as he termed it, was attributable to "old" dialects (e.g., Old English, Old Norse, Old Scottish) and that the African-derived aspects were evidence of intellectual inferiority.

> Much of his [the Negro's] talk is baby-talk. . . . [T]he slang which is an ingrained part of his being as deep-dyed as his skin. . . . [T]he African, from the

absence of books and teaching, had no principle of *analepsy* in his intellectual
furnishing by which a word, once become obscure from a real or supposed loss
of parts or meaning, can be repaired, amended, or restored to its original form.
(p. 233)

In the early 20th century, scholars such as Bennett (1908, 1909), Krapp
(1924), and Mencken (1936) continued this line of thinking about the speech
of U.S. Blacks. In the first study of Gullah (as spoken by rural and urban Black
speech communities in the coastal regions of the Southeast), Bennett (1909)
argued that

> intellectual indolence, or laziness, mental and physical . . . shows itself in the
> shortening of words, the elision of syllables, and modification of every difficult
> enunciation. . . . It is the indolence, mental and physical, of the Gullah dialect
> that is its most characteristic feature. (pp. 40, 45)

H. L. Mencken, in his famous *The American Language* (first published in
1919), wrote of the "grammatical peculiarities" in the speech of "the most ignorant Negroes" and the "confusion of persons, as in '*I is,*' '*Do she?*' '*Does you?*'"
concluding that "Black slave language may be called the worst English in the
world" (1936, p. 264). Folklorist Ambrose Gonzales (1922), in his collection of
folk stories from the Georgia-Carolinas area, was equally critical of "Black slave
language" and even attributed it to the physiognomy of African people:

> Slovenly and careless of speech, these Gullahs seized upon the peasant English
> used by some of the early settlers and by the white servants of the wealthier
> Colonists, wrapped their clumsy tongues about it as well as they could, and
> enriched with certain expressive African words, it issued through their flat noses
> and thick lips as so workable a form of speech that it was gradually adopted by
> the other slaves. (p. 10)

These conceptions of AAL were challenged in a general way by the research
of Melville Herskovits (1941) and in linguistic depth by Lorenzo Turner (1949),
whose study of Gullah was motivated by a chance encounter with two women
from the Gullah region who showed up in his class at South Carolina State
College in Orangeburg. According to Holloway and Vass (1993), this "brief
encounter would change [Turner's] life and the focus of his research for the
rest of his life" (p. ix). Turner mastered five African languages—Kongo, Igbo,
Yoruba, Krio, and Mende—and several African dialects, which he felt was necessary if he wished to understand the origin and forms of the language spoken
by Gullah Blacks. Turner's research, which spanned decades, demonstrated the

African language dimension to Gullah speech and raised the possibility of a linkage to African languages in the speech of Blacks outside the Gullah region. Even the name Gullah was determined to be an African survival, from "gula, name of a tribe in Liberia" (Turner, 1949, p. 91). (However, see also Vass [1979], who attributes the term to "Ngola or Angola," the source of significant numbers of slaves imported into South Carolina.)

Turner (1949) uncovered at least 4,000 West African words in frequent use and fundamental African survivals in sound and syntax. His work revealed that "the Gullahs . . . have used the same methods as their African ancestors in naming their children . . . names of the periods of the day, week, and year, names indicating whether the child is . . . the first, second, or third born" (pp. 40–41). Ultimately, Turner countered the baby-talk and African-genetic-inferiority myths:

> The sounds of Gullah show many striking resemblances to those of several West African languages. When the African came to the United States and encountered in English certain sounds not present in his native language, he did what any other person to whom English was a foreign language would have done under similar circumstances—he substituted sounds from his own language which appeared to him to resemble most closely those English sounds which were unfamiliar to him. (p. 240)

In what sounds like a direct response to Harrison, who had argued that the "lack" of certain sounds was evidence of African genetic pathology, Turner stated:

> The English inter-dental fricative *th* does not exist in Gullah nor in the West African languages included in this study. In pronouncing English words containing this sound, both the Gullah speaker and the West African substitute [d] and [t], respectively, for the voiced and voiceless varieties of it. (p. 245)

In a review of Turner's work, R. I. McDavid (1950), often referred to as the "dean of American dialectology," heaped lavish praise on Turner, arguing that his work should "inaugurate a new approach to the study of American Negro speech" (p. 323), for Turner had presented "a mass of evidence which should go far towards correcting . . . previous investigators" (p. 326). McDavid concluded that "Turner's book is one which no student of American English can afford to ignore" (p. 333). However, Turner's influence was to be short-lived and his work largely ignored until its revival in the 1960s.

During the 1960s and 1970s, concomitant with the fundamental social transformation that the nation was undergoing at the time, there was a virtual explosion of work on the language of U.S. slave descendants. Using the new tools of linguistic science and new analytical frameworks that had resulted from a paradigm shift in the field of linguistics, a new generation of language scholars focused their attention on AAL. Their goal was to demonstrate the systematicity of the language and to argue against the claim, coming primarily from psychology (e.g., Bereiter, 1965) that the language was evidence of cognitive deficiency in Blacks. Linguists such as Labov, Cohen, Robins, and Lewis (1968), Wolfram (1969), and Fasold (1972) presented analyses of the rule-governed behavior of speakers of what was then called "Black English," using fundamental concepts of linguistic science and, more specifically, variation theory.

Labov drew upon this linguistic research to denounce the erroneous linguistic and psychological assertions espoused by scholars such as Bereiter and Englemann (1966). In "The Logic of Nonstandard English" (1969b), Labov deftly dispelled the racist myth that AAL is illogical or ungrammatical. His decades-old study continues to serve as an antidote to false impressions about language, race, and intelligence. Labov's formulation of variable rules in AAL (1969b) was compatible with Chomsky's formal theory of linguistic competence. Thus, his efforts, along with those of other linguists of this period, introduced the study of AAL into mainstream social and scientific dialogue as a critical and legitimate line of scientific and intellectual inquiry.

Linguists working within Labov's variable linguistic paradigm postulated that speakers of AAL have in their grammatical system all the linguistic features of other speakers of American English. However, in AAL, certain features are realized differently or at a higher frequency of occurrence, or both. For example, it is common for all English speakers to occasionally reduce final consonant clusters (e.g., *las'* for *last*, or *tol'* for *told*). In the phrase *west side*, there is a tendency for speakers to reduce the final *st* in *west* to *wes' side*. Evidence suggests that Black and non-Black English speakers share this tendency, albeit with different degrees of frequency.

A similar explanation could account for grammatical forms such as copula absence (no form of the verb *to be*, as in "The coffee cold"). While copula absence is a distinctive feature of AAL, there are constraints on this usage for all speakers. Copula absence was shown to exist only in environments where copula contraction is possible. Therefore one could say, "The coffee's cold" for "The coffee is cold." However, no English speakers, including AAL speakers, delete the copula in sentence final position. All would say, for instance, "That's who he is," but never "That's who he." Further, rather than the racist explanations of old, which had posited African "inferiority" as responsible for the uniqueness of AAL, linguists argued that "the social distance between white and Black Americans must be cited as a contributing factor to the maintenance and development of distinct dialect features" (Fasold & Wolfram, 1970, p. 42). That is, racially segregated communities had resulted in corresponding linguistically distinct communities.

While the linguists of this period were in agreement about the systematic nature of AAL and clearly aligned against those espousing African American linguistic (and cognitive) deficits, there was no consensus about the linguistic origins of AAL, or agreement about the relationship between the Gullah speech communities that Turner had studied and Black American speech communities outside Gullah regions. Asserting the case for AAL as a prior Creole language, Beryl Bailey (1965) (to our knowledge, the first Black woman linguist) argued that there were differences in the "deep structure" (syntactical meaning systems) between Black and Mainstream English (ME). Bailey further maintained that there were striking similarities between Black American speech and the Jamaican Creole that was the focus of her research. It is possible to construct sentences without a copula. In the example given above, "The coffee cold," Bailey would argue that there is no "copula deletion" or "copula absence," for this formation did not have a copula to begin with. Rather, the language allows for equative-type constructions in which the copula is not obligatory.

> I would like to suggest that the Southern Negro "dialect" differs from other Southern speech because its deep structure is different, having its origins as it undoubtedly does in some Proto-Creole grammatical structure. . . . The American Negro, like the Jamaican, operates in a linguistic continuum. . . . While I claim a deep structural relationship between JC [Jamaican Creole] and CW [the "Negro English" represented in the novel *Cool World*], there has not been an identical development of the systems. (Bailey, 1965, pp. 172–175)

Another work of this era that put forth the Creolist position was Dillard's (1972) account of the historical development of AAL. Using numerous literary texts from early periods in American literature in which Black speech had been represented, journal writings by Whites, folklore collections, slave documents such as advertisements for runaway slaves, and other historical documents, Dillard reconstructed the history of AAL from its beginnings on the west coast of Africa. Like Bailey, he saw significant linguistic relationships between U.S. Black English and the Creole English of the Caribbean. Dillard argued that

> the English of most American Blacks retains some features which are common to both Caribbean and West African varieties of English. . . . Like the West Indian varieties, American Black English can be traced to a creolized version of English based upon a pidgin spoken by slaves; it probably came from the West Coast of Africa—almost certainly not directly from Great Britain. (p. 6)

It was clear that the descriptive research from linguists in this period had fundamental implications for educational policy and practice. Traditional pedagogy swept the language differences under the rug, but there were large numbers of youth who were failing school literacy tasks and who lacked the written and spoken communication skills necessary for success in the educational system. Linguists argued that the role of language differences had to be acknowledged and addressed. Bailey (1969) observed that "our approach . . . depends in large measure on a scientific and enlightened understanding of what bilingualism means, and the sociology and psychology of second language learning" (p. 153). Analyzing spoken and written patterns from 100 prefreshmen at Tougaloo College in Mississippi in the summer of 1965, she found evidence of verb patterns and other features that linked these students' language to English-based Creoles, such as her own Jamaican Creole. Contending that there was a need for "drastic revisions in our language arts curriculum as it relates to disadvantaged children," she called for instructional strategies focusing on the systematic differences between AAL and ME (1968, p. 19). Unfortunately, Bailey's untimely death prevented her from testing her linguistic and pedagogical theories.

The most crucial test of theories about the need for language pedagogy specifically designed around AAL was done in the mid-1970s by a team composed of a psychologist, a speech therapist, and an educator. Simpkins, Holt, and Simpkins, authors of the 1974 reading series *Bridge*, conducted a major research study using a reading intervention program that focused on the syntax, vocabulary, and cultural context of AAL. The team supervised 14 teachers and 27 classes, involving 540 students, in experimental (i.e., the "Bridge" reading program) and control groups (i.e., traditional reading program), over a 4-month period, in five areas: Chicago, Illinois; Phoenix, Arizona; Washington, DC; Memphis, Tennessee, and Macon County, Alabama. Using the standardized Iowa Test of Basic Skills in Reading Comprehension to assess gains in reading, the Simpkins team found that the experimental/Bridge groups made a gain of 6.2 months in their reading over the 4-month period, whereas the control/non-Bridge groups (taught with no focus on AAL and its cultural context), only gained 1.6 months in the 4 months of instruction (reported in Simpkins & Simpkins, 1981).

While research by linguists of the 1960s and 1970s focused primarily on *structure*, Smitherman's study (1977) dealt with the *use* of Black speech. Written in both AAL and ME, her work focused on secular forms (e.g., Signification/signifyin) as well as the sacred dimension of the language (Black preaching, the Traditional Black Church). In a work intended for the lay public and readers outside the field of linguistics, she located AAL in the broader context of semantics, rhetorical strategies, and linguistic-cultural practices that reflected a Black psychology and worldview. Smitherman (1977) argued that

Black speech [has] two dimensions: language and style. . . . Nina Simone sings: "It bees dat way sometime." Here the language aspect is the use of the verb *be* to indicate a recurring event or habitual condition. . . . But the total expression . . . also reflects Black English style, for the statement suggests a point of view, a way of looking at life, and a method of adapting to life's realities. To live by the philosophy of "It bees dat way sometime" is to come to grips with the changes that life bees puttin us through, and to accept the changes and bad times as a constant, ever-present reality. (p. 3)

THE SHOT HEARD FROM ANN ARBOR

Martin Luther King Junior Elementary School Children v. Ann Arbor School District Board marked a pivotal point in the AAL research tradition. Although the case did not establish a national legal precedent (because the school board chose not to appeal the ruling against it), the case did establish a linguistic precedent. For the first time, it was written into law, by way of Judge Charles Joiner's "Memorandum and Opinion," that AAL was a legitimate form of speech.

The case was the focus of media attention, both in the United States and abroad, much of it negative and distorted. One well-known journalist dissed the children's mothers by writing that "mothers whose children can't read should get the boyfriends out and get the books in" (Brown, 1979, p. 8-B). Yet the case also occasioned the brilliant, oft-quoted essay by the late James Baldwin, published in *The New York Times* shortly after Judge Joiner's ruling, "If Black English Isn't a Language, Then Tell Me, What Is?"

The *King* lawsuit was filed in federal court in July 1977 by Kenneth Lewis and Gabriel Kaimowitz, attorneys from Michigan Legal Services, on behalf of 15 Black, economically deprived children residing in a low-income housing project on Green Road in Ann Arbor, Michigan. All the students attended Martin Luther King Junior Elementary School. Within a week after filing the suit, Lewis brought Smitherman into the case as an expert witness.

Although *King* was eventually narrowed to a case about Black English, the broader issue for the single parents of the children was the school's failure to provide their children with an education. These children had been placed in learning disability and speech pathology classes (although these labels did not appropriately apply to them); they had been suspended and repeatedly retained at grade level with no intervention to redress their educational failures; and they were not learning how to read. During the course of the 2 years leading up to the trial, the mothers' intuition was corroborated by professional judgment: Their children were normal, intelligent kids who could learn if properly taught.

In the pretrial stages of *King*, Judge Joiner ruled that the case had to be focused on a single issue in the law, and he dismissed all the children's claims except one provision embodied in the 1974 Equal Educational Opportunity Act: "No state shall deny equal educational opportunity to an individual on account of his or her race, color, sex, or national origin, by . . . the failure to overcome language barriers that impede equal participation by its students in its instructional programs" (1703[f] of the EEOA). With the case now narrowly focused on language, Smitherman organized a team of scholars—linguists, educators, reading specialists, and psychologists—from around the country to testify during the trial proceedings.

On July 12, 1979, Judge Joiner ruled in favor of the children. The Ann Arbor School District was guilty of failing to take the children's language into account in the educational process, and thus the district had violated the children's right to equal educational opportunity. In his lengthy "Memorandum and Opinion," the judge quoted from linguistic research on AAL and, to a great degree, relied on this work in fashioning his ruling. The remedy that the district devised and that was approved by the court was a yearlong training program in language diversity for the teachers at King School. At the end of the year, the students who had remained at King (several had moved out of the district) had all improved in reading. To the best of our knowledge, there was no additional follow-up after this ruling.

In an effort to address the loud public concern about the "Black English" case all across the country, Smitherman convened a national symposium to discuss the implications of *King* for educational and public policy. The papers and recommendations from the national gathering of linguists, educators, and public policy experts were published by Smitherman (1981). A central thread running throughout the critiques was the inextricable relationship between Black education and American economic policy. As attorney-at-law Gabriel Kaimowitz indicated in his presentation, oppression is not merely linguistic or educational, it is also economic (Smitherman, 1981, p. 51). Recommendations that came out of various task forces at the symposium included the need for technology training for Black youth; a national language policy and a Black English awareness campaign; new terminology to replace "Black English"/"Vernacular Black English"; a call for new research on discourse patterns, especially written discourse; research on patterns of language acquisition among Black children; basic data on reading processes and habits of Black children; and greater training for teachers in linguistic diversity. Two critical recommendations in terms of educational language policy were: (1) a modification of Title VII of the Elementary and Secondary Act and use of ESEA Title I, to include projects dealing with Black English and (2) that "schools [should] use Black Language and Black Experience as a resource for teaching standard English language arts skills" (Task Force on Educational Policy, in Smitherman, 1981, p. 312).

While the national hysteria focused on the language issue, the concern of the parents was literacy and survival for their children. *King* raised the critical issue of the relationship of AAL to educational policy and public practice. If the language is systematic, as linguistic research had clearly demonstrated, then why couldn't it be used in public venues outside the "hood"? If the language was not only systematic but also useful as a language of instruction, and if tapping into the Black Language-Culture frame of reference was a significant instructional strategy to elevate the reading levels of Black youth (as the Simpkins, Holt, & Simpkins [1974] research had shown), then why were there such strong objections to using AAL as a coequal language of teaching and learning in school? Finally, since the language was used by both working- and middle-class Blacks, why was there such a great outcry against AAL and against the *King* case by members of the Black middle and professional classes? In the final analysis, such questions are not simply about language. Rather, they reflect conflicting linguistic and cultural norms. Vernacular Black dialects grew out of slavery, but mainstream forms of (White) standard English embody the language of power and economic opportunity.

RETURN TO THE SOURCE: DATA AND DEDICATION

In his analysis of *King*, Labov (1982), one of the linguists who had testified during the trial, observed that many of the most significant linguistic discoveries about AAL have resulted from the entry of scholars of African descent into linguistics:

> This action was also instrumental in bringing Black linguists into this field of research. . . . Black scholars now . . . define the role that their white allies can play in advancing the study of Black English. The significance of these events has to be seen in a larger context of the history of the Black people in America. Members of an oppressed people have entered an academic field, taken up the tools of linguistic research, and used them for the advancement of their nation. The forerunners of this movement were isolated and ignored during their lifetimes. In Lorenzo Turner's last years, he could not find anyone to take his notes and records into safe keeping; he died believing that his work was wasted and forgotten. When Beryl Bailey died, she was bitterly aware that her research was for the most part set aside, her book out of print, her contributions ignored. This is the experience of the Black scholar in the white man's world. The Ann Arbor trial marks a turning point in this dismal history. The trial was the initiative of Black people: the mothers of the Green Road children, the lawyer Kenneth Lewis, the linguist Geneva Smitherman, and many other members of the Black community. The whites who have been privileged to play an auxiliary role in this affair know that they are marginal to the success that was achieved. The only permanent advance in the condition of life in any field occurs when people

take their own affairs into their own hands. I believe that this is true of the study of Black English as it is true everywhere. (pp. 195–196)

During the decades since *King*, the major work on AAL has uncovered new insights about old language data and compelling implications for advancing the education and empowerment of U.S. slave descendants. It is no accident that these developments have come about with the emergence of a critical mass of Black linguists into the field.

Among the new insights from linguists of African descent were Baugh's (1983) findings about stylistic variation among adult speakers of AAL, who were participants in the vernacular/"street" culture of Los Angeles, Philadelphia, Chicago, and Texas. Whereas many previous studies of AAL had focused on Black Language rituals (e.g., Signification/signifyin) or had been conducted on children and school-age youth, Baugh focused on adult speakers of AAL in everyday, conversational contexts. He demonstrated their linguistic versatility in shifting from formal to informal styles depending on such factors as the topic being discussed, the social situation and the relationship between speakers. The linguistic forms, with one crucial exception, had all been documented in previous research, but that research had not tapped into the way Black speakers varied their use of these linguistic forms.

The crucial exception alluded to above was the unique semantic function of *steady*, which had not been dealt with in previous research (although it was undoubtedly in the data collected by previous researchers), as in "Ricky Bell be steady steppin in them number nines" (Baugh, 1983, p. 86). The main reason that *steady* had not appeared in previous descriptions of AAL is its similarity to ME's *steadily*. However, in AAL, *steady* has additional functions, not realized by ME speakers' use of *steadily*. Rather, *steady* indicates that the action is intense, consistent, and continuous, as in these examples from Baugh's speakers: "Your mind is steady workin," and "Them fools be steady hustlin everybody they see." While acknowledging that "Bantu languages employ aspectual markers [similar]...to that of *steady*," Baugh (1983) also notes the English influence in this semantic construction. He thus concludes that "*steady*, almost more than any other aspect of street speech, demonstrates...[the] linguistic influences [of] both African and Anglican sources" (p. 88).

Spears's (1982) research on *come* also reflected a semantic construction of AAL that had been overlooked in previous work. Contending that AAL is more different from non-Black varieties than is commonly believed by linguists, Spears argued that the verb *come* serves two semantic purposes in AAL: one as a verb of motion, the other as the semi-auxiliary *come* of indignation (e.g., "He come comin in here actin a damn fool"). Referring to this usage as a "camouflaged" form,

Spears's research also established the existence of the aspectual marker, stressed *stay*, as in "She STAY over to Alfred house," meaning "She can frequently be found at Alfred's house." His work continues to be significant for uncovering grammatical features unique to AAL that are not discussed elsewhere in the research literature.

Another important insight that emerged in the post-*King* era was the methodological issue involved in analysis of the copula, which was raised by Rickford, Ball, and Blake (1991). Copula absence, common among AAL speakers, is not found among European American speakers. Further, as Bailey (1965) has demonstrated, this verb form links AAL to Jamaican and other Caribbean Creoles. The AAL copula form, as Rickford and colleagues (1991) and Poplack (2000) independently observe, is one of the most extensively studied of any quantitative sociolinguistic variable. Rickford and colleagues (1991) discovered that there were considerable differences between previous researchers about what to call and how to count the copula. For example, does one count "are" absence, or is this to be considered a function of pronunciation (i.e., deletion of "r" after a vowel), and therefore not counted in analysis? And if "are" absence is counted, should it be collapsed with counts of "is" absence, or analyzed separately? Since variation theory depends on statistical analyses and comparisons, how to count the language variables under consideration is a crucial methodological question. By manipulating the quantitative data using three different methods of counting copula forms, Rickford demonstrated that what you count is what you get.

Another question Rickford encountered, relevant to the methodological issue, is whether AAL is diverging from ME. In the mid-1980s, Labov and associates had argued that AAL was developing on its own pathway and not converging with ME, or with other varieties of American English. (See more on the "Divergence Hypothesis" below.) Rickford theorized that if the language is indeed diverging on its own course, then one would expect younger AAL speakers to exhibit greater differences from Mainstream English than older speakers. What Rickford has called the "showcase variable" (1999, p. 62) would be a good test of this assumption. Tackling the methodological question head on, Rickford developed a more finely tuned, appropriate paradigm for counting copula forms in his study of the language of the Black community of East Palo Alto, California. He eventually observed that older speakers often appeared to be more nonstandard than younger ones, which defied previous sociolinguistic observations.

A linguistic-pedagogical line of inquiry motivated by the *King* case was research on the writing of African American students, which had been one of the key task force recommendations from the *King* symposium. In 1981, using writing samples from 17-year-old high school seniors in the National Assessment of Educational Progress (NAEP), Smitherman launched the first in a series of studies on the writing of Blacks. NAEP results comparing Black student writing from 1969 to 1979 had indicated that Blacks had improved *twice* as much as their White counterparts over the decade (although their writing scores still were not on par with those of Whites). The question that informed that work and later writing studies was the relationship between AAL and writing scores and whether AAL use in Black student essays was declining over the years. Results from the first study indicated a significant decline in AAL over the decade from 1969 to 1979 in the case of one type of writing: narrative/imaginative essays (Smitherman & Wright, 1983).

The Smitherman research team ended up examining 2,764 essays written by 17-year-old African Americans in the NAEP over a generational time span (1969–1989). Overall, the results indicated that the use of AAL forms declined, particularly in the 1980s data. For example, although copula patterns remained the same in all essay types from 1969 to 1979, these patterns declined from 1984 to 1988 (Smitherman, 1992). Another finding, based on an examination of Black discourse patterns in the essays, was a positive correlation between use of these patterns and essay score (Smitherman, 1994b). Based on these writing studies, Smitherman (1992) argued that the decline in AAL and the concomitant increase in the use of Edited/Standard Written American English raised questions about linguistic divergence:

> Thus the predictions of the 1960s and 1970s about . . . the de-Africanising of BEV [Black English Vernacular] in the direction of Standard English were not so far off the mark [contrary to the claims of] Divergence theorists. It may simply be that the manifestation of [this de-Africanising] is to be found in *writing* . . . not in the oral repertoire of the African American speech community. (p. 58; See Ball, 1999, for a critical discussion of teacher training and Black student writing.)

DIVERGENCE OR CONVERGENCE?

The "divergence hypothesis" was first raised in the work of Labov and associates, reported in a series of papers in 1983 and published by Sankoff (1986). *Divergence* referred to the theory that AAL was charting a separate course from that of White dialects in the postmodern period. Contrary to previous predictions about the impact of racial integration, increased educational opportunity, improved literacy, and the media, Labov contended that AAL had not continued to decreolize and converge toward ME. Rather, the grammar of AAL had become even more different from that of White varieties of English than had previously been the case. Basing his findings on sound changes taking place in the major population centers, and on controlled experiments whereby speakers were racially identified by virtue of phonetic features, Labov (1987) argued:

> In each of the northern cities, we find . . . an even larger group of Blacks who are isolated by increasing residential and economic segregation from the rest of the community. And here we find evidence of new grammatical features, reinterpretations of features of other dialects, and continued divergence of the tense, mood, and aspect system. (p. 6)

Independent of Labov's work, Bailey and Maynor (1989) came forth with similar claims about divergence. Whereas Labov had noted striking economic parallels to linguistic divergence, Bailey and Maynor observed that urban versus rural exposure to AAL influenced divergence trends. Butters (1989) provides one of the most thorough discussions of the entire divergence controversy, while affirming the inherent complexity of forces that affect AAL linguistic change in progress.

The divergence hypothesis was much heralded in the national media for its direct implications for educational policy. If, as the divergence camp suggested, Black speech was moving away from both White vernaculars and mainstream White speech, this could lead to the conclusion that Blacks were going backward instead of forward. As Orlando Taylor argued, a policy maker involved in funding might say something like, "Look at the millions of dollars we spent in this country in the last fifteen or twenty years to improve the quality of education for Blacks, particularly in the language arts, and look, not only can they still not talk, Professor Labov in Pennsylvania shows they talk worse" (quoted in Vaughn-Cooke, 1987, p. 12).

We would add a brief comment on the importance of personal identity in this regard. Graffiti writers of Hip Hop Culture were probably the coiners of the term *phat* (meaning excellent, great, superb), which came to be used within and beyond the African American community. Although *phat* is spelled in obvious contrast to *fat*, the pronunciation confirms that those who use it know that "ph" sounds like "f." In other words, those who first wrote *phat* diverged from ME as a result of their awareness of ME; the divergence was not by chance linguistic error. There is no single explanation to account for linguistic divergence, but Hip Hop Culture suggests that matters of personal identity play a significant role. An emerging body of scholarship on Hip Hop music is providing analyses of language and identity. For example, Alim (2002) analyzes the manipulation of AAL features—focusing in particular on copula patterns—by Hip Hop artists as a sign of the construction of what he calls a "street conscious identity." Other work in this direction includes Spady and Alim's "Modes of Being" (1999), and Alim's *You Know My Steez* (2004b), which focuses on what these scholars call "Hip Hop Nation Language" and the development of a "linguistic mode of being." Also relevant is Smitherman's "The Chain Remain the Same" (1997b).

LINGUISTIC AFRICANISMS

Some linguists in the post-*King* period have taken up the challenge of demonstrating linguistic connections between African languages and AAL. Blackshire-Belay (1996) and Smith (1998) discuss the foundations for these connections, with Blackshire-Belay proposing a "family tree of Ebonic languages," under which the variety termed *Black English* would be subsumed as a North American variety of Ebonics (1996, p. 17). Detailed grammatical analyses of specific linguistic variables that would support an African language connection are presented by Selase W. Williams (1993) and DeBose and Faraclas (1993), while Morgan (1993) argues the case with empirical research and analyses of styles of speaking.

Williams focused on the various ways that AAL speakers in Virginia, the Carolinas, and Georgia pronounce the voiceless, interdental fricative /th/ in final position, as in the word *with*, which may be rendered as *wit, wid,* or *wif.* He hypothesized that the variations could be accounted for by the particular African ethnolinguistic group(s) concentrated in a given region of the South. Speech samples were taken from Turner and from linguistic atlases and literary sources. Comparing the variant /th/ representations with the sound inventories for the dominant African language groups in these regions—e.g., Mandingo, Yoruba, Wolof—none of which have the /th/ sound, Williams (1993) argued: "Within the Afrocentric framework outlined in this paper, the varied pronunciation of word-final [Θ] is accounted for as a consequence of differential African source languages" (p. 419). He further suggested that even though some British colonists were pronouncing word-final [Θ] as [f], this "would simply have provided further reinforcement for the [f] pronunciation among those Africans who had already selected that variant on independent grounds (i.e., linguistic interference)" (p. 419).

DeBose and Faraclas (1993) propose that the term *Africanism* has to be understood as including "systems . . . holistic, meaningful patterns that underlie surface phenomena" (p. 365). Further, they contend that the search for a single African language as the source of the connection to AAL is "futile" as well as unnecessary: "While West Africa is one of the most diverse regions of the world in terms of the number and genetic affiliation of its languages, constant and intimate interethnic contact over thousands of years has forged a profound typological unity among the languages of the area" (p. 365). Using speech data from 10 AAL speakers and sample source grammars for widely-spoken languages of southern Nigeria and the West African coast, they provide extensive analyses of the verbal system of AAL, with particular attention to tense-aspect-modality and copula forms, and comparisons with the West African language systems in their study. They conclude

> The analysis of motivations for the BE [Black English] tense-aspect-modality and copula systems . . . clearly establishes that substrate patterns play a major and crucial role. . . . To ignore the role of the West African substratum in the motivation of the BE system would be analogous to trying to motivate modern English from French without acknowledging the Germanic roots of the English language. (p. 385).

Morgan (1993) makes the case for an African language connection in AAL on the basis of the existence of a "counterlanguage," a style of speaking "based on ambiguity, irony, and satire" (p. 423). She contends that enslaved Africans developed a system of communication derived from the use of ambiguity and irony in African songs and public announcements. Indirectness became a shared communication norm among the enslaved of which their masters had little knowledge. She surveys anthropological data on the function and use of indirectness in West African societies as a backdrop for the continuation of indirect speech in African America. To demonstrate the existence and extent of indirectness among contemporary African Americans, Morgan conducted a study in which 60 African and 56 European American women, ages 17–75, were questioned about a story in which indirectness and ambiguity were key. There were significant differences in the two groups' responses. Morgan concluded that "the response of the two groups of women to 'Regina's Other Story' presents a clear example of the existence of counterlanguage. . . . [T]he Black women in the study could choose between two realities or communication norms while the whites had access to only one" (pp. 430–431).

Asante (1990) also argues for communication norms or styles of speaking, rather than distinctive African words, as key to the survival of Africanisms in AAL. However, Holloway and Vass (1993)—using vocabulary lists of Bantu words found in Gullah and in Southern place-names, as well as lists of Africanisms in Black names and nicknames—contend that not only are there distinctive African word survivals, but "both West and Central African languages contributed to the diversity of Africanisms found in American English" (p. xiii).

BLACK WOMEN'S LANGUAGE

Research on AAL has generally used data drawn from males in the Black speech community. This was the case in the 1960s explosion of AAL research as well as in the post-*King* era. Morgan's work (e.g., 1989) has been a clear exception to this practice. (See also Rickford & McNair-Knox, 1994, and Alim, 2004a.) Morgan has conducted ongoing research on African American women's discourse, focusing particularly on the speech patterns of three generations of women living in Chicago.

Continuing in the tradition of linguist Claudia Mitchell-Kernan, who showcased the Sistas in her research (e.g., Mitchell-Kernan, 1971), Morgan analyzed Black discourse modes and styles of speaking among Black females. In addition to the indirectness of Black counterlanguage, Morgan (1991) argued that a particular type of "Signification/Signifyin," especially as practiced by African American women, is "reading dialect." This occurs when speakers consciously contrast or highlight obvious features of AAL or ME in order to make an unambiguous point, to "read" (verbally denigrate) a conversational partner. For instance, "It's not simply that I am cool. I be cool. In fact, I been cool (a very long time)" (Morgan, 1998, p. 265). Morgan states, "What reading dialect accomplishes is to transform the status of a lexical, prosodic, grammatical, or discourse structure that could be either AAE or AE [American English] into a framework which exploits the congruities and incongruities of each system and how they impact each other" (p. 265).

Whereas Morgan uses female subjects as her data source without necessarily highlighting their femaleness, Troutman (2000) consciously and deliberately seeks to analyze the uniqueness of African American women's language: "As creators and speakers of a particular linguistic style, African American women, in general, have developed their own language patterns based on their belief systems and social, cultural, historical, political, and religious reality" (p. 23). Troutman argues that examples of such patterns may be found in "culturally toned diminutives" (e.g., "girl" as a form of address and bonding) and in what Stanback Houston (1985) labeled "smart talk." In a study of Anita Hill's language during the Clarence Thomas Senate hearing of 1991, Troutman conducts a discourse analysis of the interaction between Hill and Senator Arlen Specter, one of the chief questioners from the Senate Judiciary Committee. Among Troutman's results is the finding that, contrary to the norm for women's talk, Hill's interruptions significantly exceed those of Specter (73% for Hill, 27% for Specter). Troutman (1995) concludes that

> Hill's conversational style . . . may be culturally toned with elements of assertive and agnostic behavior. . . . In order to win, she must actively assert her position and maintain it. . . . Hill used an assertive, confident, swift conversational style which may be characteristic of the larger speech community of African American women. (pp. 221–222)

Lanehart's (2002) *Sista Speak* maintains Morgan's cross-generational analyses, considering three generations of African American women with different cultural and linguistic orientations toward AAL and ME. Consistent with the preceding studies, Lanehart reveals a masterful array of linguistic dexterity combined with honest differences of opinion about life, language, and the role of women in African American homes and society.

AAL AND LINGUISTIC EMANCIPATION
IN GLOBAL PERSPECTIVE

Thus far we have attempted to provide a broad survey of AAL research, without straying too far outside the context of the United States. But we would be remiss if we did not acknowledge, however briefly, the role that this research has played in linguistic emancipation efforts in the broader African Diaspora and beyond. Many American readers may recall the 1996 Ebonics episode, in which the Oakland, California, School Board declared Ebonics to be the home language of 28,000 African American students in that district. However, few readers may be aware of how strongly this controversy resonated throughout English speech communities in the Caribbean and Africa. This was especially the case in Ghana and South Africa, where Black English dialects were degraded in comparison to their colonial precursors spoken by Whites who resided in Africa. Likewise, as Alexander (this volume) affirms, the quest for linguistic equality in post-apartheid South Africa parallels in significant ways the struggle to overcome racial stigmas associated with AAL and other subordinate dialects of English spoken by non-Whites in the United States. These are but two examples where linguistic and educational parallels have given rise to enhanced communication among global citizens from diverse backgrounds, to the potential benefit of all who suffer linguistic discrimination.

Our desire to collaborate on this project goes back to our first meeting at the University of Pennsylvania in 1979, when Smitherman was gathering evidence for the *King* trial and Baugh was a newly minted Ph.D. Since then our collective and independent efforts in support of the linguistic liberation of African Americans and other linguistically oppressed people have never wavered.

We have witnessed the passing of many linguistic trends, including numerous efforts by U.S. slave descendants to seek greater linguistic dignity and recognition within the larger society. We have also witnessed legal and educational trends directly related to AAL speakers, as well as other linguistic "minorities" and oppressed peoples. Along with our colleagues, many of whom we acknowledge here, we remain vigilant in our quest to overcome the negative consequences of the linguistic legacy of the African slave trade. Yet linguistic myths continue to perpetuate educational malpractice (Baugh, 1995, 1999b), linguistic profiling (Baugh, 2000b), and the continued denial of individuals' right to their own language (Smitherman, 2000). It is these linguistic barriers, and their racially motivated existence, that we ultimately seek to overcome.

CHAPTER 9

If Our Children Are Our Future, Why Are We Stuck in the Past?

Beyond the Anglicists and the Creolists and Toward Social Change

Sonja Lanehart

There are two dominant perspectives on the history and development of African American English (AAE) held by two distinctive groups: (1) Anglicists, mostly non–African American scholars who spend much of their time arguing that AAE is a dialect of British English, and that Africans in America who created AAE forgot their native culture and language upon arrival here, and (2) Creolists, mostly African American scholars who spend much of their time arguing that AAE derived from contact between Blacks and Whites and the cultures and languages they brought to their contact situation. In other words, the latter group holds that Africans in America maintained aspects of their languages and cultures in adapting to their oppressive environment, while the former claims that Africans in America either did not value their cultures enough to preserve them, or else they did not have the ability to do so (G. Bailey, 2001; Mufwene, 2000; Poplack, 2000; Rickford & Rickford, 2000; Smitherman, 1977; Winford, 1997, 1998).

I find it interesting that the predominantly African American group (the Creolists) tends to apply knowledge about AAE to educational, social, and political problems, while the predominantly non–African American group (the Anglicists) does not. This is not to say that no non–African American linguists have contributed to improving the educational, social, and political landscape for African Americans. There are many who have (i.e., Adger, Christian, & Taylor, 1999; Labov, 2001; Wolfram, Adger, and Christian, 1999). However, I question the efficacy and intentions of the long-standing debate about the history and development of AAE, when right now we have African American children who are discriminated against because of their language—the essence of who they are—and graduating with high school diplomas they cannot read. It is time to stop quibbling over the particulars of dialect and creole when we as linguists can contribute to a greater cause. We have a constituency that is more likely to benefit from research on the contemporary sociolinguistic and educational issues involving AAE than they are from the AAE origins debate.

For as long as I can remember, I have been told about the Anglicists and the Creolists as if they were the Cowboys and the Indians, or the Good Guys and the Bad Guys, or the North and the South. You get the picture. Although there have been other "camps" in the origins debate, and more recent ones (the Ebonicist and divergence positions, for example), the two main positions remain the same (see Bailey & Maynor [1989], Baugh [2000a], Fasold et al. [1987], and Perry & Delpit [1998] for a full description of the divergence and Ebonicist hypotheses). I have now been a researcher in the area of language use in the African American community long enough to have friends in both camps. I even have friends who are fence straddlers, who change camps periodically, or who refuse to identify with either. I have seen this debate take place as an undergraduate student at the University of Texas, as a graduate student at the University of Michigan, and now as a faculty member at the University of Georgia. I have gone from being told about the stories to living them firsthand.

When I tell people outside the field about AAE, they seem dumbfounded that anyone would believe that AAE is not historically rooted to Africa, since the people who speak it are. I have been involved in research groups and projects that aimed to determine whether AAE is a dialect of British English or an English and African creole, and I have tried to convince myself that such questions are important. Ultimately I do not feel the evidence exists that can support either side beyond reasonable doubt. And besides, it does not matter what the outcome of this storied debate may be.

Some people believe it might be helpful to prove that AAE is an English and African creole so that it could be classified as a foreign language and receive bilingual-education funding. That was reportedly one strategy of the Oakland Unified School District Board in its 1996 Ebonics Resolutions, though they later denied it. In any case, I do not buy that argument. The Gullah speakers off the coast of Georgia and South Carolina have not benefited much from their special linguistic designation. In fact, during the Oakland Ebonics controversy, the GeeChee people of those islands got no publicity at all, even though there is no controversy among linguists about the origin, status, or nature of their language—it is an English and African creole. The point remains, what do those people need today? What do AAE-speaking children need in terms of education and language policy? If the "great origins debate" were resolved today, how would we be better off? Would we be closer to helping AAE-speaking children learn to read and write? Would we be closer to helping them learn critical thinking skills?

Would we be closer to giving them better schools with better facilities, better funding, and better opportunities? I do not think so. That is a problem I cannot get past. And that is why I can no longer engage in the origins debate.

I recently spoke with a non–African American researcher during a conference about her research in reading with AAE-speaking children. I commented that we are still trying to determine why African American and other inner-city children cannot read, despite all the research that linguists, sociolinguists, psychologists, reading researchers, and other scholars have done. We know that we can help these children learn to read. We have been told as much by top scholars on numerous occasions at our scholarly conferences. And yet, instead of working together for a useful cause, we have spent a good bit of our resources working to answer a question that primarily serves the egos of a few instead of the needs of the many. This has gone on for decades and I am greatly perplexed by it.

I am reminded that a house divided cannot stand. Although there are a number of linguists, including several African Americans, engaged in research that benefits or directly addresses the educational needs of AAE-speaking children, some of those scholars are also involved in the origins debate. That means that their attention is divided. We are all busy in our scholarly pursuits, and most of us are often over committed. Does it really make sense, therefore, to engage in fruitless arguing when there is something more fruitful on the table?

HOW DID WE GET HERE?

I realize that, in the beginning, linguists waged the origins debate in order to combat poor scholarship and to remedy years of neglect on the subject of language use in the African American community, as if the debate itself would legitimize the study of AAE. However, just because they started the debate does not mean we have to continue it. There is no longer a need to justify the study of language use in the African American community. There are ample reasons already. We are at a crossroads, and we got here, in part, because of lost time and lost causes.

A few years before *Brown v. Topeka Board of Education* (1954) was being battled, Lorenzo Dow Turner had written *Africanisms in the Gullah Dialect* (1949). Of course, other studies about language use in the African American community had been written before that landmark decision, but this was rigorous scholarship written by an ingroup member, quite unlike much of what had been published before. The fact is that much of the so-called scholarly work on African American language use had been written by non-Blacks, and none of it had the kind of impact that Turner's work did. It was a pivotal piece, and it left a lasting impression on all subsequent scholarship in the area. Turner's achievement reminds me of other stories. Students of color have told me about professors who have told them that they could not study their community because they were too close to it, as if that would somehow taint the quality of their work—or worse, deprive it of all value. I have never heard European American Whites tell me similar stories. How can people of color alone be too close to their communities? I have to wonder, because that is the impression I get when I look at the research history of language use in the African American community. I am not suggesting that non–African Americans should not investigate our community, but, as the saying goes, "Nobody can tell my story like I can." (How different the stories are when the lion finally gets to tell them.) If *we* do not investigate our own communities with the vision and insight that we have, who will?

In *Sista, Speak!* (Lanehart, 2002), I examine the language, literacy, and identities of five working- and middle-class African American women across three generations of my family. All were born and raised in the South. I focus on the matriarch, Maya; Maya's fourth-oldest child, Grace; Maya's eighth and youngest child, Reia; and Grace's two children, Deidra and Sonja (me). Each narrative proceeds with the women telling about their background, education, language, and literacy and concludes with a discussion of their goals and possible selves.[1] I may be accused of bias, since these are stories of women in my family and one of the stories is my own. But then, who else is studying us the way we ought to be studied—and who else can tell our stories like we can? I know these stories are not unique. I have heard them repeated in the lives of many women and I felt they needed to be told.

In telling these stories, I learned much about the education of Black folk, and I am still learning. The stories of my family that center around the periods before and after the *Brown* (*Brown I* in 1954 and *Brown II* in 1955) decisions have provided a puzzle for me that oddly coincides with my Anglicist-Creolist conundrum. The narratives of Grace and Reia in particular strike me as instructive. Grace went to school before, during, and after the *Brown* decisions. Below is an excerpt from her narrative in which she describes her education:

> During the time when I was going to school, we were not integrated back then. All of my teachers was Black. There was no White teachers at that school. All the Blacks went to school together and all the Whites went to school together. You didn't even see a White person. You walked the streets all day going to school and coming from school. You were not gonna see a White person in that area. Because they had they own area. . . . No White people lived around us. None. They were like ten, fifteen, twenty miles away and that was a long ways because we didn't have transportation hardly. . . . Everybody had their own area of town. And that's the way it was back then when I was growing up. . . .

I always felt that Whites got a better education than Blacks. We always got their hand-me-down books and different stuff like that. And being Black—I think they taught different things in their school than they taught in our school. And I still say that.

And I'ma tell you another thing. I was telling that to Reia today. You know when you were talking about Simon did a better job on his test, on the English, than you did and stuff like that? And what I still can't get her to see those tests are not designed for Black people. They're designed for White people. I don't care how smart you are, they're not designed for you to pass. Now I don't know how you passed it, but I'm telling you. They design things for them . . .

And I think a lot has to do with the teachers. I really do. I don't know if Black teachers— I'm sure they probably grew up some of them in the same manner that I did and by them not knowing I'm sure they went through a lot of hard times too and they did the best they could do. I can say my mother did the best she did raising me. I feel they did the best they could do. But I always felt that the other races got a better education than we got for some reason. And I don't know what manner it was, how they were taught or what. But we were always left behind. And I'm sure it's because of race. They will not let you catch up with them. And that's why they didn't want integration I'm sure. (Lanehart, 2002, pp. 47–48)

Grace wanted a better education than what she was getting in the South, that is, an equal education to that of the Whites, but she did not really want to go to school with Whites. That should not come as a surprise, since all throughout her schooling she was not in the company of Whites. Her generation did not have a problem being segregated; they had a problem being dehumanized, mistreated, and taken for granted.

Reia went to school a decade after the *Brown* decisions. However, she still went to all-Black elementary schools, because she lived in all-Black neighborhoods during that time. Her situation changed when she took advantage of the desegregation opportunities that *Brown* provided. Because she was a very bright student, she started going to magnet schools. Here is an excerpt from Reia's narrative about her own education:

I went to all Black schools until the second half of my sixth grade when we moved out to where we live now, where Maya 'nem live now. That's when I started going to interracial schools. . . . I only had Black teachers all the way through the sixth grade. Maybe when I went to the interracial school my teacher was Black, it was a Black man. From there, when I started junior high school, that's when I started White teachers.

I didn't notice any difference [between Black teachers and White teachers] until I got in high school. Cause even in junior high school it was probably half and half—half Black teachers half [White teachers] . . . And I really didn't see any blatant differences, to be truthfully honest with you, until I got to high school and it was really for the most part just one of my math teachers where there was a blatant difference in the way she treated Black students and the [White students]. She was very prejudiced obviously. That wasn't very subtle with her. It was pretty obvious that she treated the White students [different] and she helped 'em out more. Like when they came up to her desk to ask questions or if they asked questions while she was standing at the board, she answered their questions and seemed that [she] really enjoyed answering. But like if we raised our hand [or] didn't understand something, she'd get an attitude and kinda like she made you feel dumb and stupid. And that was in Geometry and I had taken Algebra One and I made straight A's in Algebra One. I was halfway teaching the class in Algebra One and that was under a White teacher. But when I took Geometry, by the end of the first school year, that first half of the school year, I had a D in Geometry. . . . And the woman—this was God sent. But she got sick or something happened where she couldn't finish off the rest of the school year so we had to get transferred and I was transferred back to the Algebra teacher that I had and I ended up getting a B in Geometry for that school year. But it's like I didn't even get the foundations. My foundation wasn't really established that well but I still got in there and did well and I know I woulda made straight A's in Geometry. I would have liked Geometry a lot better if I'da had a teacher that wasn't like her—that wasn't prejudiced and thought we were all stupid and dumb. And I had her for English too. I had her for one of my English classes. And I was an honor roll student. I was on the Dean's list. . . . All the White kids got A's and B's in the class. Everybody Black got a C and below. I got the highest grade in the class and it was a C. And there was one girl who made straight A's. She gave the girl a F. You got straight A's and you got a F in English. In English? Excuse me, for crying out loud. I mean English is not that hard. But that's what I mean about it was a blatant difference. . . . For the most part [I think the schools that I went to were good schools for learning and that they prepared me for my road to college]. I mean even Roosevelt, the all Black school. . . . But I thought they were good schools. And you know, I'm glad I went to all-Black schools to be truthfully honest with you. I'm glad I did because I didn't have to deal with any racial issues per se cause all my teachers were Black; all the students were Black. (Lanehart, 2002, pp. 72–74, 76)

In comparing the narratives of Grace and Reia, both women preferred segregated Black schools. The difference was that Grace did not have a choice in the matter. Another difference was that Grace wanted access to better education but could not get it. Reia had that access and used it. However, there was a change in what *better* meant, a change that came about as a result of the *Brown* decisions.

Baugh (2000a) relates a statement made by Professor Richard Wright of Howard University during a guest appearance on *The Gordon Elliot Show* in

January 1997. Wright's comments echo what Grace and Reia have to say about race in schools before and after the *Brown* decisions:

> I wanted to make a statement that the whole problem of Black children going to school and not learning standard English is a relatively recent phenomenon. It is not the case that Black people used to go to school [and they] came out the way they went in, okay? I went to school during the 1940s and 50s. We didn't go to school as speakers of Black English. We went to school understanding that the purpose of school was to clean up whatever you took in. . . . Since desegregation you've had to deal with the weight of color. When we went to school, we just went to school. You didn't go to school as a Black child, you just went to school as a child. . . . The weight of race is something Black people have to carry today. When I went to school I did not carry the weight of race. . . . During the period of segregation there was not such a thing in your mind as you were going to a Black school. . . . You were simply going to school and the assumption was that you were going to school to learn because you had something to do there you couldn't do away from school, and that's learn something. (pp. 109–110)

This excerpt reinforces a recurring message in Baugh (2000a): This nation will not heal and cannot move forward educationally, socially, or politically until it redresses not only the linguistic consequences of slavery in the United States, but all consequences. In other words, as long as there is racism and its effects, there will be those who question the efficacy of the *Brown* decisions because of the rise of racialization in schools that took place afterward. Likewise, there will also be some who point out the potential benefits of educational resegregation for Black students in the K–12 levels—benefits that Reia and Professor Wright describe as a haven of resilience-building for Blacks.

With the implementation of *Brown* and the desegregation of schools, I think education opened up for non-European Americans. But educators did not necessarily care about them, accept them, or teach them in as nourishing and supportive environment as they needed—an environment that *all* children need. As Grace has said on many occasions, Blacks did not mind being in segregated schools; they just wanted good schools. And good schools *can* be all Black.

Spears (2001) talks about his experience growing up in all-Black neighborhoods and going to all-Black schools in those neighborhoods, which he refers to as the "Golden ghettoes":

> *Golden ghetto* is a term that brings out the positive aspects of large Black communities during segregation and has been used by prominent Black social scientists, such as St. Clair Drake (1945), who wanted to focus attention on the vibrant, positive impact of businesses, organizations, and institutions in such communities. Golden ghettoes were multi-class, so at least one of their features

was that Black children growing up had an abundance of role models. . . . The high school was excellent in terms of the education it provided students. It ranked with celebrated all-Black high schools, of which there were many, such as Dunbar in Washington, D.C. Classes were often named by the professions conspicuously taken up by their members. For example, the class right behind me was the "doctor class" (roughly 6% of the class became physicians). All of the teachers and administrators were quite willing to insert themselves into students' lives to make sure they succeeded. When students who were thought to have great potential were backsliding, they were often called out in public and talked to with directness. Most important is that teachers knew how to get and keep students' attention and respect. They knew what kind of speech would be effective and the specific situations in which it would be effective. There was never a dull moment because all the faculty, administrators, and staff accessed regularly a wide range of Black speech genres to do their job and often employed them theatrically. Persons who did not grow up in these communities would find the teachers' and administrators' behavior scandalous; cause for contract termination if not lawsuits. None of the students thought their behavior was anything out of the ordinary and it would never have occurred to us to complain to parents about it. The parents, had we done so, would have asked what we had done to elicit that behavior. Since such direct speech behavior was always purposeful, the parents would have agreed with the school teachers and administrators. Indeed, the parents engaged in the same kinds of speech behavior themselves. (pp. 251–252, 254–255)

Not only can segregated schools work, but the language and discourse patterns of Blacks in those segregated schools can work too, as Michèle Foster (2001) has shown. So why don't they work now? Why did we have *Martin Luther King Junior Elementary School v. Ann Arbor School District* (1979), a.k.a. the Black English Trial (see R. W. Bailey, 1983), and the Oakland Ebonics controversy of 1996–1997,[2] if it really is okay to talk to Black children using the language of their home in school? Why did teachers before *Brown* know it was okay, but teachers afterward do not? Is it really about the language, or is it about the people who speak the language?

The controversy over the divergence hypothesis indicated that AAE speakers did not need to learn a language of wider communication from Whites. They could just as well learn it from Blacks who spoke a language of wider communication. In those Golden ghettoes, where else did those "doctor" and "lawyer" classes learn to speak so well if they were segregated? That is why this is not just about the education of African Americans, but their language as well. That is why the work of scholars like Smitherman (1977, 1994, 2000), Delpit (1995), and Foster (2001) matters. How could it not matter? If something about the way a preschool African American boy walks alerts a non–African American teacher that the child is too aggressive and should be in special education, as Audrey Mc-Cray has suggested, what do you think the child's language suggests?[3] It is no secret that AAE-speaking children get put in special education routinely because of the way they talk. Linguists can do something about that. Even if teachers do not know any better, we do. We know that the language used in the African American community is not a sign of stupidity or the need for special education. The teachers from those African American communities before desegregation, who taught their children a language of wider communication, who cared for them and did "the best they could"—they knew it too. So why don't teachers know it now?

CONCLUSIONS: HOW YA GONNA BE?

I still have more questions than answers. But I want you to have questions too—because, as I tell my students, you need a question before you do your research and determine your research methods. Balkin (2001), who examines what *Brown* "should have said," states something that cannot go unexamined:

> The effective compromise reached in the United States at the beginning of the 21st century is that schools may be segregated by race as long as the segregation is not due to direct government fiat. Furthermore, although *Brown I* emphasized that equal educational opportunity was a crucial component of citizenship, there is no federal constitutional requirement that pupils in predominantly minority school districts receive the same quality of education as students in wealthier, largely all-white districts. (p. B12)

After reading Balkin's assessment, there was no doubt in my mind that a decision needed to be made. How could it not be about the quality of education? Was that not the whole point? If it was not about the quality of education, then that makes *Brown* about Black people wanting to be closer to White people or something. I don't think so. I do not think Black people or people of color overall have such an inferiority complex that they cared more about keeping company with White people than about the quality of education they deserved and needed, and still need now. We are still at a crossroads, and it is time once again to make a change—to make a real difference.

As much as I would like to think that these words will help bring about the death of the AAE-origins debate, I hope that I have at least conveyed that things might have been better at one point for AAE-speaking children, for culturally Black children, and that they can be better still. AAE-speaking children should be able to attend schools where teachers know their language and discourse patterns and recognize their speech for the rich resource that it is, not as a deficit or a sign of mental deficiency. Culturally Black parents should be able to visit their children's schools and not be afraid that teachers will shame them because of their educational level or culture. As Baugh (2001) has indicated, it takes the cooperation of parents, teachers, and students to make education work. That will not happen unless *all* parties are valued and respected.

Without question there is much to glean from the Golden ghettoes. Clearly that is somewhere to look for the better. But I also think that Grace's and Reia's stories are places to look, too. Although Grace tells of growing up with inferior schools, she also tells of growing up in a community of people she wanted to be among. Reia relates something similar. The people were not the problem. Equality and access were problems. What was "better" about their situations was not the education they received—there was obvious room for improvement there—so much as the caring, understanding, nurturing, and camaraderie they saw in their communities. All that makes a community a community makes what Grace, Reia, Arthur Spears, and Richard Wright describe better than what I see today—despite the progress we have supposedly made. We can do better.

I want those reading this to know that linguists can make a difference informing other scholars, educators, and the public that language use in the African American community is vibrant and here to stay and that most of its speakers do not care if it is a dialect of British English or an English and African creole. Linguists can use their resources to help culturally Black, AAE-speaking children learn to read and write, excel in critical literacy and thinking skills, and accomplish other creative endeavors if they choose to accept that mission and give up the origins debate. What matters is what any of us are doing for the plight of AAE speakers, right here and right now.

NOTES

1. "Possible selves represent individuals' ideas of what they might become, what they would like to become, and what they are afraid of becoming. . . . [T]he pool of possible selves derives from the categories made salient by the individual's particular sociocultural and historical context and . . . by the individual's immediate social experiences" (Markus & Nurius, 1986, p. 954).

2. See Perry & Delpit (1998) for a critique of the Ebonics controversy. See Baugh (2000a) for a detailed exegesis of the controversy.

3. Special education scholar Audrey McCray's (2000) conference paper titled "There's Something About the Way He Walks" examined problems African American males have in schools by something as innocuous as the way they walk. I would suggest you could do a similar study titled "There's Something About the Way He [or She] Talks"—though, of course, language is not innocuous.

CHAPTER 10

Mother-Tongue Education and the African Renaissance, with Special Reference to South Africa

Neville Alexander

It was during the political transition of South Africa that I first met Geneva Smitherman and came to appreciate just how much our approaches to language policy coincided. She strode into my circle of friends and associates at a time when, as South Africans of a radical cast of mind, many of us were ambivalent about the African American scholars we had come across during the apartheid years. It ought to be remembered that we had been isolated for decades and few of us had actually met an African American person in the flesh. Because of our opposition to the pro-apartheid policies of the U.S. administration, we were naturally suspicious of any Americans, Black or White, who did not expressly condemn their own government. But even so, it soon became clear that here was a kindred spirit, one who had come to many of our own insights about language and education, albeit by a different trajectory. I particularly appreciated her aggressive stance on the relationship between language policy and progressive social change during the 1996 Ebonics controversy, and I was impressed by the way her words echoed what many people were saying about the educational situation here in South Africa. It is this parallel, and what it has to do with the so-called African Renaissance, that I wish to discuss here.

The African Renaissance was first propounded in 1998 by South African President Thabo Mbeki (1998) as a comprehensive pan-African social, political, and cultural program of action. In recent discussions on what this concept might mean, scholars from diverse countries and disciplines have pointed out the contradiction, not to say absurdity, of an African Renaissance that does not promote the development and official use in high-status domains of indigenous African languages. After all, the European Renaissance of the late 14th through 16th centuries is inextricably associated with the emergence of the modern languages of that continent. The events of that historic period transformed the technology, the knowledge, and the consciousness of the time, and simultaneously initiated the broadening of democracy and the waning of feudalism. All this could only be effected through the languages that the majority of people actually spoke, rather than the remote Latin lingua franca of the intellectual minority.

It is all the more surprising that those who proclaim the so-called African Renaissance do not appear to have given a moment's thought to this issue. Even those scholars who are sensitive to the language question have tried to finesse their neglect by suggesting that the English, French, or Portuguese they use is infused with the idioms and syntax of indigenous African languages. In this way, they say, they are using European languages to give expression to their African way of seeing things. Thus Makgoba (1999) is fully aware of the paradox of the following statement:

> Language is not simply a means of communication or expression, but a corpus of knowledge of a people. While most contributors in this volume are Africans who speak one African language or another, none has used an African language in their writing. We have all used the African idiom and borrowed English as a means of writing. Our nuances, impressions, and interpretation of the English language are rooted in our African languages, experiences and meanings. Can African people champion their renaissance through the medium of foreign languages? This is perhaps one of the greatest challenges to African people. Language is culture and in language we carry our identity and our culture. Through language we carry science and technology, education, political systems and economic developments. The majority of the African people, about whom the rebirth or reawakening is about [sic], live in their indigenous languages throughout their lives.

This is not necessarily a false way of representing a complex reality. On the other hand, few of the African intelligentsia have had the courage to go as far as Ngugi wa Thiong'o, who now writes in Gikuyu, his mother tongue, even though his work is usually translated into English and other European languages. While I would agree that Ngugi's is an extreme either-or position, the fundamental thrust of his argument, as expounded in his essay "The Language of African Literature" (1986), is unanswerable. Borrowing the words of David Diop, Ngugi makes the point in the simplest possible terms: "Surely in an Africa freed from oppression it will not occur to any writer to express, otherwise than in his rediscovered language, his feelings and the feelings of his people" (p. 20).

Ngugi acknowledges, however, that merely writing in an African language is not going to transform the oppression and marginalization of African people. Hence, his frank caveat:

Writing in our languages per se—although a necessary first step in the correct direction—will not itself bring about the renaissance in African cultures if that literature does not carry the content of our people's anti-imperialist struggles to liberate their productive forces from foreign control; the content of the need for unity among the workers and peasants of all the nationalities in their struggle to control the wealth they produce and to free it from internal and external parasites. (p. 29)

How exactly to go from the current dominance of colonial languages in Africa to that future scenario where indigenous languages are dominant is a complicated question, one that involves many more aspects of language planning, language policy development, and language policy implementation than we have room to address here. In what follows, therefore, I will focus on the difficulties of language medium policy and mother-tongue education (MTE) in post-apartheid South Africa.

LANGUAGE MEDIUM POLICY IN
SOUTH AFRICA IN THE 20TH CENTURY: MILNERISM

The history of language medium policy in South African education during the 20th century is shot through with bitter conflict. At the beginning of the century, that arch imperialist Sir Alfred Milner instituted a policy of systematically anglicizing the White Afrikaans-speaking people of the country. In Milner's mind, this strategy amounted to an undeserved bonus for the defeated Afrikaners. In the aftermath of the Anglo-Boer War (1899–1902), which Great Britain won only after a titanic struggle, Milner saw it as one of his reconstruction tasks "to ensure the dominance of the British element, politically and culturally. Therefore instruction through the Dutch language was not to be allowed in the government schools: 'Dutch should only be used to teach English, and English to teach everything else'" (Davenport & Saunders, 2000, p. 239).

The dialectic of South African history turned this fateful policy decision into a reason for continuing the war by other means. The development and promotion of the Afrikaans language became one of the major planks in the political platform of Afrikaner nationalism. A secret society called the Afrikaner Broederbond set about mobilizing White Afrikaans-speaking people for the "repossession" of what they had come to think of as "their country." Their efforts gave rise to one of the most successful language-planning exercises of the 20th century. The "miracle of Afrikaans," as ideologues later called it, refers to the rapid development and adoption of the language in all high-status domains, especially as a language of instruction at institutions of higher education. This sudden transformation marked a significant turning point not only for the history of apartheid South Africa, but also for post-apartheid language planning.

During the Milnerist period, MTE (in Afrikaans) was practiced almost solely in private schools—virtual seedbeds of Afrikaner nationalism. By 1934, bilingual (English-Afrikaans) education had become the norm in almost all schools reserved for Whites. Following 1948, however, when the apartheid government gained political office, MTE (known in South Africa by its Afrikaans equivalent, *moedertaalonderwys,* in order to emphasize its racist intent) was imposed on all schools, including those of the African majority. In theory, MTE was in line with the most progressive postwar pedagogy, as reflected by UNESCO's statements on the subject in the early 1950s. However, as it was used by the racist White minority in South Africa, MTE foisted the inferior curriculum of Bantu education on an entire people as part of a reactionary process of retribalization and Afrikanerization of the country. The result was to effectively tarnish the concept of MTE in the eyes of most Black South Africans. Indeed, this unintended consequence of the Afrikaner nationalist agenda is possibly the most debilitating legacy of apartheid in our nation's history.

VERWOERDISM

As happens so often in history, the oppressed became the oppressor. The very same Afrikaners who had seen tens of thousands of their own massacred under the cynical policies of British imperialism conceived and implemented even more sinister policies at the expense of those South Africans who were not White. The result was a lethal curricular cocktail, one that eventually gave rise to a generation of Black youths for whom the Molotov cocktail was the only effective antidote to Bantu education.

In a nutshell, the policy that Werner M. Eiselen and Hendrik F. Verwoerd, the near-Nazi fathers of Bantu education, inflicted on the unsuspecting pupils of the country decreed that all African language–speaking children should be taught in their mother tongue for the first 6 (later 8) years, after which time there would be a switch to both English and Afrikaans as the languages of teaching. The policy and its implementation evolved over time, but its overall effect was devastating. Parents, teachers, and students became increasingly dissatisfied and alienated until, in the mid-1970s, the system lost all credibility and finally imploded on June 16, 1976. On that day, thousands of children in Soweto demonstrated against the government's Bantu education policy. Police opened fire, sparking off a nationwide cycle of protest and subsequent repression. Those events drew the attention of media worldwide and provoked strong international criticism.

The tragic irony of the children's revolt is that the language medium policy that was subsequently introduced as a conciliatory measure to improve the educational situation in the direction that Black people seemed, misguidedly, to be demanding, turned out to be a case of the cure being worse than the disease. According to Heugh (2001), the 1979 Bantu Education Amendment Act led to the scrapping of the regulation that enforced the switch to both Afrikaans and English as media of instruction in Black schools at the junior secondary level.

> Schools and parents could choose either Afrikaans-medium or English-medium from the 5th year onwards. Secondly, the use of mother tongue medium was further reduced from 6 years after 1975 to 4 years after 1979. A switch in medium would now take place in the 5th year. It is this particular decision/compromise which has unintentionally catapulted South African education towards disaster and turned it into a system that fails the majority of learners. (p. 26)

It is my view that the language attitudes that were reinforced among Black people as a result of this experience are the main reason for the problems in the South African educational system today.

A FEW HOME TRUTHS ABOUT LANGUAGE MEDIUM IN EDUCATION

In order for us to understand why this is such a crucial matter, it is necessary to recognize that language is the basis of all learning. If a student does not understand the language in which he or she is being taught (or communicated with more generally), no learning can take place. Axiomatically, human beings learn best in the language or languages of which they have the best command (i.e., the mother tongue, the language in which the child is socialized by his or her parents and family.) This is particularly the case during the first few years of schooling, when the transition is made from the informal learning environment of the home to the formal drills of the classroom. In most countries today, students are taught a second language of wider communication. In Africa, this second language becomes the primary language of instruction in higher education. This is why, on the African continent, language medium policy in education has become the central educational issue, followed closely perhaps by teacher education and development.

It is generally accepted among educators that the self-confidence of the learner is vital to success in school. Anyone who lacks proficiency in the language of instruction is, *ipso facto,* disadvantaged. Such an individual cannot be spontaneous and is seldom in a position to enjoy the learning process. Above all, severe limitations are placed on the creativity and initiative of that individual when the link between term and concept has to be mediated by a process of halting self-translation. Among other things, this is the cause of the widely observed reticence displayed by most second-language speakers in conversational settings. Nowhere are more children placed in this ball-and-chain situation than in Africa. This is, in my opinion, one of the most damaging legacies of colonialism. The fact that even postcolonial regimes continued using the colonial language (English, French, or Portuguese) as the "official" language, and as the language of teaching after the first few years of primary school, is the main reason for the mediocrity of Africa's intellectual production during the 20th century. This disastrous heritage has to be addressed systematically if the economic, political, and social aspects of the so-called African Renaissance are to have any viability.

One of the more obvious consequences of the current situation is that the higher-education institutions of most African countries are oriented outward, mostly toward Europe but increasingly toward the United States. All high-level academic and professional personnel are either foreign or else recruited from the sliver of intelligentsia trained in the North who have acquired the requisite proficiency in the languages of power, despite the handicaps of the African educational system. These are well-known facts among African scholars. Only a few courageous people have spelled out some of the less obvious but nonetheless enduring consequences of this reality (Djité, 1993; Prah, 1995, 1997). The time has come for the political and cultural leadership of the continent to acknowledge the nonmaterial reasons why economic development programs in African countries routinely fail. Insights such as the following should inform the goals of the African Renaissance, specifically those of the New Program for African Development (NEPAD), which is supposed to represent its economic dimension:

> It needs to be emphasized that the adoption and process of technological assimilation is hardly a viable proposition if it is not translated or adopted into the endogenous cultural base, so that it is organically integrated into the endogenous knowledge system and builds on to the existing cultural fund. . . . [The] more a technological package is couched in the indigenous language of the user, the more likely it is to catch on and succeed. . . . Technology that is merely consumed as an end product requires little integration into the productive culture of the user. The fact that it stands outside the production system of the consumer may increase its exchange value, but it remains more used than understood. The language of its construction continues to be irrelevant to its consumption. It is at best vaguely accessible to an elite reproduced in the image of the west and structurally divorced from native or mass culture. (Prah, 1997, p. 30)

The propositions I have stated here all point to one inescapable conclusion: Unless MTE is rehabilitated at all levels of the educational systems of African countries, the myth of Afro-pessimism propagated by the Western media will become a self-fulfilling prophesy. The African giant will remain chained to the ground in torpid slumber, even as it is racked by internal conflict of suicidal—indeed genocidal—potential.

LANGUAGE MEDIUM POLICY
IN THE NEW SOUTH AFRICA

The self-inflicted wound of an educational system based on a foreign language threatens to continue hemorrhaging in post-apartheid South Africa. However, the prospects for a positive outcome are more favorable now than ever. The material infrastructure and trained human resources that the apartheid state handed over to the democratically elected government in 1994 are of a much better quality than any other African country was "fortunate" enough to receive from a retreating colonial master. Moreover, we have been able to learn from the experiences of other African countries.

The deservedly admired language provisions of the current South African constitution are the result of a political compromise between the leaders of the African National Congress and the (Afrikaner) National Party. The latter would have been unable to sell the negotiated settlement of 1993–1994 to its constituency if the language-rights issue had not been settled to their satisfaction. Although not all the provisions are the result of the passionate commitment of the Afrikaners to their language, this passion led to the constitutional provision for 11 official languages and the promotion of multilingualism as one of the defining characteristics of being South African. While it is true that during the liberation movement there was a general acceptance of societal multilingualism, it is also true that what I have referred to as "static maintenance syndrome" prevailed throughout most of the movement (Alexander, 2002). With a few laudable exceptions, most of the middle- and working-class leadership of the movement believed that the salvation of South Africa would come through the medium of English and the proliferation of that language among the people.

In practice, the prevalence of these language attitudes among the elite has led to the promotion of a unilingual (English-only) policy in the public sector, and in most of the private sector as well. The resistance of Afrikaans-speaking people to this policy of de facto anglicization ranges from racist illusions about the superiority of the White minority to the more sensible realization that the future of Afrikaans as a language is tied up with the development of other indigenous African languages and the enhancement of their status in South African society. This is increasingly seen not merely as a matter of the democratic gains of the liberation struggle, but also as a necessary condition for the economic development and unification of the country as a multicultural polity. The fact is that, in a country where the native English-speaking population is small, it will probably take centuries for the majority of the "common people" (i.e., the urban and rural poor) to acquire the proficiency needed to use English as an instrument of empowerment. Whether such a development is even desirable is another question, considering how few South Africans actually have to communicate on an international level. Be that as it may, assuming that the spread of English as the global language is inevitable for the foreseeable future, for most people in the world it will remain a second, third, or completely foreign language. It is therefore self-limiting and self-destructive for African elites to impose a foreign language on their own people as the "official" one. In the long run, such a course of action can only lead to tyranny and exploitation of the worst kind.

The struggle between those of us who see the promotion of multilingualism (including English as one of a package of language resources) as the best strategy for social transformation and those who favor English-only can be seen in the tensions around language medium policy in education. The position of the latter group is captured in the following counterintuitive statement made by people who are deservedly considered to be among South Africa's progressive educationalists:

> It would seem that modernisation in South Africa, and the inexorable urbanisation in particular, is undermining the possibilities for the first alternative (bilingual models of education N.A.) and that the more realistic option is a straight-for-English approach, except in linguistically homogenous classes where there is little exposure to English outside the classroom or where parents expressly request an alternative. Under these conditions, a research priority could be to examine the minimum requirements for successful teaching in English in South African schools—the teachers' English language competence, the books and materials required, the most effective ways of bridging the learners' language and English and other possible forms of support. (Taylor & Vinjevold, 1999, pp. 225–226)

Against this elitist, middle-class position, we hold to the radical view that in the present phase of its development, post-apartheid South Africa, like most of Africa, should implement an additive bilingual educational system. Such a system would include a range of language options approximating a dual-medium ideal, but tailored to the particular conditions prevailing in a given region or locality. It is our view that knowing English is a wonderful and important asset, especially since 1945. But knowing English should not lead to the destruction of other languages, and it should not become an instrument of individual and group disempowerment. If it does, then it is time to reflect on how we can transform it into a means of empowerment. Bilingual education is one such strategy. It is necessarily a transitional strategy, because once the local languages have acquired sufficient power and are used as regularly in high-status functions as English is today, the need for bilingual education (or, more precisely, dual-medium education) will fall away. People may wish to retain it because of perceived advantages, or they might opt for an English-medium approach. Either way, they would be in a position to make an informed choice. To put the matter differently, far-sighted language policy and planning is important to the consolidation of democracy.

In a Mephistophelian twist of historical logic, the question of whether a genuinely democratic, multicultural South Africa will emerge from the post-apartheid turmoil may depend on the manner in which Afrikaans-speaking intellectuals and professionals deploy the linguistic and academic resources they accumulated in pursuit of their racist agenda from the 1940s to 1980s. If Afrikaners use the skills and knowledge they acquired through "White" affirmative action under apartheid in order to educate and empower their Black counterparts, and generally to raise levels of literacy and training among those who were "left behind," we have every reason to hope that a relatively stable and positive outcome can be realized.

THE BOTTOM LINE

The economic, social, and psychological costs of the existing system, where the mother tongue effectively disappears after the first few years of primary schooling, are demonstrably enormous. In terms of illiteracy, criminal activities, and other social pathologies, the connections are obvious to those carrying out the most cursory of investigations. Language medium policy is one of several factors that help explain the devastating drop-out and failure rates in South Africa and most other African educational systems. In fact, there can be no doubt that it is *the* critical factor because, as I have said, language is the most important instrument by means of which human beings learn. The Project for the Study of Alternative Education in South Africa (PRAESA) has estimated that with an average annual failure rate of 50% in the examination for the school-leaving certificate, South Africa is wasting something on the order of R 3 billion (approximately 470 billion U.S. dollars) every year. The saddest part of this situation is that the Black, African-language-speaking children are the main victims of this irrational system. The only students who enjoy the full benefits of MTE from the cradle to the university and beyond are those whose mother tongue is either English or Afrikaans.

In short, language medium policy reinforces all the other inherited mechanisms that exacerbate the social and racial inequality built into the system.

Once all has been said, the simple question remains: Is it better for a new government committed to social transformation to perpetuate an educational system based on a language that is effectively foreign to most of its citizens, or should it turn the system around over time in order to base it on the mother tongues of the people?

The answer would seem obvious.

Afterword

Geneva Smitherman

Back in the day when I was an 18-year-old graduate student, impatient with what I then called the "turtle-slow progress of social change," I remember being part of a small group of folks listening to a Black scholar-activist who was also a professor at a prestigious university. Holding forth about Black people's quest for empowerment, he was trying to impart to us the lessons of the Blood. With the arrogance so characteristic of youth, I boldly interrupted this Elder's flow with an impertinent query: "Black liberation, yeah, yeah, we all down wit that. But what do *you* teach up in Mainstream University?" He calmly and quietly replied, "Every course I teach, I teach the same thing."

Lookin back over my long, hard journey, over the stony road my generation has trod, I too always teach the same thing. It has never been just about the language. And never about language in some narrow structural sense, but language as discourse, rhetoric, and cultural practice. My work, my mission, inside and outside the Academy, has always been about the speech and the speakers. I stepped out on faith in the power of the Word and the People.

My extended, rural-Tennessee, sharecropping family was part of that 20th-century great migration of Black people out of the American South to the "Promised Land" of the North and West. As the daughter of a Baptist preacher man, I was baptized in the linguistic fire of my people, and I went on to study and write about that fire as a linguist and cultural critic in the Black Arts and Black Studies Movements. Although I became an academic, I never stopped talkin that talk of the speech community that gave me birth. That's one of the things that has enabled me, as anthropologist Faye Harrison might say, to hear out of more than one ear. There was a time, though, when school and society made me feel ashamed of the way I and my family and friends spoke. We talked too "loud," "dropped" word endings, "broke" verbs, and sounded "country"—even those of us who ain nevah even live in the "country." But through the Black Arts Movement, I learned that language is a people's identity, culture, and history, and that with words, to borrow from Ishmael Reed, you could not only "empty the riverbeds of their content," you could even "raise the dead."

The Black Arts Movement. The Black Studies Movement. The Black Liberation Movement. THE MOVEMENT. As political scientist Ron Walters has convincingly argued, it spanned the period from 1960 to 1980. It was a catalyst that brought about fundamental change in a whole lot of Black people. Like, there was a time—as Don L. Lee wrote—when if somebody hadda call us Black, we "woulda broke his right eye out, jumped into his chest, talked bout his momma, lied on his sister and dared him to say it again." But like the old Bluesmen sang, the thangs we usta do, we don't do no mo.

To be sure, linguistic myths and misconceptions about African American Language yet live. But an honest summary of our language history over the past 3 decades warrants the conclusion that progress has been made. The brilliant works in this book speak volumes to that progress. Black scholars are now large and in charge. Yes, thangs done change on the language front. Recall that once upon a time—in 1963 to be exact—a scholar published an article in the *Journal of Negro Education* proclaiming that "Black Dialect" was the "last barrier to integration"—I mean, like whoa! We no longer have to fight for the linguistic legitimacy of African American speech. With the post-1960s global spread of African American Language and Culture, particularly what H. Samy Alim calls HHNL (Hip Hop Nation Language), we have made inroads even on the public language front. Everyone today understands the dialectical pull of language and identity and the implications of those final *g*'s that I was adamant about representin in *Talkin and Testifyin* back in 1977. We must continue to be vigilant about language as an instrument of social transformation, not only for Black people, but for all peoples everywhere.

Back in the day, the postmodern version of the Reparations Movement was just getting under way. Now with a Harvard Law School professor on board and leading public intellectuals like Randall Robinson solidly behind the call for reparations, it is time for linguists to make some input. I'm talkin bout linguistic reparations, about those lost African languages that U.S. enslavement destroyed. As John Baugh notes in the introduction to this volume, Black Americans are the only racial/ethnic group in the United States in which the first generation did not speak its native tongue. What is the cost? How should this language loss be repaid? I submit this as a challenge for the new generation of Black Language scholars to take up.

Another road I want to see a new generation of linguists travel is toward multilingualism. I want to see a campaign for Black people to become fluent not only in African American Language and the Language of Wider Communication, but also in Spanish, Arabic, Xhosa, Yoruba, Swahili, Zulu, Twi, Gĩkũyũ, and other languages. Why settle for one or two when we can speak so many?

Those of us on the language battlefield in the Academy and in K–12 educational systems must take the campaign to the people on the ground. We have done some of this, but we need much more. It is crucial that folks outside

Academia know and see and hear the beauty and truth of the Black Sound. It was clear during the late 1990s controversy generated by the Oakland, California, Ebonics Resolution that our labor in the vineyard had borne fruit among everyday people (which was not the case during *King* and the "Black English" controversy of the late 1970s). In several community forums, folks indicated that it made sense for Blacks to keep "our Ebonics lingo" (as one community leader in Chicago put it) even as we learn "Standard English and other languages." Of course the sound and fury of the ill-informed media took many of us by surprise. In the next round, we must take complete charge. Don't let nobody else define our linguistic reality. Bumrush the media.

In this millennium, we need to move the language conversation to the higher ground of the collective—locally, nationally, and globally. I urge collaboration not only with other language scholars, but also with scholars across disciplines and regions. As I have experienced in my work with European, Caribbean, and now South African scholars, technology makes it possible to forge connections, partnerships, work teams, research endeavors—any time, any place, anywhere, with anybody.

Much remains to be done. We have only begun to understand the linguistic contributions of Black women. Hip Hop is a barely explored reservoir of linguistic riches. The language and literacy education of Black youth haunts and challenges us. And the struggle for equal language rights continues. Anyway, the race is not to the swift, but to those who endureth until our change done come.

The wisdom of the Elders demands that we stay steady on the case. In our research and pedagogy, Beryl Bailey cautions us against slavish devotion to one research methodology or language paradigm. She calls upon us to "modify the orthodox procedures" and "to adopt some completely unorthodox ones" when necessary. Frantz Fanon teaches us that "to speak is to assume a culture," and those of us blessed with education and social advancement must continue to speak in a way that makes it plain that nothin done change. W. E. B. Du Bois teaches us that education is not the same as training; education must be about us and the language that we use and understand. The goal of education is not to make a living, but to make a life. As I have learned from the Elders and the sacrifices of many thousands gone, the role of the linguist and the cultural critic—indeed, the role of all scholars and intellectuals—is not just to understand the world, but to change it. The contributors to *Talkin Black Talk: Language, Education, and Social Change* share this vision, and their collective efforts bring us one step closer to achieving equal language rights.

Geneva Smitherman/Dr. G

March 2006

References

Adger, C., Christian, D., & Taylor, O. (1999). *Making the connection: Language and academic achievement among African American students.* Washington, DC, & McHenry, IL: Center for Applied Linguistics and Delta Systems.

Adger, C., Wolfram, W., & Detwyler, J. (1993). Language differences: A new approach for special educators. *Teaching Exceptional Children, 26*(1), 44–47.

Alexander, N. (2000). *English unassailable but unattainable: The dilemma of language policy in education in South Africa.* (PRAESA Occasional Papers No. 3). Cape Town, South Africa: Project for the Study of Alternative Education in South Africa/University of Cape Town.

Alexander, N. (2001). Bilingual education as a necessary transitional strategy in post-colonial Africa. In J. Pfaffe (Ed.), *Local languages in education, science, and technology* (pp. 16–28). Zomba: Centre for Language Studies, University of Malawi.

Alexander, N. (2002). *Ordinary country: Issues in the transition from apartheid to democracy in South Africa.* Oxford, UK: Berghahn.

Alim, H. (2002). Street-conscious copula variation in the Hip Hop Nation. *American Speech, 77,* 288–304.

Alim, H. (2003). On some serious next millennium rap ishhh: Pharoahe Monch, Hip Hop poetics, and the internal rhymes of *Internal Affairs. Journal of English Linguistics, 31,* 60–84.

Alim, H. (2004a). Hip Hop Nation language. In E. Finegan & J. Rickford (Eds.), *Language in the USA.* (pp. 387–409). Cambridge, MA: Cambridge University Press.

Alim, H. (2004b). *You know my steez: An ethnographic and sociolinguistic study of styleshifting in a Black American speech community.* (Publications of the American Dialect Society No. 89). Durham, NC: Duke University Press.

Alim, H. (2004c). Hearing what's not said and missing what is: Black language in White public space. In C. B. Paulston & S. Keisling (Eds.), *Discourse and intercultural communication: The essential readings.* Malden, MA: Blackwell.

Alim, H. (2005). Critical language awareness in the United States: Revisiting issues and revising pedagogies in a resegregated society. *Educational Researcher, 34*(7), 24–31.

Alim, H. (2006). *Roc the mic right: The language of hip hop culture.* New York: Routledge.

Anderson, E. (1993). Rap music in the classroom? *Teaching English in the Two-Year College, 20,* 214–221.

Anderson, R. C. (1985). Role of the reader's schema in comprehension, learning, and memory. In H. Singer & R. B. Ruddell (Eds.), *Theoretical models and processes of reading* (3rd ed.) (pp. 372–384). Newark, DE: International Reading Association.

Angelou, M. (1971). The thirteens. *Just give me a cool drink of water 'fore I diiie* (pp. 46–47). New York: Random House.

Applebee, A. N. (1979). Children and stories: Learning the rules of the game. *Language Arts, 56*(6), 641–646.

Asante, M. K. (1990). African elements in African American English. In J. E. Holloway (Ed.), *Africanisms in American culture* (pp. 19–33). Bloomington: Indiana University Press.

Au, K. H., Carroll, J. H., & Scheu, J. A. (1997). *Balanced literacy instruction: A teacher's resource book.* Norwood, MA: Christopher-Gordon.

Baer, H., & Singer, M. (1992). *African American religion in the twentieth century: Varieties of protest and accommodation.* Knoxville: University of Tennessee Press.

Bailey, B. (1965). Toward a new perspective in Negro English dialectology. *American Speech, 40*(3), 171–177.

Bailey, B. (1968). Some aspects of the impact of linguistics on language teaching in disadvantaged communities. In A. L. Davis (Ed.), *On the Dialects of Children* (pp. 570–578). Champaign-Urbana, IL: National Council of Teachers of English.

Bailey, B. (1969, Spring/Summer). Language and communicative styles of Afro-American children in the United States. *The Florida Foreign Language Reporter, 46,* 153.

Bailey, G. (2001). The relationship between African American vernacular English and White vernaculars in the American South: A sociocultural history and some phonological evidence. In S. L. Lanehart (Ed.), *Sociocultural and historical contexts of African American English* (pp. 53–92). Amsterdam, The Netherlands: John Benjamins.

Bailey, G., & Maynor, N. (1989). The divergence controversy. *American Speech, 64*(1), 12–39.

Bailey, R. W. (1983). Education and the law: The *King* case in Ann Arbor. In J. W. Chambers, Jr. (Ed.), *Black English educational equity and the law* (pp. 1–28). Ann Arbor, MI: Karoma.

Balkin, J. M. (2001). *What Brown v. Board of Education should have said: The nation's top legal experts rewrite America's landmark civil rights decision.* New York: New York University Press.

Ball, A. (1995). Text design patterns in the writing of urban African-American students: Teaching to the strengths of students in multicultural settings. *Urban Education, 30*(3).

Ball, A. (1999). Evaluating the writing of culturally and linguistically diverse students: The case of the African American vernacular English speaker. In C. R. Cooper & L. Odell (Eds.), *Evaluating writing: The role of teachers' knowledge about text, learning, and culture* (pp. 225–248). Champaign-Urbana, IL: National Council of Teachers of English.

Ball, A. (2000). Empowering pedagogies that enhance the learning of multicultural students. *Teachers College Record, 102*(6), 1006–1034.

Ball, A. (Ed.) (2006). *With more deliberate speed: Achieving equity and excellence in education: Realizing the full potential of* Brown v. Board of Education. 2006 Yearbook of the National Society for the Study of Education. Malden, MA: Blackwell.

Ball, A., & Alim, H. (2006). Preparation, pedagogy, policy, and power: *Brown*, the *King* case, and the struggle for equal language rights. In A. Ball (Ed.), *With more deliberate speed: Achieving equity and excellence in education: Realizing the full potential of* Brown v. Board of Education. 2006 Yearbook of the National Society for the Study of Education. Malden, MA: Blackwell.

Bamgbose, A. (2000). Language and the African renaissance: Lessons from the South African experience. In E. Wolff (Ed.), *Working documents of the panel on language policy in Africa: The African renaissance as a challenge for language planning*. Leipzig, Germany: Institut für Afrikanistik.

Baraka, A. (1966). Expressive language. *Home* (pp. 166–172). New York: William Morrow.

Baraka, A. (1969). W. W. In C. Major (Ed.), *New Black poetry* (p. 78). New York: International.

Baraka, A. (1970). The nation is like ourselves. *It's nation time* (pp. 7–11). Chicago, IL: Third World Press.

Baratz, J., & Shuy, R. (Eds.). (1969). *Teaching Black children to read*. Washington, DC: Center for Applied Linguistics.

Baugh, J. (1983). *Black street speech: Its history, structure, and survival*. Austin: University of Texas Press.

Baugh, J. (1995). The law, linguistics, and education: Educational reform for African American language minority students. *Linguistics and Education, 7*, 87–105.

Baugh, J. (1998). Linguistics, education, and the law: Educational reform for African American language minority students. In S. Mufwene, J. Rickford, G. Bailey, & J. Baugh (eds.), *African-American English: Structure, history, and use* (pp. 282–301). London: Routledge.

Baugh, J. (1999a). Considerations in preparing teachers for linguistic diversity. In C. Adger, D. Christian, & O. Taylor (Eds.), *Making the connection: Language and academic achievement among African American students* (pp. 81–96). Washington, DC, & McHenry, IL: Center for Applied Linguistics and Delta Systems.

Baugh, J. (1999b). *Out of the mouths of slaves: African American language and educational malpractice.* Austin: University of Texas Press.

Baugh, J. (2000a). *Beyond Ebonics: Linguistic pride and racial prejudice.* New York: Oxford University Press.

Baugh, J. (2000b). Racial identification by speech. *American Speech, 75,* 362–364.

Baugh, J. (2001). Applying linguistic knowledge of African American English to help students learn and teachers teach. In S. L. Lanehart (Ed.), *Sociocultural and historical contexts of African American English.* (pp. 319–330). Amsterdam: John Benjamins.

Baugh, J. (2006). Linguistic considerations pertaining to *Brown v. Board*: Exposing racial fallacies in the new millennium. In A. Ball (Ed.), *With more deliberate speed: Achieving equity and excellence in education: Realizing the full potential of* Brown v. Board of Education. 2006 Yearbook of the National Society for the Study of Education. Malden, MA: Blackwell.

Beck, I. L., McKeown, M. G., Hamilton, R. L., & Kucan, L. (1997). *Questioning the author: An approach for enhancing student engagement with text.* Newark, DE: International Reading Association.

Bennett, J. (1908). Gullah: A Negro patois. *South Atlantic Quarterly, 7,* 332–347.

Bennett, J. (1909). Gullah: A Negro Patois. *South Atlantic Quarterly, 8,* 39-52.

Bereiter, C. (1965). Language program for culturally deprived children. In *Language programs for the disadvantaged.* Champaign-Urbana, IL: National Council of Teachers of English.

Bereiter, C., & Engelmann, S. (1966). *Teaching disadvantaged children in preschool.* Engelwood Cliffs, NJ: Prentice Hall.

Blackshire-Belay, C. A. (1996). The location of Ebonics within the framework of the Africological paradigm. *Journal of Black Studies, 27,* 5–23.

Bloom, B. S. (1956). *Taxonomy of educational objectives: The classification of educational goals, by a committee of college and university examiners.* New York: Longman.

Bowie, R., & Bond, C. (1994). Influencing future teachers' attitudes toward Black English: Are we making a difference? *Journal of Teacher Education, 45,* 112–118.

Boyd, T. (1997). *Am I Black enough for you? Popular culture from the 'hood and beyond.* Bloomington: University of Indiana Press.

Boyle, J. R. (1996). The effects of a cognitive mapping strategy on the literal and inferential comprehension of students with mild disabilities. *Learning Disability Quarterly, 19,* 86–98.

Bronstein, A., Dubner, F., Lee, P., & Raphael, L. (1970, December). *A sociolinguistic comment on the changing attitudes toward the use of Black English and an experimental study to measure some of those attitudes.* Paper presented at the 56th annual convention of the Speech Communication Association, New Orleans, LA.

Brooks, C. (1985). *Tapping potential: English and language arts for the Black learner.* Champaign-Urbana, IL: National Council of Teachers of English.

Brown, J. (1979, June 22). Don't segregate kids for "Black English." *Detroit News,* 1B, 8B.

Brown, R., Pressley, M., Van Meter, P., & Schuder, T. (1996). A quasi-experimental validation of transactional instruction with low-achieving second grade readers. *Journal of Educational Psychology, 88*(1), 18–37.

Brown, S. (1995). UnwRapping rap: A literacy of lived experience. Paper presented at the Conference on College Composition and Communication. Washington, DC.

Brown v. Board of Education, 347 U.S. 483 (1954).

Bruner, J. (1960). *The process of education.* Cambridge, MA: Harvard University Press.

Bullins, E. (1971). *The duplex: A Black love fable in four movements.* New York: William Morrow.

Burling, R. (1973). *English in Black and White.* New York: Holt-Rinehart.

Butters, R. R. (1989). *The death of Black English: Divergence and convergence in Black and White vernaculars.* New York: Peter Lang.

Calfee, R., Chambliss, M., & Beretz, M. (1991). Organizing for comprehension and composition. In W. Ellis (Ed.), *All language and the creation of literacy* (pp. 79–83). Baltimore, MD: Orton Dyslexia Society.

Calfee, R. C., & Patrick, C. L. (1995). *Teach our children well.* Stanford, CA: Stanford University Alumni Association.

Calfee, R. C., & Wolf, S. (1988). *The BOOK.* Stanford, CA: Project READ, Calfee Projects.

California Department of Education. (1999). *Reading/language arts framework for California public schools, kindergarten through grade 12.* Sacramento, CA: Author.

Carter, P. (2005). *Keepin' it real: School success beyond Black and White.* Oxford: Oxford University Press.

Chambers, J., Jr. (1983). *Black English educational equity and the law.* Ann Arbor, MI: Karoma.

Chomsky, N. (1957). *Syntactic structures.* The Hague, The Netherlands: Mouton.

Chomsky, N. (1965). *Aspects of the theory of syntax.* Cambridge, MA: MIT Press.

Christie, P. (1985). *The right to learn: The struggle for education in South Africa.* Johannesburg, South Africa: SACHED/Ravan Press.

Chuska, K. (1995). Improving classroom questions: A teacher's guide to increasing student motivation, participation, and higher-level thinking. Bloomington, IN: Phi Delta Kappa Educational Foundation.

Cobb-Scott, J. (1985). Language and the teaching-learning process. In C. Brooks (Ed.), *Tapping potential: English and language arts for the Black learner*. Champaign-Urbana, IL: National Council of Teachers of English.

Covington, A. (1975). Teachers' attitudes toward Black English. In R. Williams (Ed.), *Ebonics: The true language of Black folks* (pp. 40–54). St. Louis, MO: Robert Williams & Associates.

Cummings, J. (1989). *Empowering minority students*. Sacramento: California Association of Bilingual Educators.

Darling-Hammond, L. (1985). Equality and excellence: The educational status of Black Americans. New York: College Board.

Darling-Hammond, L. (2000). How teacher education matters. *Journal of Teacher Education, 51*, 166–173.

Davenport, R., & Saunders, C. (2000). *South Africa: A modern history*. London: Macmillan.

De La Cruz, A. (1991). *The woman who outshone the sun*. San Francisco: Children's Book Press.

DeBose, C. E. (1992). Codeswitching: Black English and Standard English in the African American linguistics repertoire. *Journal of Multilingual and Multicultural Development, 13*, 157–167.

DeBose, C. E. (2001a, January). The African American literacy and culture project. Lecture presented at the annual meeting of the Linguistic Society of America, Washington, DC.

DeBose, C. E. (2001b, October). The status of Variety X in the African American linguistic repertoire. Lecture presented at New Ways of Analyzing Variation Panel Discussion, Raleigh, NC.

DeBose, C. E. (2005). *The sociology of African American language: A language planning perspective*. New York: Palgrave Macmillan.

DeBose, C. E., & Faraclas, N. (1993). An Africanist approach to the linguistic study of Black English: Getting to the roots of the tense-aspect-modality and copula systems in Afro-American. In S. S. Mufwene (Ed.), *Africanisms in Afro-American language varieties* (pp. 364–387). Athens: University of Georgia Press.

Delpit, L. (1995). *Other people's children: Cultural conflict in the classroom*. New York: The New Press.

Dillard, J. L. (1971). The creolist and the study of Negro non-standard dialects in the continental United States. In D. Hymes (Ed.), *Pidginization and Creolization of Languages* (pp. 393–408). London: Cambridge University Press.

Dillard, J. L. (1972). *Black English: Its history and usage in the United States*. New York: Random House.

Djité, P. (1993). Language and development in Africa. *International Journal of the Sociology of Language,100/101,* 149–166.

Drake, S. C. (1945). *Black metropolis.* New York: Harcourt Brace.

Du Bois, W. E. B. (1961). *The souls of Black folk.* Greenwich, CT: Fawcett. (Original work published 1903)

Du Plessis, H., & Du Plessis, T. (Eds.). (1987). *Afrikaans en taalpolitiek: 15 Opstelle.* Pretoria, South Africa: HAUM.

Duncan-Andrade, J. (2004). Your best friend or your worst enemy: Youth popular culture, pedagogy, and curriculum in urban classrooms. *The Review of Education, Pedagogy, and Cultural Studies, 26*(4), 313–337.

Dunjwa-Blajberg, J. (1980). *Sprache und politik in Südafrika: Stellung und funktion der sprachen unter dem apartheidsystem.* Bonn, Germany: Informationsstelle Südliches Afrika.

Dyson, A. H. (2003). *The brothers and sisters learn to write: Popular literacies in childhood and school cultures.* New York: Teachers College Press.

Dyson, M. (1993). *Reflecting Black.* Minneapolis: University of Minnesota Press.

Fairchild, H., & Edwards-Evans, S. (1990). African American dialects and schooling: A review. In A. Padilla, H. Fairchild, & C. Valadez (Eds.), *Bilingual education: Issues and strategies* (pp. 75–86). Newbury Park, CA: Sage.

Fanon, F. (1967). *Black skin, White masks.* New York: Grove Press.

Fasold, R. W. (1972). *Tense marking in Black English: A linguistic and social analysis.* Washington, DC: Center for Applied Linguistics.

Fasold, R. W. (Ed.) (1987). Are Black and White vernaculars diverging? Special issue of *American Speech, 62*(1).

Fasold, R. W., Labov, W., Vaughn-Cooke, F., Bailey, G., Wolfram, W., Spears, A. K., & Rickford, J. (1987). Are Black and White vernaculars diverging? Papers from the New Ways of Anazlzing Variation XIV Panel Discussion. *American Speech, 62*(1), 3–80.

Fasold, R. W., & Shuy, R. (1970). *Teaching Standard English in the inner city.* Washington, DC: Center for Applied Linguistics.

Fasold, R. W., & Wolfram, W. (1970). Some linguistic features of Negro dialect. In R. W. Fasold & R. Shuy (eds.), *Teaching Standard English in the inner city* (pp. 41-86). Washington, D.C.: Center for Applied Linguistics.

Fasold, R. W., & Wolfram, W. (1975). Some linguistic features of Negro dialect. In P. Stoller (Ed.) *Black American English: Its background and its usage in the schools and in literature* (pp. 49–83). New York: Dell.

Faustin, C. (1994). Bush medicine. In C. Powling (Ed.), *Faces in the dark: A book of scary stories.* New York: Kingfisher.

Finegan, E. (1980). *Attitudes toward English usage: The history of a war of words.* New York: Teachers College Press.

Fisher, C. J., Fox, D. L., & Paille, E. (1996). Teacher education research in the English language arts and reading. In J. Sikula, T. J. Buttery, & E. Guyton (Eds.), *Handbook of research on teacher education*. New York: Simon & Schuster.

Fisher, M. (2003). Open mics and open minds: Spoken word poetry in African Diaspora participatory literacy communities. *Harvard Educational Review, 73*(3), 362–389.

Fishman, J. A. (1980). Bilingual education, language planning and English. *English World Wide: A Journal of Varieties of English, 1,* 11–24.

Foster, M. (2001). Pay leon, pay leon, pay leon, paleontologist: Using call-and-response to facilitate language mastery and literacy acquisition among African American students. In S. L. Lanehart (Ed.), *Sociocultural and historical contexts of African American English*. (pp. 281–298). Amsterdam, The Netherlands: John Benjamins.

Frisk, P. J. (1992). Rap music and the first-year writing curriculum. Paper presented at the Annual Meeting of the Conference on College Composition and Communication. Cincinnati, OH.

Fuller, H. (1971). Towards a black aesthetic. In A. Gayle (Ed.), *The Black aesthetic* (pp. 3–12). New York: Doubleday.

Gee, J. (1996). *Social linguistics and literacies: Ideology in discourses*. London: Taylor & Francis.

Giovanni, N. (1970). Ego tripping. *Re: Creation* (pp. 37–38). Detroit, MI: Broadside Press.

Gonzales, A. (1922). *Black border*. Columbia, SC: The State Company.

Gorodnov, V. (1988). *Soweto: Life and struggles of a South African township*. Moscow, Russia: Progress.

Gramsci, A. (1971). *Selections from the prison notebooks*. New York: International.

Green, L. (1993). *Topics in African American English: The verb system analysis*. Unpublished doctoral dissertation, University of Massachusetts, Amherst.

Green, L. (1995). Study of verb classes in African American English. *Linguistics and Education: An International Research Journal, 7,* 65–81.

Green, L. (2001, January 6). *Recent advances in research in African American English: Patterns-based approach and descriptive analysis*. Paper presented at the Linguistic Society of American Convention, Washington, DC.

Gumperz, J., & Hymes, D. (Eds.). (1972). *Directions in sociolinguistics: The ethnography of communication*. New York: Holt-Rinehart.

Guskin, J. (1970, March). *Social perceptions of language variations: Black dialect and exceptions of ability*. Paper presented at the American Research Association Conference, Minneapolis, MN.

Guthrie, J. T. (1985). Story comprehension and fables. In H. Singer & R. B. Ruddell (Eds.), *Theoretical models and processes of reading* (3rd ed.) (pp. 434–476). Newark, DE: International Reading Association.

Harrison, J. A. (1884). Negro English. *Anglia, 7,* 232–279.

Heath, S. B. (1982). Questioning at home and at school: A comparative study. In G. Spindler (Ed.), *Doing the ethnography of schooling: Educational anthropology in action* (pp. 103–131). New York: Holt, Rinehart & Winston.

Heath, S. B. (1983). *Ways with words: Language, life, and work in communities and classrooms.* Cambridge: Cambridge University Press.

Herskovits, M. (1941). *Myth of the Negro past.* Boston: Beacon Press.

Heugh, K. (2000). *The case against bilingual and multilingual education in South Africa.* (PRAESA Occasional Papers No.6). Cape Town, South Africa: Project for the Study of Alternative Education in South Africa/University of Cape Town.

Heugh, K. (2001). A history of mother tongue and bilingual education in South Africa. In PRAESA and UFSIA, *Mother tongue education, with special reference to South Africa and Belgium.* Cape Town, South Africa: Project for the Study of Alternative Education in South Africa.

Hicks, P. T. (1987). The relationship between an oral rhythmic style of communication (rap music) and learning in the urban preschool. Paper presented at the Annual Meeting of the Association for Education in Journalism and Mass Communication, San Antonio, TX.

Hilliard, A. G. (1999). *SBA: The reawakening of the African mind.* Gainseville, FL: Makare.

Hirson, B. (1981). Language in control and resistance in South Africa. *Journal of African Affairs, 80,* 219–237.

Hollie, S. (2000). *African American students as Standard English language learners: An alternative approach.* Los Angeles: University of Southern California.

Holloway, J. E., & Vass, W. K. (1993). *The African heritage of American English.* Bloomington: Indiana University Press.

Honeman, B. (1990). Rationale and suggestions for emphasizing Afrocentricity in the public schools. Paper presented at the Conference on Rhetoric and the Teaching of Writing, Indiana, PA.

Hughes, L. (1940). *The big sea.* New York: Hill & Wang.

Hughes, L. (1961). Feet live their own life. *The best of Simple* (p. 3). New York: Hill & Wang.

Hymes, D. (1972). Models in the interaction of language and social life. In J. Gumperz & D. Hymes (Eds.), *Directions in sociolinguistics: The ethnography of communication* (pp. 35–71). New York: Holt-Rinehart.

Jackson, A. (2006, April). Critical hip hop pedagogy: A Black cultural studies approach to college composition. Paper presented at the American Educational Research Association, San Francisco, CA.

Johnson, K. (1971, May). Teacher attitudes toward nonstandard Negro dialect. *The Education Digest, 36*(9), 45–48.

Kane-Berman, J. (1978). *Soweto: Black revolt, White reaction.* Johannesburg, South Africa: Ravan Press.

Killens, J. O. (1971). *The cotillion, or One good bull is half the herd.* New York: Trident.

Knight, E. (1968). Hard Rock returns to prison from the hospital for the criminal insane. *Poems from prison* (pp. 11–12). Detroit, MI: Broadside Press.

Knight, E. (1971). I sing of Shine. *The Black poets* (pp. 209–210). New York: Bantam.

Krapp, G. P. (1924). The English of the Negro. *American Mercury, 33,* 16–25.

Labov, W. (1969a). Contraction, deletion, and inherent variability of the English copula. *Language, 45,* 715–762.

Labov, W. (1969b, Spring/Summer). The logic of non-standard English. *Linguistic-cultural differences and American education: Special edition of the Florida Foreign Language Reporter, 7,* 60–74, 169.

Labov, W. (1972). *Language in the inner city: Studies in the Black English vernacular.* Philadelphia: University of Pennsylvania Press.

Labov, W. (1982). Objectivity and commitment in linguistic science: The case for the Black English trial in Ann Arbor. *Language in Society, 11,* 165–201.

Labov, W. (1987). Are Black and White vernaculars diverging? *American Speech, 62*(1), 5–12.

Labov, W. (2001). Applying our knowledge of African American English to the problem of raising reading levels in inner-city schools. In S. L. Lanehart (Ed.), *Sociocultural and historical contexts of African American English* (pp. 299–318). Amsterdam, The Netherlands: John Benjamins.

Labov, W., Cohen, P., Robins, C., & Lewis, J. (1968). *A study of the non-standard English of Negro and Puerto Rican speakers in New York City: Vol. 1. Phonological and grammatical analysis.* Cooperative Research Project No. 3288. New York: U.S. Office of Education.

Labov, W., & Harris, W. A. (1986). De facto segregation of Black and White vernaculars. In D. Sankoff (Ed.), *Diversity and diachrony* (pp. 1–24). Amsterdam, The Netherlands: John Benjamins.

Ladson-Billings, G. (1994). *The dreamkeepers: Successful teachers of African American children.* San Francisco: Jossey-Bass.

Ladson-Billings, G. (1995). Toward a theory of culturally relevant pedagogy. *American Educational Research Journal, 32*(3), 465–491.

Lanehart, S. L. (2002). *Sista, speak! Black women kinfolk talk about language and literacy.* Austin: University of Texas Press.

Lee, C. (1993). *Signifying as a scaffold for literary interpretation: The pedagogical implications of an African American discourse genre.* Champaign-Urbana, IL: National Council of Teachers of English.

Lee, D. (1968). *Black pride.* Detroit, MI: Broadside Press.

Lee, D. (1969a). But he was cool or: he even stopped for green lights. *Don't cry, scream* (pp. 24–25). Detroit, MI: Broadside Press.

Lee, D. (1969b, December). Directions for Black writers. *The Black Scholar, 1,* 53–57.

Lee, D. (1969c). *Don't cry, scream.* Detroit, MI: Broadside Press.

Lee, D. (1969d). Don't cry, scream. *Don't cry, scream* (pp. 27–31). Detroit, MI: Broadside Press.

Lee, D. (1969e). From a Black perspective. *Don't cry, scream* (p. 34). Detroit, MI: Broadside Press.

Lee, D. (1969f). Gwendolyn Brooks. *Don't cry, scream* (pp. 22–23). Detroit, MI: Broadside Press.

Lee, D. (1969g). Malcolm spoke / who listened. *Don't cry, scream* (p. 33). Detroit, MI: Broadside Press.

Lee, D. (1969h). Poem to complement other poems. *Don't cry, scream* (pp. 36–38). Detroit, MI: Broadside Press.

Lee, D. (1969i). The revolutionary screw. *Don't cry, scream* (p. 57). Detroit, MI: Broadside Press.

Lee, D. (1969j). *Think Black.* Detroit, MI: Broadside Press.

Lee, D. (1970a). Blackman: An unfinished history. *We walk the way of the new world* (p. 22). Detroit, MI: Broadside Press.

Lee, D. (1970b). *We walk the way of the new world.* Detroit, MI: Broadside Press.

LeMoine, N. (2001). Language variation and literacy acquisition in African American students. In J. Harris, A. Kamhi, & K. Pollock (Eds.), *Literacy in African American communities.* Mahwah, NJ: Lawrence Erlbaum Associates.

LeMoine, N. (2003). The impact of linguistic knowledge about African American language/Ebonics on teacher attitude toward the language and the students who speak it. Published doctoral dissertation, University of Southern California.

LeMoine, N., & Los Angeles Unified School District (1999). *English for your success: A language development program for African American students.* Maywood, NJ: Peoples Publishing Group.

Lester, J. (1969). Stagolee. *Black folktales* (p. 129). New York: Grove Press.

Lukens, R. J. (1999). *A critical handbook of children's literature.* New York: Addison-Wesley.

Macklis, K. (1989). Fifth graders "rap" English elements. *The Reading Teacher, 42,* 340.

Maddahian, E., & Sandamela, A. (2000). *Academic English mastery program 1998–1999 evaluation report.* Los Angeles, CA: Los Angeles Unified School District Research and Evaluation Unit.

Mahiri, J., & Sutton, S. S. (1996). Writing for their lives: The non-school literacy of California's urban African American youth. *Journal of Negro Education, 65*, 164–180.

Major, C. (1994). *Juba to jive: A dictionary of African American slang.* New York: Penguin.

Makgoba, M. (Ed.) (1999). *African Renaissance: The new struggle.* Cape Town, South Africa: Mafube/Tafelberg.

Markus, H., & Nurius, P. (1986). Possible selves. *American Psychologist, 41*, 954–969.

Martin Luther King Junior Elementary School Children v. Ann Arbor School District Board, 473 F. Supp. 1371 (1979).

Mbeki, T. (1998, August 13). [Statement on the African Renaissance.] Speech presented at the Gallagher Estate, Johannesburg, South Africa.

McDavid, R. I. (1950). [Review of the book *Africanisms in the Gullah dialect,* by Lorenzo Turner]. *Language, 26,* 323–333.

McDavid, R. I. (1951). The relationship of the speech of American Negroes to the speech of Whites. *American Speech, 26*(1), 3–17.

McDavid, R. I. (1967). Historical, regional, and social variation. *Journal of English Linguistics, 1*(1), 25–40.

Meacham, S., & Anderson, T. (2003). Hip hop as literacy. Paper presented at the American Educational Research Association, Chicago, IL.

Meier, T. (1999). The case for Ebonics as part of exemplary teacher preparation. In C. Adger, D. Christian, & O. Taylor (Eds.), *Making the connection: Language and academic achievement among African American students* (pp. 97–114). Washington, DC, & McHenry, IL: Center for Applied Linguistics and Delta Systems.

Mencken, H. L. (1936). *The American language* (4th Ed.). New York: Alfred A. Knopf.

Milford, J. A. (1992). Rap lyrics: Instruments for language arts instruction. *The Western Journal of Black Studies, 16* (2), 98–102.

Mitchell-Kernan, C. (1970) *Language behavior in a black urban community.* Unpublished dissertation, University of California, Berkeley.

Mitchell-Kernan, C. (1971). *Language behavior in a Black urban community.* (Language Behavior Laboratory Monograph No. 2). Berkeley, CA: University of California-Berkeley.

Mitchell-Kernan, C. (1972). Signifying and marking: Two Afro-American speech acts. In J. J. Gumperz & D. Hymes (Eds.), *Directions in sociolinguistics* (pp. 161–179). New York: Holt, Rinehart & Winston.

Mkalimoto, E. (1969). Energy for a new thang. In C. Major (Ed.), *New Black poetry* (p. 90). New York: International.

MME Productions. (1993). *MME report: Reaching the hip-hop generation.* (Robert Wood Johnson Foundation, I.D. No. 18762). Philadelphia: MME Productions.

Morgan, M. (1989). *From down south to up south: The language behavior of three generations of Black women residing in Chicago.* Unpublished doctoral dissertation, University of Pennsylvania.

Morgan, M. (1991). Indirectness and interpretation in African American women's discourse. *Pragmatics, 1,* 421–451.

Morgan, M. (1993). The Africanness of counterlanguage among Afro-Americans. In S. S. Mufwene (Ed.), *Africanisms in Afro-American language varieties* (pp. 422–435). Athens: University of Georgia Press.

Morgan, M. (1998). More than a mood or an attitude: Discourse and verbal genres in African American culture. In S. S. Mufwene, J. Baugh, & J. R. Rickford (Eds.), *African American English: Structure, history, and use* (pp. 251–281). New York: Routledge.

Morgan, M. (2001). "Nuthin' but a g thang": Grammar and language ideology in hip hop identity. In S. L. Lanehart (Ed.), *Sociocultural and historical contexts of African American English* (pp. 187–209). Amsterdam, The Netherlands: John Benjamins.

Morrell, E. (2002). Toward a critical pedagogy of popular culture: Literacy development among urban youth. *Journal of Adolescent & Adult Literacy, 46*(1): 72–77.

Morrow-Pretlow, T. (1994). Using rap lyrics to encourage at-risk elementary grade urban learners to read for pleasure. Ed.D. Practicum, Nova Southeastern University, Fort Lauderdale, FL.

Mufwene, S. (2000). Some sociohistorical inferences about the development of African American English. In S. Poplack (Ed.), *The English history of African American English* (pp. 233–263). Oxford: Blackwell.

National Centre for Curriculum Research and Development. (2000). *Language in the classroom: Towards a framework for intervention.* Pretoria, South Africa: Department of Education.

National Education Policy Investigation Research Group. (1992). *Language: Report of the NEPI Language Research Group.* Cape Town, South Africa: OUP/NECC.

Ngugi wa Thiong'o. (1986). The language of African literature. *Decolonising the mind: The politics of language in African Literature* (pp. 4–33). London: Heinemann.

Oakes, J. (1985). *Keeping track: How schools structure inequality.* New Haven, CT: Yale University Press.

Ogbu, J. (1978). *Minority education and caste: The American system in cross-cultural perspective.* New York: Academic Press.

Ogbu, J. (1992, November). Understanding multicultural education. *Educational Researcher, 21,* 5–14, 24.

O'Meara, D. (1983). *Volkskapitalisme: Class, capital, and ideology in the development of Afrikaner nationalism, 1934–1948.* Johannesburg, South Africa: Ravan Press.

Orfield, G., & Yun, J. T. (1999). *Resegregation in American schools.* Cambridge, MA: The Civil Rights Project at Harvard University.

Palinscar, A. S., & Brown, A. L. (1984). Reciprocal teaching of comprehension-fostering and comprehension-monitoring activities. *Cognition and Instruction, 1,* 117–175.

Paris, S. G. , Wixson, K. K., & Palinscar, A. S. (1986). Instructional approaches to reading comprehension. *Review of Research in Education, 13,* 91–128.

Pearson, P. D., & Camperell, K. (1994). Comprehension of text structures. In H. Singer & R. B. Ruddell (Eds.), *Theoretical models and processes of reading* (3rd ed.) (pp. 323–342). Newark, DE: International Reading Association.

Peitzman, F., & Gadda, G. (1991). *With different eyes: Insights into teaching language minority students across the disciplines.* Los Angeles: UCLA Publishing.

Perry, T., & Delpit, L. (1998). *The real Ebonics debate: Power, language, and the education of African American children.* Boston: Beacon Press.

Plessy v. Ferguson, 163 U.S. 537 (1896).

Poplack, S. (Ed.) (2000). *The English history of African American English.* Oxford: Blackwell.

Prah, K. (1995). *Mother tongue for scientific and technological development in Africa.* Bonn, Germany: German Foundation for International Development.

Prah, K. (1997). The language factor in the scientific and technological development of Africa. In of Arts, Culture, Science and Technology, *The feasibility of technical language development in the African languages.* Pretoria, South Africa: DACST.

Prince, A. P. (2006). Structuring access to learning opportunities in American high schools. Unpublished dissertation, Stanford University.

Reed, I. (1970). *19 Necromancers from now.* New York: Doubleday.

Richardson, E. (2003). *African American literacies.* New York: Routledge.

Richardson, E. (2006). *Hiphop literacies.* New York: Routledge.

Rickford, A. (1999). *I can fly: Teaching reading and narrative comprehension to African American and other ethnic minority students.* Lanham, MD: University Press of America.

Rickford, A. (2001). The effect of cultural congruence and higher order questioning on the reading enjoyment and comprehension of ethnic minority students. *Journal of Education for Students Placed at Risk, 6*(4), 357–387.

Rickford, A. (2002). The effects of teacher education on reading improvement. *Journal of Reading Improvement, 38*(4), 147–169.

Rickford, A., & Rickford, J. (1995). Dialect readers revisited. *Linguistics and Education: An International Research Journal, 7*(2), 107–128.

Rickford, J. (1977). The question of prior creolization of Black English. In A. Valdeman (Ed.), *Pidgin and creole linguistics* (pp. 199–221). Bloomington: University of Indiana Press.

Rickford, J. (1997). Unequal partnership: Sociolinguistics and the African American speech community. *Language in Society, 26,*161–197.

Rickford, J., Ball, A., & Blake, R. (1991). Rappin on the copula coffin: Theoretical and methodological issues in the analysis of copula variation in African American vernacular English. *Language Variation and Change, 3,* 103–132.

Rickford, J., & McNair-Knox, F. (1994). Addressee-and topic-influenced style shift: A quantitative sociolinguistic study. In D. Biber & E. Finegan (Eds.), *Perspectives on register: Situating register variation within sociolinguistics* (pp. 235–276). Oxford: Oxford University Press.

Rickford, J., & Rickford, R. J. (2000). *Spoken soul: The story of Black English.* New York: John Wiley & Sons.

Ronkin, M., & Karn, H. (1999). Mock Ebonics: Linguistic racism in parodies of Ebonics on the internet. *Journal of Sociolinguistics, 3*(3), 360–380.

Rosenblatt, L. M. (1991). The reading transaction: What for? In B. M. Power & R. Hubbard (Eds.), *Literacy in process* (pp. 114–127). Portsmouth, NH: Heinemann.

Rouch, R. L., & Birr, S. (1984). *Teaching reading: A practical guide of strategies and activities.* New York: Teachers College Press.

Ruddell, R. (1999). *Teaching children to read and write: Becoming an influential teacher.* Needham Heights, MA: Allyn & Bacon.

Sanchez, S. (1970a, January/February). Queens of the universe. *The Black Scholar,* 30–34.

Sanchez, S. (1970b). *We a baddDDD people.* Detroit, MI: Broadside Press.

Sankoff, D. (Ed.) (1986). *Diversity and diachrony.* Amsterdam, The Netherlands: John Benjamins.

Sarup, M. (1989). *An introductory guide to post-structuralism and postmodernism.* Athens: University of Georgia Press.

Scholtz, J. (1965). *Die Afrikaner en sy taal 1806–1875.* Cape Town, South Africa: Nasou Bpk.

Shakur, T. (1999). *The rose that grew from concrete.* New York: MTV/Pocket Books.

Simpkins, G., Holt, G., & Simpkins, C. (1974). *Bridge.* Boston: Houghton Mifflin.

Simpkins, G., & Simpkins, C. (1981). Cross-cultural approach to curriculum development. In G. Smitherman (Ed.), *Black English and the education of Black children and youth: Proceedings of the National Invitational Symposium on the* King *decision* (pp. 221–240). Detroit, MI: Wayne State University Center for Black Studies.

Sims, R. (1975). Black children and the language arts: A call for reform. In R. L. Williams (Ed.), *Ebonics: The true language of Black folks* (pp. 22–27). St. Louis, MO: Williams & Associates.

Skutnabb-Kangas, T. (2000). *Linguistic genocide in education—or worldwide diversity and human rights?* Mahwah, NJ: Lawrence Erlbaum Associates.

Smith, E. (1975). Ebonics: A case history. In R. L. Williams (Ed.), *Ebonics: The true language of Black folks* (pp. 77–85). St. Louis, MO: Williams & Associates.

Smith, E. (1998). What is Black English? What is Ebonics? In. L. Delpit & T. Perry (Eds.), *The real Ebonics debate: Power, language, and the education of African American children.* Boston: Beacon Press.

Smith, F. (2001, December 3). WAT goed op koers ondanks slakkegang. *Die Burger.*

Smitherman, G. (1973, May–June). White English in blackface, or who do I be? *Black Scholar, 5,* 3–15.

Smitherman, G. (1977). *Talkin and testifyin: The language of Black America.* Boston: Houghton Mifflin.

Smitherman, G. (Ed.) (1981). *Black English and the education of Black children and youth: Proceedings of the National Invitational Symposium on the* King *decision.* Detroit, MI: Wayne State University Center for Black Studies.

Smitherman, G. (1983). What go round come round: *King* in perspective. In C. Brooks (Ed.), *Tapping potential: English and language arts for the Black learner* (pp. 41–62). Washington, DC: National Council of the Teachers of English.

Smitherman, G. (1992). Black English, diverging or converging? The view from the National Assessment of Educational Progress. *Language and Education, 6*(1), 47–61.

Smitherman, G. (1994a). *Black talk: Words and phrases from the hood to the Amen Corner.* Boston: Houghton Mifflin.

Smitherman, G. (1994b). "The blacker the berry, the sweeter the juice": African American student writers. In A. H. Dyson & C. Genishi (Eds.), *The need for story: Cultural diversity in classroom and community* (pp. 80–101). Champaign-Urbana, IL: National Council of Teachers of English.

Smitherman, G. (1997a). Black language and the education of Black children. One mo once. *The Black Scholar, 27*(1), 28–35.

Smitherman, G. (1997b). "The chain remain the same": Communicative practices in the Hip Hop Nation. *Journal of Black Studies, 28*(1), 3–25.

Smitherman, G. (1999). Language policy and classroom practices. In C. Adger, D. Christian, & O. Taylor, (Eds.), *Making the connection: Language and academic achievement among African American students* (pp. 115–124). Washington, DC, & McHenry, IL: Center for Applied Linguistics and Delta Systems.

Smitherman, G. (2000). *Talkin that talk: Language, culture, and education in African America.* New York: Routledge.

Smitherman, G., & Baugh, J. (2002). The shot heard from Ann Arbor: Language research and public policy in African America. *The Howard Journal of Communications, 13*(1), 5–25.

Smitherman, G., & Wright, S. (1983, March). *Black student writers, storks, and familiar places: What can we learn from the National Assessment of Educational Progress?* Paper presented at the Convention of the Conference on College Composition and Communication, Detroit, MI.

Spady, J., & Alim, H. (1999). Modes of being. In J. Spady, C. Lee, & H. Alim (Eds.), *Street conscious rap*. Philadelphia: Black History Museum.

Spady, J., Dupres, S., & Lee, C. (1995). *Twisted tales in the hip hop streets of Philly*. Philadelphia: Black History Museum/Umum/Loh Press.

Spears, A. (1982). The Black English semi-auxiliary *COME. Language, 58*(4), 850–872.

Spears, A. (Ed.) (1997). *Race and ideology: Language, symbolism, and popular culture*. Detroit, MI: Wayne State University Press.

Spears, A. (1998). African American language use: Ideology and so-called obscenity. In S. S. Mufwene, J. Baugh, & J. R. Rickford (Eds.), *African American English: Structure, history, and use*. New York: Routledge.

Spears, A. (2000, January). *Stressed "stay."* Paper presented at the Linguistic Society of America Convention, Chicago, IL.

Spears, A. (2001). Directness in the use of African American English. In S. Lanehart (Ed.), *Sociocultural and historical contexts of African American English* (pp. 239–259). Amsterdam, The Netherlands: John Benjamins.

Stanback Houston, M. (1985). Language and Black woman's place: Evidence from the Black middle class. In P. A. Treichler, B. Stafford, & C. Kramarae (Eds.), *For alma mater: Theory and practice in feminist scholarship* (pp. 177–191). Chicago: University of Illinois Press.

Steele, C. (1992, April). Race and the schooling of Black Americans. *The Atlantic Monthly, 269*(4), 68–78.

Stewart, W. A. (1967). Sociolinguistic factors in the history of American Negro dialects. *Florida Foreign Language Reporter, 5*, 1–7.

Stewart, W. A. (1968). A Sociolinguistic typology for describing national multilingualism. In J. Fishman (Ed.), *Readings in the sociology of language*. The Hague, The Netherlands: Mouton.

Strother, K. E. (1994). Livin' phat on the 'cool tip': Hip hop rhetoric—the language of a muted group. Paper presented at the Annual Meeting of the Speech Communication Association, New Orleans, LA.

Taylor, H. (1991). *Standard English, Black English, and bidialectalism: A controversy*. New York: Peter Lang.

Taylor, J. (1983). Influences of speech variety on teachers' evaluation of reading comprehension. *Journal of Educational Psychology, 75*, 662–667.

Taylor, N., & Vinjevold, P. (1999) *Getting learning right: Report of the President's Education Initiative Research Project*. Johannesburg, South Africa: Joint Education Trust.

Taylor, O. (1975). Black language and what to do about it: Some Black community perspective. In R. L. Williams (Ed.), *Ebonics: The true language of Black folks* (pp. 28–39). St. Louis, MO: Williams & Associates.

Tierney, R. J., & Pearson, P. D. (1981). Learning to learn from text: A framework for improving classroom practice. In E. Dishner & T. Bean (Eds.), *Reading in the content area: Improving classroom instruction* (pp. 87–103). Dubuque, IA: Kendall/Hunt.

Trabasso, T. (1993). The power of the narrative. In F. Lehr & J. Osborn (Eds.), *Reading, language, & literacy: Instruction for the twenty-first century*. Hillsdale, NJ: Erlbaum.

Troutman, D. (1995). The tongue or the sword: Which is master? In G. Smitherman (Ed.), *African American women speak out on Anita Hill–Clarence Thomas*. Detroit, MI: Wayne State University Press.

Troutman, D. (1997). Black women's discourse. In T. van Dijk (Ed.), *Discourse as social interaction* (pp. 148–156). London: Sage.

Troutman, D. (2000, October). "We be strong women": A womanist analysis of Black women's sociolinguistic behavior. Paper presented at New Ways of Analyzing Variation (NWAVE) Conference, East Lansing, MI.

Troutman, D. (2002). "We be strong women": A womanist analysis of Black women's sociolinguistic behavior. In M. Houston & O. Davis (Eds.), *Centering ourselves: African American feminist and womanist studies of discourse* (pp. 99–122). Cresskill, NJ: Hampton Press.

Turner, L. (1949). *Africanisms in the Gullah dialect*. Chicago, IL: University of Chicago Press.

U.S. Department of Education. (1999). *National assessment of educational progress 1998 reading report card for the nation and states* (NCES 1999–500). Washington, DC: Government Printing Office.

Van den Broek, P., & Trabasso, T. (1986). Causal networks versus goal hierarchies in summarizing text. *Discourse Processes, 9,* 1–15.

Van Keulen, J. E., Weddington, G. T., & DeBose, C. E. (1998). *Speech, language, learning, and the African American child*. Needham Heights, MA: Allyn & Bacon.

Vass, W. K. (1979). *The Bantu speaking heritage of the United States*. Los Angeles: University of California Center for Afro-American Studies.

Vaughn-Cooke, F. (1987). Are Black and White vernaculars diverging? *American Speech, 62*(1), 12–32.

Whorf, B. (1956). *Language, thought, and reality*. Cambridge: MIT Press.

Wiley, T. G. (1996). Language planning and policy. In S. L. McKay & N. H. Hornberger (Eds.), *Sociolinguistics and language teaching* (pp. 103–147). New York: Cambridge University Press.

Wiggins, G., & McTighe, J. (1998). *Understanding by design*. Alexandria, VA: Association for Supervision and Curriculum Development.

Williams, M. (1983). *The velveteen rabbit*. New York: Random House.

Williams, R. L. (Ed.). (1975). *Ebonics: The true language of Black folks*. St. Louis, MO: Williams & Associates.

Williams, S. (1993). Substantive Africanisms at the end of the African linguistic disaspora. In S. S. Mufwene (Ed.), *Africanisms in Afro-American language varieties* (pp. 406–422). Athens: University of Georgia Press.

Williamson, J. (1975). A look at Black English. In R. L. Williams (Ed.), *Ebonics: The true language of Black folks* (pp. 11–21). St. Louis, MO: Williams & Associates.

Winford, D. (1997). On the origins of African American vernacular English—A creolist perspective. Part I: The sociohistorical background. *Diachronica, 14,* 305–344.

Winford, D. (1998). On the origins of African American vernacular English—A creolist perspective. Part II: Linguistic features. *Diachronica, 15,* 1–55.

Winter, J. (1988). *Follow the drinking gourd*. New York: Knopf.

Wolff, E. (2000). The notion of the "African Renaissance" as developed in speeches by South Africa's President Thabo Mbeki in 1998/1999. In E. Wolff (Ed.), *Working documents of the Panel on Language Policy in Africa: The African renaissance as a challenge for language planning*. Leipzig, Germany: Institut für Afrikanistik.

Wolfram, W. (1969). *A sociolinguistic description of Detroit Negro speech*. Washington, DC: Center for Applied Linguistics.

Wolfram, W. (1999). Repercussions from the Oakland Ebonics controversy: The critical role of dialect awareness programs. In C. Adger, D. Christian, & O. Taylor (Eds.), *Making the connections: Language and academic achievement among African American students* (pp. 61–80). Washington, DC, & McHenry, IL: Center for Applied Linguistics and Delta Systems.

Wolfram, W., Adger, C., & Christian, D. (1999). *Dialects in schools and communities*. Mahwah, NJ: Lawrence Erlbaum.

Wolfram, W., & Schilling-Estes, N. (1998). *American English: Dialects and variation*. Malden, MA: Blackwell.

Wolfram, W., & Thomas, E. R. (2002). *The development of African American English*. Oxford, UK: Blackwell Publishers.

Wright, R. (1936). Big Boy leaves home. *Uncle Tom's children* (pp. 16–61). New York: Harper & Row.

Wright, R. (1937). *Black boy*. New York: Harper & Row.

About the Editors
and Contributors

Neville Alexander, a political activist and educator, has lectured at numerous universities and is author of *One Azania, One Nation* (1979) and *An Ordinary Country* (2003). In 1980, he was appointed Cape Town Director of the South African Committee on Higher Education (SACHED). He currently is the director of the Project for the Study of Alternative Education in South Africa (PRAESA) at the University of Cape Town and is a recognized leader in the struggle for equal language rights in South Africa and beyond.

H. Samy Alim is an Assistant Professor of Anthropology at UCLA and is author of *Roc the Mic Right: The Language of Hip Hop Culture* (2006) and *You Know My Steez: An Ethnographic and Sociolinguistic Study of Styleshifting in a Black American Speech Community* (2004), and coauthor of *Street Conscious Rap* (1999). His research interests include language and race, global Hip Hop Culture (particularly in the Arabic-speaking world), and diversifying approaches to language and literacy development.

John Baugh is the Margaret Bush Wilson Professor in Arts and Sciences at Washington University in St. Louis, where he directs the Program in African and African American Studies. He is the author of *Beyond Ebonics: Linguistic Pride and Racial Prejudice* (2000), *Out of the Mouths of Slaves: African American Language and Educational Malpractice* (1999), and *Black Street Speech: Its History, Structure, and Survival* (1983).

Charles DeBose is a professor of English at California State University, East Bay. He is author of *The Sociology of African American Language* (2005) and coauthor of *Speech, Language, Learning, and the African American Child* (1998) as well as numerous book chapters, journal articles, and reviews in the areas of African American language, sociolinguistics, and pidgin-creole studies. His 1975 dissertation from Stanford University focused on the creole language Papiamentu.

Sharroky Hollie, a national consultant in culturally and linguistically responsive teaching and learning, is an assistant professor in teacher education at California State University, Dominguez Hills. He is cofounder of the Culture and Language Academy of Success in Inglewood, California, an independent school that supports students' development of cultural and linguistic knowledge and awareness of themselves, their community, the nation, and the world as an entrée to a standards-based, academically rigorous, and intellectually stimulating curriculum.

Sonja L. Lanehart is the Brackenridge Endowed Chair Professor of Literature and Humanities at the University of Texas–San Antonio. She is the author of *Sista Speak! Black Women Kinfolk Talk About Language and Literacy* (2002) and editor of *Sociocultural and Historical Contexts of African American English* (2001). Her research interests include language use and literacy in the African American community, language and identity, and the educational applications of sociolinguistic research.

Noma LeMoine is author of *English for Your Success: A Language Development Program for African American Children Grades Pre-K–8—A Handbook of Successful Strategies for Educators* and is a nationally recognized expert on issues of language variation and learning in African American and other students for whom standard English is not native. She is currently the director of the Los Angeles Unified School District's Academic English Mastery and Closing the Achievement Gap Branch, as well as the director of the Academic English Mastery program, which supports teachers in effectively incorporating linguistically responsive pedagogy into instructional practice.

Angela E. Rickford is an Associate Professor of Education at San Jose State University. She is a reading specialist whose research is in the area of teaching literacy to ethnically diverse student populations. She is the author of *"I Can Fly": Teaching Narratives and Reading Comprehension to African American and Other Ethnic Minority Students* (1999) and several articles. She has served as a reading consultant for Bay Area reading companies and is currently the director of the Early Literacy Project, a federally funded Grant Project at San Jose State University.

Sonia Sanchez is a poet, mother, activist, and professor. She is the author of 16 books, as well as a contributing editor to *Black Scholar* and the editor of two anthologies. Her poetry books include *Homecoming* (1969), *We a BaddDDD People* (1982), *Wounded in the House of a Friend* (1995), *Does Your House Have Lions* (1997), and *Like the Singing Coming off the Drums* (1998). She has held the Laura Carnell Chair in English at Temple University and was the recipient of the Robert Frost Medal and the Langston Hughes Medal for poetry. Her forthcoming memoir, *Defiant Trespass*, is highly anticipated.

Geneva Smitherman (aka "Dr. G") is University Distinguished Professor of English and director of the African American Language and Literacy Program at Michigan State University. She is the author of numerous articles and several books on language and education, including *Talkin and Testifyin: The Language of Black America* (1977), *Black Talk: Words and Phrases from the Hood to the Amen Corner* (2000), *Talkin That Talk: Language, Culture, and Education in African America* (2000), and *Word from the Mother: Language and African Americans* (2006). She is also director of the My Brother's Keeper Program in Detroit.

Arthur K. Spears is Professor and Chair of the Anthropology Department at the City College and is a member of the doctoral faculty in the Linguistics and Anthropology Programs at the Graduate Center, both branches of the City University of New York (CUNY). His most recent book is *Black Linguistics: Language, Society, and Politics in Africa and the Americas* (coeditor; 2003). His forthcoming books are *The Haitian Language* (coeditor) and *Black Language in the English-Speaking Caribbean and U.S.* (editor).

Index